THE MISCHIEF-MAKER

WRITTEN BY: DONNA GENE STANKEY

CO-AUTHORED BY: RAMONA HAMMEL

ISBN (eBook):   978-1-956742-20-6
ISBN (Paperback):   978-1-956742-21-3

Contents

Dedication

This book is dedicated to my mother:
Donna Gene (Setterington) Stankey.

It is thanks to you that your children have a wonderful historical account of the Setterington Family. We appreciate all your long hours of collecting stories from the relatives, and the research that you put into this book so that we could get to know them better. Also thank you for your love of history and wanting to preserve a piece of it for all to read.

Acknowledgements

I would also like to acknowledge; my friend, Andrea Howard, who has helped me with all her computer knowledge to make this publication possible; Sue Hardaker, from the Elsie Historical Society, for her help getting me information and pictures; my sister, Rita, who I would call with questions about events in the book since I could no longer ask our mother; my husband, Randy, who was very patient with me while going through the process of getting the book published. Thank you all.

Author's Note

The *Mischief-maker* continues the story of my father's life which began in *Rate*. The Setterington family lived in Mary Smith's house in Elsie for about five years. The *Mischief-maker* covers this period of time.

The more I learned about Dad's life, the more compassion I felt for my grandmother. I don't think Dad ever intentionally caused his mother to worry, nor did he intend to make more work for her, it just seemed to happen. The old expression "hindsight is better than foresight" often applied to his misadventures. I always felt Grandma hated having to doctor his various hurts.

My information came from both Dad and Aunt Blanche; sometimes, Uncle George would add tidbits when I was talking with Aunt Blanche. My greatest task was assembling all the material in chronological order. In some instances, the order may not be entirely correct, but I did my best, often consulting other records for dates.

Grandma and I always talked a lot when I had to stay with her after school until my ride came. This was the days before busses, and the boys I rode with played sports, so I was at Grandma's until 5:00 or 5:30 each school day afternoon. There were questions I never asked, and I regret that, but between the age of nine and fourteen, I was more likely to sit and listen. 1 have often wished I had asked her about her step-brothers and if she knew much about her father's and mother's early life. Children were not supposed to interrupt their elders.

Both Dad and Aunt Blanche were good at descriptions, and they often explained how something made them feel. Some of the words chosen may sound alien to you who read this, but often the words are not mine, but are the exact words used by Dad or Aunt Blanche.

In many ways, their generation expressed themselves differently than people do now. Besides, they lived in a rural community and many expressions centered around farming and raising livestock. Words that were used, names of farm machinery and other equipment, are not in the small dictionaries of today. I am not always certain of my spelling, but Dad was hardly the one to ask. He once told me, "I hate to write letters. After I know what I want to say, I have to think of how to say it in words I can spell." The computer kicked up the word "milch." Apparently, the word is no longer used to designate cows that produce milk which the farmer sells as opposed to a beef cow who provides only enough milk to feed her calf.

If you wonder at the spelling and lack of punctuation in the letter from Horatio to Millie, it is because I have the letter, and I copied it exactly as written.

CHAPTER 1

Ralph sat on the front porch of the gray house which looked as though it had grown rather than been built, tossing a stick for Bruno to fetch. His mind was wandering; he performed the task of throwing the stick automatically, absently rewarding the dog with a pat on the head and a "Good boy, Bruno. Fetch it again."

Jeepers, they'd been in town over a week now, and Ralph found that he was bored. It wasn't that he didn't have friends because he did, but so far he hadn't found life in the village of Elsie one-quarter as interesting as life on a farm. Pa had only kept one cow, two driving horses, and a work team, and of course, Ralph was expected to help with chores same as always only now it took hardly any time at all. Ralph cleaned stables for the horses, led them out to water, and fed them, but as had been their usual way, Pa took care of the cow; that is unless he specifically told Ralph to feed her when he expected to be late.

Rate missed his best friend, Don (Curly) Sherman. The boys had lived on adjacent farms and had been buddies, always wandering the woods together, traipsing along the riverbank together, looking forward to the day when their fathers would feel they were old enough to own rifles. Pa had told Rate twelve, and Mr. Sherman had said that sounded like a pretty good age to him too. Then, maybe after that, they'd get a shotgun so they could hunt ducks, and grouse, and even those pesky old crows which were such a nuisance to farmers.

It wasn't that he couldn't go to any woods or a river because he could. North of town there were plenty of woods and a creek; to the west, there was the Maple River with some mighty good fishing at the dam by the gristmill. Only somehow, it just wasn't the same walking in someone else's fields.

Blanche. She was the reason they'd made the move. Now that Grandmother and Grandfather Setterington had moved to South Lyons, Blanche had no place to stay so she could go to town to school. She'd been too good for the little, one room, country school where he had gone. Ma and Pa just always catered to her. Course he had heard Ma tellin' Blanche the other night that it was all well and good for her to have friends, but she also had to remember that she still had duties to perform around the house. Pa had never said one word which was typical. Pa just never said a thing if Blanche shirked her work, but let him slack off, and Pa was on his back first thing. Never seemed quite fair, but he supposed it was because he was a boy, and he guessed more was expected from a boy than a silly, old girl.

He knew Ma hadn't been sorry to have her bossy mother-in-law move away since she didn't have to put up with Lovina's fault-finding nearly as often now. Grandmother had been the reason Blanche had had to go to town to school, and Ralph had a suspicion Grandmother had been the one to suggest they move into town to accommodate Blanche. Not that Pa would ever admit he still did whatever his mother or father suggested; course Ma knew, and there were times when she let Pa know how much it rankled that he let his mother interfere in their lives.

Actually, it hadn't made all that much difference to Ralph whether his grandparents were around or not. Even at the age of ten, he was still afraid of both grandparents; neither of them had ever given him a reason not to fear them; they were stern, domineering, quick to criticize, and laughed all too seldom. Regardless, he worshiped his grandfather; it was for his grandfather that his father had nicknamed him Rate.

Horatio Setterington was an impressive personage, to others as well as the lad. He stood ramrod straight, his shoulders were broad and square, his six foot, two inch frame was wiry and even at his age--he was past sixty--he carried a look of strength; his thinning hair was steel gray as was the neatly trimmed Vandyke; his eyes were black and piercing although the crinkles at the corners sometimes softened their intensity because he was not completely devoid of humor; in fact, Horatio enjoyed seeing a good joke played as well as the next person.

Seemed funny how Pa had always done whatever his parents wanted. Uncle John sure had done whatever he wanted no matter how Grandmother ranted at him. Pa had plenty of backbone except when he came up against his parents; then, he was quick to knuckle under. He supposed both Grandmother and Grandfather approved of Pa's new job. Pa was working selling farm implements for Mr. Pierce for nine dollars a week. Didn't seem like all that much money to Ralph. Pa still had a large flock of sheep, and of course, he hadn't sold the farm, he was only renting it to Mr. Onstott; Ralph thought he'd heard Pa say that he had only rented the eighty where they had lived which meant there would still be hay to put up on the north eighty and the south forty. Bet Pa would never give up trading horses either; he'd heard it said that horse trading was born in a person like being tall or having blue eyes.

Milford Setterington and Mina Smith had been married in 1885, and after a short wedding trip to Manistee, had moved onto a farm three miles west and one-half mile north of Elsie which they had purchased from Horatio. Millie had seemed content on the farm and prices had been better of late than they had been some of the years. Even Miney was not sure why her husband had decided to leave the farm. It was 1904, and their income had been better this year than the year before. She knew when Millie had sold off the pigs, the cows--they had kept one to have their own milk- and the young cattle, he had banked the money saying he was well pleased with the amount he had received.

Much as Miney was loath to admit it, her husband was often so close mouthed she just never knew what he was thinking. Didn't do her one mite of good to question him either since he was not one to be coerced into saying one word against his will. Miney, who was always quick to voice her opinion on anything as long as her in-laws weren't within hearing distance, found this trait of Millie's difficult to understand.

"Well, Bruno, we'd best get the chores done afore Pa gets home. C'mon."

Ralph got up from the steps and headed across the street to the barn. At least Bruno would go this far with him. Funny thing about that darned dog, couldn't call him off the property in any direction except to cross the street to the barn, or to follow a rig if it was going out to the farm. Well, that wasn't quite all. Every time Pa was coming home from the farm, Bruno would prick up his ears, cock his head and listen, then take off west on a dead run. Pa always said Bruno met him just as he turned the corner by the village cemetery, and that was two blocks away. He never met Millie at any other time, only when he was returning from the farm.

Somehow, it always rankled Ralph that the dog was so obvious in showing his affection for Millie. After all, who'd picked the 150 quarts of strawberries just so he could buy the pup, and who'd always taken care of him? Course he had to admit that Bruno took his part if he and Pa was to scuffle, and on the farm, the dog had followed Rate wherever he went. It was only here, in town, that he refused to go anywhere with the boy, coax all he might; Bruno often laid at the edge of their lot watching in the direction Ralph had left, waiting patiently for his return. Now, he ran willingly enough with the boy, jumping at his side to playfully catch his arm, as they went to the barn.

Ralph had to clean the stables by forking the manure into a wheelbarrow, taking the load out, and dumping it on a pile behind the barn. He also had to lead each horse to the tank for a drink, bed them down well with fresh straw and fork fresh hay into their mangers. In the morning, he gave them a ration of oats in their grain box as well. He usually gave them a quick curry job to keep their coat clean. Of course, if one was going to be harnessed, she was curried and brushed until her coat shone. Rate liked horses, so instead of slacking on this job, he was more likely to spend extra time doing the task exceptionally well.

Pa usually took care of the cow. Once in a while he might tell Rate to clean her stall and feed her, but that was only if he was going to be extra late. Pa always took care of milking her too; the cow gave them more than enough milk for their needs. Miney had asked Millie what he intended to do when the cow freshened again; as it was, the cow was going dry and come February and March, they'd have to buy milk until the cow had her calf. Miney knew that even if they kept the calf for a short time, the cow would give more milk than they needed. Although Millie had offered no comment, she had had the thought that just maybe one of their neighbors might buy the extra milk. She knew Mother Setterington had once sold milk when they kept a cow, so perhaps she could do the same. That way, she could have a little extra money to buy a few things for the house--a new oilcloth for the kitchen table, or new curtains for the living room since the old ones had literally fallen to pieces the last time she washed them, and try as she might, she had not been able to mend them so it didn't show. She had brought this to Millie's attention, but there again, he hadn't quite seen her point of view. Now, selling milk was a possibility to consider.

The warm sunny days of September gradually gave way to the colder, crisper days of October. The trees had divested themselves of much of their finery and the air was permeated with the aromatic smell of burning leaves. Fall was well on its way.

Halloween was almost here. Ralph and his playmates had overheard some of the older boys discussing the mischief they were perpetrating. Rate knew for certain that a good many outhouses would be tipped over, buggies removed from barns to be found elsewhere, even a horse or a cow tied in strange places; nothing was done with intent to destroy anything--it was just an inconvenience for the persons who happened to own the items involved. Of course, most of the menfolk just seemed to expect this sort of shenanigans to take place; therefore, they took the whole prospect with complete aplomb. Many, no doubt, remembered occasions from their own boyhood when their escapades had aggravated the old folks.

One night, when Millie seemed in an affable mood, Ralph had asked his father a question.

"Pa, when you was young, did you ever do anything for fun on Halloween?"

Millie chuckled, thought a moment, then smiling faintly said, "There was a time or two that I seem to recall."

"What did you do?"

"There was this one time in particular, I mind. There was this old man we boys didn't like atall because he never had a sense of humor and couldn't take no joshin'. He always raised a big patch of watermelons, and of course, we fellows did like to coon a watermelon now and again. Most people never cared since we'd only take one or two from any one patch and were always particular not to destroy any of the others. Well, old man Skutt didn't hold with this notion so he always kept a shotgun handy. Loaded with rock salt, it was. Rock salt isn't exactly dangerous, but it sure can sting. Sometimes, we'd sneak around his place, then make some noise, just to hear him rant and rave and shoot at where he thought we were.

"Anyways, a bunch of us got together and planned what we was gonna do weeks ahead of time. On Halloween, we took his wagon, which happened to be loaded with bags of grain, from the barn, dismantled it, and put it back together straddle the ridgepole of the barn. Took nearly all night to do it because we had to be that careful. We wrapped blankets around the pieces so they wouldn't sound so loud hitting the side of the barn as we pulled them up. I can tell you, boy, it was hard work to be so quiet, and it was cloudy that night so it was mighty difficult to see. We even hauled the grain up and put it in the wagon just like we had found it."

"How'd he ever get it down?" asked Ralph in wonder.

"Danged if I know. We didn't care about that, and none of us dared show our face around there to find out 'cause we knew he'd be madder'n a wet hen. If he hadn't always been such an old grouch, we just might have offered to help him get it down. Guess we all felt he had it coming."

Millie paused a moment. Ralph was quiet, surmising that his father had another tale to tell.

"John had a strange experience one year not long before he was married. How funny it was depended on which side of the fence you was on. Seems he was coming home, rather late, on foot. Don't recollect where he'd been, but he came upon some boys putting a buggy in those maple trees in front of Tillie

Lance's house. Well, John thought the whole affair comical so he offered to give the boys a hand. The lads accepted his offer, and with some big galoot like John helping, the work went much easier and faster. When they finished, the boys took off and John went on home.

"Come the next day--" Millie broke off laughing heartily. "Come the next day, John went to use his buggy, and it wasn't there." Millie laughed again. "Don't know why, but John had an inkling what had happened. He went over to Tillie's and sure enough, it was John's buggy settin' up there in those trees nice as you please." Now, Millie laughed uproariously, and the tears ran down his cheeks. "I'd have given a week's wage to have seen John's face when he realized he'd helped put his own buggy in the trees. Guess for a moment, he was mad clean through, and it was probably a good thing he hadn't been able to tell who the boys were, it bein' so dark an' all. By the time he got that buggy down, he'd regained his sense of humor and laughed at himself. John never was too smart in some ways. Imagine helping to put your own buggy into a tree without recognizing it. He got just what he deserved."

Ralph laughed with his father. Bet that had been a sight for sore eyes, Uncle John mad over something. Usually, Uncle John had a real sense of humor, more so than Pa, and a whole lot more than Grandfather. He guessed part of the reason his grandfather and Uncle John didn't get on very well was because of Uncle John's irresponsible ways.

"Pa, can I go Halloweening?"

"No."

"Ain't I big enough?" he asked wistfully.

"Not yet, you're not."

Well, that ended that. It would do no good to explain to his father that some of his friends were being allowed to go out; Pa would simply say those boys weren't his responsibility.

"Did you ever do anything else?" Disappointment crept into his voice in spite of him trying to sound casual.

"I suppose I did. Can't rightly remember everything, you know. There was the time Orrin Dunham and I climbed the belfry to the school and turned the bell upside down. We had the damndest time keeping it in that position. Anyway, we filled it with water. That took some doin', let me tell you, gettin' those pails up there without spilling it all over the floor below. Couldn't have no light and didn't want to make enough noise so we'd get caught.

"We had a man who was principal of the school, and he also helped the schoolmistress teach grades seven through eleven. We knew that he was the one who always rang the bell. Well, the next morning with the first jerk of the bell rope, he got a good drenching. We were lucky he never found out who did it, or he'd have skinned us alive and nailed our hides to the fence. Kids sure did think it funny, him standin' there like a drowned rat, but you never saw a man look so full of rage. Thought he was like to die of apoplexy, his face got that red."

When Ralph had gone upstairs to bed, Miney, who had been silent during all of Millie's storytelling, spoke to her husband.

"Millie, I do wish you wouldn't fill Ralph's head with ideas of mischief. He has enough ideas of his own without you giving him any more."

"Now, Miney, it don't hurt none. Rate just wanted to know what I did when I was younger, so I told him. That don't mean he will try to do the same thing." He gave a hearty chuckle. "I'm sure that when the time comes, Rate will be able to think of his own ideas. Leastwise, he's done all right so far, hasn't he?"

He gave his disgruntled wife an amused grin.

"Milford, you just encourage him to get into some sort of devilment."

"All's I want is for him to be an average boy. I don't want some prissy acting sissy for a son."

"Well! I never thought I was trying to make him into a sissy. I've doctored all his hurts and put up with his mischievous ways without punishing him very often--at least not since he got older. I just want him to have respect for other people's property and feelings."

"All right, Miney, I get your point, so just keep still."

There. Millie had gone and done it again. Sometimes, he treated her like a child, always telling her to keep still when he didn't want to talk. Of course, he would never raise any objections to his mother when she voiced *her* opinion. Well, just wait until Ralph got into trouble over some prank, then she'd see what Millie had to say. She'd even take pleasure in reminding him it was his own fault.

Since they were now living in town, Miney had been giving considerable thought to Blanche's piano lessons. Miney had been giving the girl lessons for quite some time, but it seemed as though Blanche progressed at a snail's pace. Perhaps what she needed was someone outside the family as a teacher. Not that Miney wasn't capable because she had been teaching other children since before she was married; however, it did occur to her that Blanche might not be trying all that hard since her teacher was only her mother. Miney was of the opinion that all young girls should learn to play the piano; in her estimation, playing the piano well was equally as important as cooking, baking, and sewing.

"Blanche, I talked with Mabel Wooley today, and she is more than willing to take you on as one of her pupils."

"Ma," sighed her daughter, "I just don't think it is going to make one whit of difference. I just don't think it is in me to play the piano."

"Nonsense, child. Of course you can. It will make a difference having Mrs. Wooley for your teacher instead of your mother."

"How come you can teach someone else's kids?"

"Guess I don't rightly know," admitted Miney, giving her daughter a thoughtful look. "I just don't understand why you find it so difficult."

"Neither do I, but I do. Maybe if I liked to play the piano better, I could get the hang of it easier. I like to sing, and one day when Hazel and I were singing, Mrs. Hamilton told me I had a very sweet voice."

"Did she now? Ma's always thought that, and so does Ralph for that matter. But don't you *want* to learn to play the piano?" asked a puzzled Miney, her daughter's remark a complete mystery.

Somehow, Miney could not envision a life without being able to sit down and play some hymns. She remembered when she was a child at home how her father would sing with her when she played; Pa had had such a nice, rich baritone. Music had been a very important part of their life. Pa had been the one to teach her how to let him harmonize with her when they sang since she had a lovely soprano voice; she sighed remembering those moments with nostalgia.

Blanche looked at her mother a long moment, mulling the question over in her mind, before choosing her words carefully for a reply.

"I'm not really sure. I like to hear music, but I can take it or leave it when it comes to playing it. Perhaps if it came easier, but I can practice and practice and my fingers are all thumbs so I still make mistakes. I'm not like that in other things. My sums always came easily and I've been told I write well, and I find spelling comes easy too. Music is the only thing that seems so difficult. But I'll try." Blanche looked at her mother indecisively, clenched her teeth a moment, then spoke once again. "Ma, promise me that if Mrs. Wooley doesn't think I'm doing very well after a few weeks you'll let me quit," beseeched the young girl.

"All right, Blanche. We'll see what Mabel thinks after a few lessons."

The next week Blanche dutifully started taking piano lessons from Mabel Wooley. Mabel was Fern Wooley's sister-in-law since she was married to Fern's brother, Bert. Fern was Blanche's very best friend so it made her wonder if it would be proper to call Mrs. Wooley "Mabel" because, of course, that is what Fern called her, or whether she should call her Mrs. Wooley because she was about fifteen years older than Blanche. The problem was settled at the first lesson when Mabel said, "Goodness, Blanche, you don't have to be so formal with me.

I know you and Fern are the best of friends and you don't say 'Mr.' Wooley, you call him Bert."

Blanche laughed and felt much more at ease.

After several weeks of lessons, Blanche had made virtually no progress. If she managed to keep her fingers on the right keys, the time was always wrong. Mabel set a metronome in action to do Blanche's counting for her. Somehow, the steady click, click, click of the metronome made Blanche nervous and when she concentrated so hard to play in time with the instrument, she invariably struck the wrong keys and that flustered her even more.

It was finally a mutual agreement between Miney, Mabel, and of course, Blanche, that the music lessons be discontinued. This decision came as a complete relief to Blanche. Although Miney did her best to hide her disappointment, Blanche realized how badly her mother felt, but she felt as though she really had given it an honest effort. Well, like Ma was always saying, some things were just a God-given talent, and when it came to playing the piano, God had certainly passed Blanche by. She was glad that Ma had finally admitted that her daughter simply did not have this talent and nothing Miney could do would ever give it to her.

November came with its gray, dull days, cold nights that brought a scum of ice to the watering tanks and the edges of the smaller streams; the hint of winter was certainly in the air when Millie decided it was time the sheep from the south forty should be driven back to the barn on the eighty for the winter months. This year, he would have to take care of them himself since the renter was not moving onto the farm until the first of March. Oh, well, sheep could be fed and watered once a day and most likely be all right. He had plenty of feeders, and once filled with hay, Millie knew it would last the flock for the entire day.

It was Friday night when Millie spoke to his son who as usual sat with his nose buried in a book; Rate was an avid reader and his most cherished possessions were his books. Miney had read to him as a very small child and had laughed because Ralph had been in such a hurry to learn to read for himself.

"Rate, you'd best get to bed early because we are going to move the sheep tomorrow. I want to get an early start."

"All right, Pa. I just want to read another chapter. Is that all right?"

"Just so's you understand you have to get up early," said Millie, nodding his head.

"I do, Pa, and I'll get up when you call," promised Ralph.

In fact, Rate hated to put the book down; he was in an especially interesting part, so he sneaked in an extra chapter. If Millie surmised this, he kept his counsel although he noted the lateness of the hour when Ralph finally closed the book and went upstairs to go to bed.

Ralph was dreaming. He and Bruno were running in the lane, back of the barn, headed for the ditch. The dog barked and jumped and ran in circles around his young master. Then Ralph heard his father's voice, coming from a great distance, faint and indistinct. "Rate!" Only the one word. Ralph stirred in his sleep. He half roused himself, listened a moment, heard nothing but the wind blowing a tree branch against the house, opened his eyes and noted the darkness of the room. Must have been dreaming, he thought. It's too early for Pa to have called. With those thoughts, he snuggled down under the thick quilts once again and immediately dropped into a deep slumber.

Rate awoke with a start! Jeepers, Pa had just come through the open doorway, and it had been his heavy tread on a squeaky floorboard that had brought Ralph out of his tranquility. Rate made a lunge for the side of the bed away from his father, but his movements were too slow encumbered as they were by the bedclothes. Just as his feet cleared the covers, Millie's huge hand closed about one ankle. Without a word, Millie started for the door. Rate grasped frantically for the foot of the bed; his fingers narrowly missed their objective. Rate hit the floor with a thud. Nor did Millie stop there. With that one foot firmly locked in his hand, he crossed the room, went out the door, and down the hall. Rate's nightshirt had pulled up exposing his bare buttocks to the rough flooring, scraping off a patch of skin here and there. The worst part was yet to come. Down the back stairs which led to the corner of the dining room by the kitchen they went, with poor Ralph bumping and banging on each step.

He felt like crying out. Each bump was worse than being struck with a paddle. Once he hit directly on his tail bone and felt the pain race through his lower extremities. However, he bit his lip and uttered not even a muffled sound. He'd not give Pa the pleasure of knowing how much he was hurting. What a relief when they reached the bottom. His behind felt numb, like he'd never have any feeling there ever again.

Millie abruptly relinquished his hold on Rate's foot.

"You've fifteen minutes to eat your breakfast, get dressed, and get out to the barn."

With that ultimatum, Millie stalked out of the house.

Miney had put Ralph's bowl of oatmeal on the table as she had watched her son being dragged into the kitchen. She dared not voice either her disapproval or her concern for her son.

"Here, Ralph, eat your breakfast while it's hot. Then you can get dressed."

"1--I'm not hungry, Ma. I'll just go get dressed."

"Nonsense. You'll feel better after you get some hot food in you. Didn't you hear him call?" she asked sympathetically.

"I guess not. I was dreamin', and I just thought it was part of my dream."

Rate sat down gingerly, and for once Miney made no admonishing remarks as he wolfed down his food.

"Does it hurt much?"

"Naw. It's kinda numb right now."

From the worried frown on her face, he knew his mother was concerned. Ma was never one to condone what she termed severe physical punishment, so he knew she had not approved of her husband's method; it was just that there was nothing she could do about it. No use to make her feel badly. Bet his hind end would be sore later on. Drat it all anyhow. Pa just never was one to call more than once, or wait for an answer which would show that he had heard his father. Still, if it had been Blanche, Pa wouldn't have done that to her; he would have thought nothing about calling her a second time. Guess after this he'd just have to be more careful about listening.

Whether a result of this experience or not, but in the years to come, on more than one occasion Ralph was to slip quietly down the stairs in the dark of night, cautiously skirt a couple of chairs in his advance to the stove which sometimes glowed a dull red through the isinglass in the door; then he would note with satisfaction that his father's shoes still stood by the side of the stove where Millie put them each night just before retiring. Never again was he to fail to respond to that single word, "Rate," no matter what time of night came the call. He became a light sleeper as if a part of him was afraid to sleep because it must be ready to answer his father's summons. Here again Millie demanded and was awarded instant obedience. Ralph never bore his father any degree of resentment, he simply accepted the discipline as being for his own benefit.

It was Saturday evening, and Mina knew that Blanche had been invited to a party at Hazel Hamilton's. However, Blanche had shown no indication that she was going any place; although seemingly preoccupied and not very talkative, she had helped with supper and had dried the dishes; now, she sat at the table with a book. Ralph was in the kitchen rubbing tallow on his high tops to waterproof them since one could expect snow in quantity any day now. Millie was reading the Owosso paper, paying no attention to anyone; Miney had brought the rug she was crocheting nearer the oil lamp setting in the middle of the library table.

The family always sat here nights especially in the coldest weather since this room was always cosy-warm. It not only had its own stove at one end, but it got heat from the kitchen as well. Had they had company, they would have sat in the parlor; they only had a fire in that room if someone came to visit, otherwise the heavy curtains were drawn across the archway to help conserve fuel. During the winter, they only used the back stairway, and the only heat upstairs came from a small register in the floor of each room which allowed a small portion of the heat from the room below to filter through. It was never enough to keep the temperature above freezing during the truly bitter winter months.

Finally, Miney decided she had perhaps got the dates mixed up and Blanche must be going to a party next week. Seemed odd that she had made such a mistake, she usually kept dates straight.

"Blanche."

"Yes, Ma."

"Weren't you supposed to be going to a party over to Hamilton's tonight?"

"Well, Hazel gave me an invitation," she hedged.

"Why aren't you getting ready? It must be nearly time for it to start."

"I'm not going, that's why I'm not getting ready."

"Not going? Did you and Hazel have a falling out?"

"Oh, Ma, of course not. I'm just not going. That's all there is to it," she stated somewhat emphatically.

"Would you mind telling me why?" asked a confused Miney.

Blanche took a deep breath, looked her mother squarely in the eye and said, "All right. Since you asked, I'll tell you. When the young people give parties, sometimes they play games, but lately they mostly play cards, and sometimes they dance. You have made it perfectly clear to me that I am not to play cards *or* dance so that leaves me to sit by myself doing nothing while the others have a good time. I'm not going to any more parties, not ever," she stated resolutely.

"Goodness, Blanche, you've said nothing before." "You've never asked before," she countered.

"I didn't realize that so many of the young people did these things. Why, Blanche, most of those you go around with are good Christians. Well, leastways they've always attended Church regularly, either the Baptist or the Methodist. How in the world can they condone card playing and dancing? Do their parents know?" Miney asked in disbelief. Surely she was no more strict than any good Christian parent should be.

Blanche remained silent.

"Blanche, dearest, you know how the Church feels about such things. The devil is just waiting to pounce on us at any sign of weakness so we have to be extremely careful. I don't like to have you miss out on the fun, but--"

Her voice trailed off. Miney did not like to deny her daughter anything. Of course, she remembered that she and Millie had at one time played cards at their Grange meetings, and it had seemed harmless fun, but Father Setterington had found out about it and had made her see that card playing was the devil at work.

Millie looked up from his paper, his face completely expressionless.

"Blanche, there is no need for you to sit here when you could be out enjoying yourself. Now you hurry up and get your clothes changed. You go to your party. If they play cards, you learn to play cards, and if they dance, you learn to dance. You are only young once."

"But, Millie--"

"Miney, keep still. Blanche isn't going to miss out on having friends just become of some silly notion of the Church."

"Well, I never!"

"Oh, Pa, thank you."

Blanche hurried to her father's chair, threw her arms around his neck and gave his cheek a kiss. It was an unaccustomed display of affection, and Millie patted her arm clumsily, almost embarrassed by his daughter's actions. Since she had budded into womanhood, Millie had stopped putting his arm around her or giving her a kiss, he felt she was too grown up for that, and it made him more than a little uncomfortable to be demonstrative although there were times when he would liked to have shown her some affection. There was no doubt that he loved his daughter dearly.

"Blanche, you just enjoy yourself like everyone else."

"I will, Pa, I will."

Blanche took a kerosene lamp down from the shelf in the kitchen, carefully removed the chimney, touched the lighted match to the wick, then replaced the chimney as the flame burned higher; she went up the stairs to her bedroom to change into her best dress, the one she usually wore to Church.

Miney looked at her husband who had gone back to his reading, deliberately avoiding her eyes. It wasn't often Millie just out and out rescinded one of her rules. From the set look to his face, she knew it would do absolutely no good to try to discuss the matter with him. When he had spoken, there was no changing his mind. What would Mother and Father Setterington think? Goodness, there she was worried about what her in-laws would say completely forgetting that since they had moved away from Elsie, they weren't likely to find out. Besides, she'd just tell them it was their son's idea, and they could just speak to him about it. After all, since she was an obedient wife, the matter was out of her hands.

To be perfectly honest, Miney had to admit that her parents had never actually said that either dancing or card playing was wrong. Miney had grown up with people who did neither just like Pa had never associated with anyone who drank. Now, she had heard that Rate Setterington--as Horatio was most often called--had not always been that particular, and that when Millie was but a lad, Horatio had drunk his whiskey in a saloon and had even attended dances. Of course, all that was before Father had got religion. Now, he was completely against drinking, smoking, dancing, *and* card playing. Pa had never really voiced his opinion in these areas she supposed because he had never felt it to be necessary. They just hadn't associated with people who did these things.

Pa hadn't smoked either, but he had chewed tobacco. Oh, how Miney remembered that dirty, old spittoon. Just the thought made her wrinkle her nose as she recalled how she hated cleaning it. The older he got, the more inconsiderate he had been. Why if Pa had sat in a chair, he expected Ma to have his spittoon right beside that particular chair. If he moved to another chair, he expected his wife, or a daughter, or just anyone to move the spittoon; if not, he would spit on the floor. Miney had even had to keep a spittoon at the farm because some days her father arrived before dinner and didn't leave until after supper. Most of the time he spent pouring over the Bible, and then he'd question her. If she gave a wrong answer, he made a note of the passage she should study; she knew she would be questioned on this particular passage in the near future. And all the while the spittoon had to be kept handy.

She also remembered how her father had always badgered a new preacher. Pa was always the first one in the congregation to invite the preacher for dinner after Sunday services; then, he'd proceed to bring up passages from the Bible and start asking all manner of questions. Usually, the poor man became completely confused, embarrassed, and apologetic much to her father's delight.

Since Pa had never really said anything about card playing, perhaps as long as there was no betting, there was no evil. That must be it--it was simply that some people used them for betting and therein lay the sin. Perhaps Millie hadn't been as wrong as she thought. She still couldn't reconcile herself that dancing was permissible. She knew being that close and familiar with a boy so as to touch while dancing boded no good, but then, Blanche was a good girl. Well, there was absolutely nothing she could do about the situation because Millie had spoken, and she knew for certain nothing could make him change his mind. She'd learned long ago how adamant Millie could be.

Ralph had remained as quiet as a church mouse listening to his parents and Blanche. By golly, Pa never said a great deal, but when he spoke, it sure counted. He could tell by Ma's tone of voice that she was mighty upset with Pa. Not that it would make any difference to Pa. One thing sure, his folks never argued much. It was blamed hard to argue all by yourself and that's what would have to happen; Pa just said what he had to say, and then told Ma to keep still. He knew it was difficult for his mother to bite her tongue and shut her mouth when there was so much more she wanted to say. Still, Ma could do it. Guess she must have learned the futility of trying to change her husband's mind when they was first married. Rate did wonder if Pa had been quite as stubborn when he had been courtin' Ma or whether it was a side of him that he sort of sprung on her after they was already wed. Maybe some day he'd ask Ma.

Now that he was getting older, Rate noticed that his mother was more likely to talk to him. Sometimes, she even drew him into a conversation when Blanche was around. Course Ma had always been interested in his school work, and she was glad he enjoyed reading. He'd heard her tell Aunt Lorin one day that when Ralph has his nose in a book, you just don't know he's around. Maybe she just liked it because he kept quieter when he was reading.

Golly, if Blanche was going to get to learn to play cards, he wondered if this applied to him too. Probably not, was the discouraging thought. Somehow, there often seemed to be one set of rules for Blanche and an entirely different set for him. Well, he could always hope. Dancing was for sissies, but cards--well, that just looked like a lot of fun. Maybe he'd just never bother to ask and simply take it for granted that what Blanche could do, he'd be permitted to do too. It was like walking on thin ice--if he was careful, no one would ever know the difference.

CHAPTER 2

Soon the nights became colder, the temperature dropped into the lower teens and failed to get above freezing during the day. Thus far, the snow had held off with only a few flurries now and then; therefore, the ground was still almost bare. Since it had been an unusually wet fall, there was a sizable pond of water just south of town which was now a smooth lake of ice. Rate had learned to skate out there last year because it was frozen long before the millpond was safe. However, it had not been flooded nearly as large as it was this year.

Each night after school, a group of boys and girls went out there to skate. The boys were forever playing crack-the-whip, even if the girls did complain. Girls were just sissies and didn't like to play rough games. Sometimes, when the boys felt in a congenial mood, they let the girls skate unmolested at one side of the pond while they dominated the larger portion. Even this little space satisfied the girls since they usually skated for a much shorter length of time than the boys, and they didn't play games.

Some of the larger boys were the ones who did the "cracking." That meant that when the line of boys held hands and skated along, they were the lead ones, and then they would suddenly stop, giving a hard pull to swing the line of boys around. Now, the lads on the very end of the line fairly flew across the ice, traveling a much greater distance than the rest.

On one of these occasions, Ralph was the tail end. When the whip cracked, he went skimming gloriously over the smooth ice. Oh, no! He was too close to the edge of the pond and was fast running out of ice. He turned his skates sideways to stop, but the tug of the boy beside him was too much. His skates struck the bare, frozen ground. As his hand was pulled from his companion's grasp, he attempted to run over the rough earth, lost his balance and down he went. Ouch! Ohmigosh, his knee hurt. It felt like someone had stuck a hot iron on it. Oh! Oh! He rolled on the ground clasping his knee in his hands.

In his fall, he had struck his knee on a sharp, frozen lump of dirt which had a jagged hunk of ice embedded in it. His friends gathered around, not knowing what to do to help. Finally, the initial pain lessened and he flexed the leg several times. It hurt, but he guessed he'd live. When he tried skating back across the pond, the knee throbbed. He hated to admit he was hurt, but he took off his wooden-top skates, fastened the straps together, slung them over his shoulder, and headed for home, trying his best not to limp--at least until he was out of sight of his friends.

By the time he arrived home, his knee was swollen and the pain was constant.

Miney noticed he was limping, but when she asked about it, Ralph said it wasn't much. He was in no mood for his mother's fussing, telling him that he should be more careful. She just never did understand why a fellow did the things he did.

A few days later, an abscess had formed, and since Rate could not bend his leg, Miney took him to the doctor. His knee was so painful he could hardly put his weight on that leg to hobble around. Doc Brown had looked at it, prodded it here and there adding greatly to Rate's discomfort, then said he guessed they'd best wait a day or two to see if it would break by itself. He suggested putting hot, moist heat on it several times a day. If it didn't break or dissolve, he'd have to lance it. He loaned Rate some crutches, and that was that.

Rate was to learn that it took some skill to handle himself on crutches. Worst of all was the flight of steps to go up at school to get him onto the main floor where his classroom was. His friends were sympathetic, but a few seemed to view the situation with levity. Then, there were those with a sadistic nature who wanted to torment him while he could do nothing to defend himself.

Bion Clement was one of the latter. He walked up to Rate and asked what had happened that he was on crutches. Rate explained. Bion asked, "This the one that's sore?" and delivered a swift kick to the very spot where the abscess had formed. Ralph could not refrain from crying out in pain.

George Lusk and Bud Grell wanted to catch Bion after school and give him a trouncing to pay him back, but Ralph told them he'd rather settle his own score. He looked upon Bion as somewhat of a sissy since Bion didn't often play the rougher games with Ralph and his cronies even though he was a good-sized lad.

A day later, Ralph Boone, who was known as the school's bully, got in his lick. A brawny lad with perhaps more brawn than brains, he never picked on any of the fellows his own size, he made sure they were smaller or couldn't fight back; he was at least three years older than Ralph. Just as Rate started down the steps to leave school at the west side of the building, Boone appeared running down the hall.

"Git outta my way, limpy," he called.

With that Boone gave Rate a shove which sent the young boy sprawling down the remaining steps.

"Told ya t' git outta the way, di'n't I?"

"Ralph Boone, you just wait. Someday I'll be big enough to black your eyes for this."

"Wanna make somethin' of it now?" bristled the bully. "Told you, I'll wait until I'm bigger. You'll see."

Boone laughed and ran out the door.

Rate's knee sure hurt. Brownie (Volney) McNall helped him get his books and crutches, then held the door while Ralph swung though.

The abscess was slowly dissolving which relieved some of the pressure making it feel some better. However, it was still mighty sore. The kick delivered by Bion hadn't helped, and now he had really banged it a good one falling down those cussed steps. Well, one day he'd get even with both Bion and Boone. Course Boone was a big fellow and was older; still, there'd come a time when Ralph was sure he would settle the score.

Millie had been doing Ralph's chores while the boy had to use crutches. A couple of nights ago, Ralph had walked around the house without the crutches, but Millie noticed tonight that Ralph was indeed favoring that right leg once more.

"Knee hurt?"

"Some," admitted Ralph.

"Thought it was gettin' better. What did you do?"

"Two things, I guess. Yesterday, Bion Clement just came up and kicked me on the knee, and then today, that Ralph Boone shoved me down the stairs just as I was coming home, and I banged it then."

"You do anything about it?"

"Told 'em both I'd get even one day, and I will. Course Boone is a big fella so I might have to wait a while," he conceded.

Millie nodded his head in agreement.

"Milford Setterington, I can't believe my ears. You were just encouraging your son to fight," exclaimed Miney.

Millie gave her a steady look, then said, "That's right. Both boys took advantage of him when he couldn't fight back. An eye for an eye, you know."

"Fighting solves nothing," she said, ignoring his Biblical reference.

"Blacking their eyes would make them think twict before they ever took advantage of him again," Millie pointed out.

"But I don't like to have him fighting like some common ruffian. He does enough of that now without you encouraging him. I've lost count of the black eyes he's had not to mention the torn clothes and missing buttons."

"Just never mind, Miney. It's nothing a woman would understand anyways." Of course, this ended the discussion even if Miney still seethed underneath.

After a few moments of quiet, Ralph ventured a question.

"Pa, someone at school said that his pa had worked for Grandfather hauling lumber. I never knew Grandfather had anything to do with lumber. Didn't he just run a general store and livery stable?"

"When he and my grandfather first came here from Canada, that's what they owned. Then, along with the livery stable, they did a lot of teaming. There were lots of little communities around which needed supplies and Pa furnished a team and wagon to haul freight. A man could rent just a team, a team and wagon, or a team, wagon, and man by the day. Pa accommodated them any way they wanted and charged a good price for the service, you can bet your bottom dollar on that.

"But he did get involved in lumber. He and a man named Potter bought lumber by the section from the government. Pa's father, John Setterington, owned a mill in Canada while Pa was growing up so Pa knew the lumber business inside and out. Potter had a mill in north where he sawed the logs; then, Pa and Potter had this agreement that when they paid their help, only part of the pay was in cold, hard cash, the rest was in due bills which could only be used in Pa's store to buy groceries and supplies. Never thought that was quite fair--forcing them to trade at Pa's. I asked Pa bout it once and he just told me that it was good business. Couldn't argue that any.

"I worked for Pa one year driving a team and hauled cured lumber from the mill to St. Johns. You realize that was afore the railroad had come through here to Ovid, so St. Johns was the nearest railhead to haul to. Why in those days there would sometimes be a hundred teams go through Elsie in one day, all loaded with lumber. I could carry 3,000 board feet of lumber to the load. I had it better than most because I'd come from the mill to Elsie in one day, stay overnight at home, then go to St. Johns the next day. I was paid a dollar per thousand so I got three dollars for each trip. Why, boy, I felt I was making money hand over fist. Course the team and wagon belonged to Pa, and I had no expenses, so I guess that was a pretty fair wage." Millie gave a hearty chuckle. "Besides, Pa never paid me in any of them gol-durn due bills, just gave me the cash.

"I was already plannin' on marryin' your Ma, so I saved the most of it to help buy us a farm. Pa had given me to understand that when I was ready to get married, he'd have a piece of property that he'd sell to me for a good price. Pa didn't know that I'd had my eye on any particular piece, but I had.

"I'll admit that the eighty didn't look like much the first time I saw it. Pa had traded Sherm Page forty acres of cleared land for that hundred and sixty acres of half forest and half swamp. The only building was the upright part of the house which was a barn at the time up on the south corner. Why, boy, I helped clear that land, helped drain where the buildings stand, and watched Pa supervise the digging of the ditch right through the trees. Even dug my share assessed by the Drain Commissioner which was on the next farm north. I've watched every stump taken out and helped put in all those rails for fences. Oh, yes, I knew what piece of land I wanted, so I hung onto my money like I was never going to see any more."

"Weren't you afraid Grandfather would sell it to someone else?"

"There were times when I gave it thought although I knew he wanted to put up some buildings because he'd be able to get a much better price. Believe me, Pa always looks at all the angles when there is money to be made. Well, anyway, when I was sure your Ma was going to marry me even though we hadn't set the date, I spoke to Pa about it, and just like he said, he gave me a good price on it. It's a good farm, Rate, and I was lucky Pa had got it in the first place."

Ralph didn't say anything, and Millie picked up the paper he'd been reading. Ralph wondered how they had moved the barn from the south line fence to become the upright of the house. Must have been a tremendous job. Had Grandfather already built the barn and that old granary and sheep shed before Pa had bought the place? Pa hadn't been too clear about that, and sometimes, Rate hated to interrupt to ask questions.

Guess probably Pa was right when he said it was a good farm because their crops were as good as any of their neighbors--better than some. Rate knew this for a fact. When it was threshing time or corn husking time, it was easy to see which farm had produced the best.

But then, if it was such a good farm, why in heck had Pa wanted to move into town? Blanche. Just because his sister couldn't drive back and forth like other girls, they had to move into town to make things easier for her.

Course he had to admit that Blanche didn't really ask to be coddled; there was many a time when Blanche would have preferred to do something herself, but Ma hadn't figured she should. In all fairness, Blanche could be mighty determined, and if she had to or wanted to, she could handle a horse right well. Fact was, he felt she was more reliable than Ma because Ma only wanted someone like Gyp or Old Mikey to drive because neither one ever got scared or hardly ever moved faster than a fast walk.

He guessed it wasn't exactly his sister's fault that Pa and Ma showed so much partiality. Sometimes, he felt that when she did something especially nice for him it was to help atone for their parent's behavior.

Ralph began to think of the farm; he wished they were going to move back come spring. Guess the place had changed a lot since Pa had owned it. First of all, there was only eighty acres now since Pa had sold the north eighty to his brother, John. That north eighty hadn't had any buildings on it so Uncle John had traded it back to Grandfather, and Grandfather still owned it although Pa worked it for him.

Rate remembered when the granary and tool shed had been built; the old granary had been moved onto the north eighty for a couple of years and then Pa had sold it to Ezz Garrett who'd moved it across the road and used it as a barn for a while.

From the time Ralph could remember, the field south of the house and north of the barn had been clear and tillable. Some of the trees in the orchard were still young although he never remembered the time when they had not produced fruit. Grandfather had set out most of the trees, but Pa had added the crabapple trees and the pear tree.

Back of the ditch was still uncleared except for about five acres south of the lane next to the ditch. Most of the timber had been cut on the south side, but the stumps still dotted the field, and in some cases, there were old logs from trees which had been blown down many, many years ago. Of course, Pa had been working on burning out the stumps, but it all took time. The sheep kept the pesky brush from taking over. Nature sure did work hard to reclaim the land; no sooner were the huge trees gone when here came the brush popping up all over the place. Made a man work, work, work, to cut the timber, clear the stumps, haul off the stones--of which there were plenty--and get it ready to plow. Even though Ma complained about how much trouble sheep were at lambing time, they did a mighty important job for the farmer. In fact, most farmers had at least a small flock for that very purpose since not many farms were completely cleared as yet.

No getting around it, Rate knew he was going to miss the farm. He liked seeing things grow. This watching things grow didn't exactly apply to a garden though because he didn't like having to hoe rows of vegetables or potatoes. Ma usually did the weeding herself since she said he and Blanche couldn't tell the vegetables from the weeds. Ralph grinned at this. He hated weeding even more than hoeing, so he had made sure a few vegetables came out with the weeds correctly assuming his mother would hesitate to ask him to weed anything again.

It wasn't that he didn't like vegetables because he did although peas and corn were the best. He liked turnips--if they were raw, that is. He often cut through the garden, pulled up a turnip, cut off the root, perhaps washed it in the stock watering tank if it was a little too dirty, and holding it by the leafy top, began to munch away. The tops he always threw to the pigs. He always felt Ma spoiled a perfectly good turnip by cooking it. He liked squash too, but with leaves that big, he could hardly use the excuse he thought it was a weed. Guessed he just felt working in a garden was beneath a man's dignity; he felt that men had much more important jobs to do, and that garden work was for women.

There was nothing beautiful about a garden, but a field of wheat billowing in the gentle breeze, or the particular shade of green which only oats get when they are first headed out, or maybe the beards on a field of barley--now, that was something worth looking at. Rate heaved a sigh. No use to think of such things now, he'd just have to make the best of the situation just as it was.

The winter proved to be a mighty cold one. The January thaw forgot to put in even a brief appearance, and February stayed near zero or the low teens even though there were days when the sun shone brilliantly from a blue-gray sky. In fact, it was setting a record for the coldest February that was to last for over seventy years.

Rate had finally recovered so he could once more go skating. Now, in midwinter, the boys usually went to the millpond where they often skated a mile or so up the winding river. At least there wasn't any chance of running out of ice when they cracked the whip here; naturally, Ralph had not given up the game just because of his accident. His mother's admonitions to be careful fell on a deaf ear, and he skated as vigorously as before. What was a little pain compared to the fun of skimming over the windswept ice, the glorious feeling of the wind at his back, a giant hand helping to push him ever faster.

Spring came late, but when the days finally did warm, they sometimes went unseasonably warm and the piles of snow left in record breaking time. George Onstott moved onto the farm the middle of March, so Millie no longer had to trek to the farm each and every day. George could now take care of the sheep which was a good thing since lambing time was rapidly approaching.

With the nearing of planting season, Millie became very busy selling farm implements for Mr. Pierce, and he also was much more active trading horses on the side. Somehow, this business of trading horses never had any appeal for Ralph. First of all, if he liked a horse--and he did have his favorites--he certainly didn't want to get rid of that horse just to fatten his purse with a few dollars. Besides, he'd often seen Grandfather and Pa shake their heads in wonder and laugh because Uncle John didn't know good horseflesh when he saw it, and Uncle John was always getting took on his trades. Course Pa often said that John was too damned stubborn to learn.

He never wanted to admit his Pa or his brother knew more about horses than he did. In fact, Uncle John was even more stubborn than Pa or Grandfather, if that was possible. At least Pa and Grandfather were never stubborn if it meant losing money. Course Pa would never admit he was wrong about anything; somehow, he'd manage to crawl out of the situation looking as though he'd been right all along.

With spring, when the streets were once more dry and solidly packed instead of being squishy and full of ruts, everyone brought out bicycles that had been stored for the winter.

Rate wanted a bicycle. He had learned to ride Bud Crell's at recess time in the school yard last fall, but he wanted one of his own. He guessed he'd ask Pa for one--it was a mighty fine bike they had bought Blanche a few years back. Seemed like they should feel he deserved a new bicycle too.

Ralph had hesitatingly approached his father. Millie had been his usual taciturn self and had hardly answered the lad, so Rate had no indication whether his father was receptive to the idea or not. He knew better than to press the matter further.

Then, came the day when Millie arrived home soon after school was out for the day.

"Rate," bellowed Millie from the street. "Where in thunderation are you?"

"Here, Pa," said Ralph coming from the back of the house munching on one of his mother's over-sized cookies. "What do you want?"

"Get on over here and find out."

Ralph dutifully trotted over to the wagon.

"There," said Millie. "I found you a bicycle today. Stopped by to see Charlie Randall and this kid came by pushing this here bicycle. Asked him if he'd sell it. Said he'd take a dollar fifty for it, so I took it before he changed his mind. 'Pears like I made a good deal. Well, boy, cat got your tongue? What do you think of it?"

Ralph looked at the battered, rusted bicycle, with the peeling paint, which rested on the wagon bed. He could not keep the crestfallen look from momentarily sweeping over his face. Then, he regained his composure, smiled at his father and said, "It's fine, Pa. Just fine. I'll get it out now and take it for a spin afore I do my chores. Thanks a lot." He spoke with much more enthusiasm than he felt.

Why had Pa bought him this hunk of junk when Blanche had rated a shiny new bicycle? It just seemed that no matter what, Blanche always came out best. The older they got, the more Pa favored Blanche. Course Ma had always showed partiality, but he figured that was just 'cause Ma liked girls best. 'Sides, everyone knew Ma hadn't even wanted any children much less a boy who was forever getting into mischief and getting himself hurt. Ma had always been good to him unless one counted against her all those switchings she had given him when he was younger. However, at first Pa had treated both him and Blanche with nearly the same consideration. In fact, he had been very vocal about his good luck to have a son to carry on the family name.

Now, the gulf was perceivably widening; the more Ralph tried to please his father, the less he succeeded. Milford never gave Rate a word of praise for any job no matter how well done. As might be expected, Millie was quick to voice disapproval, or even ridicule his son when Ralph attempted something which ended in failure. Seemingly, he never fully realized that the boy had feelings, that the barbs penetrated instead of bouncing off unnoticed.

The strangeness of this was that many times when Millie talked of his youth, he reiterated that Horatio had been a most difficult taskmaster, never praising, always condemning, and often punishing severely. It would have seemed plausible that Milford would not have followed so closely in his father's footsteps since they were distasteful to him.

However, the Setterington characteristics were deeply ingrained and apparently were to be passed from generation to generation with little or no modification. John, Millie's brother, was perhaps the exception. John's hatred for his father not only colored his thoughts, but warped his actions; he wanted to be anything he thought would irritate his father. John never felt this strongly about his mother; therefore, the possibility that what he did also distressed her, never occurred to him; he was far too busy planning his campaigns in the war against his father. No matter what position Horatio took on any issue, John was to be found aligned with the opposition. It was from these confrontations with his father he derived a sadistic sort of pleasure. To everyone else, he was known as a good-natured, good-hearted, fun loving, easy-going man who sometimes lived from hand to mouth with not a care in the world because he lived under the assumption that sooner or later something better would come along; therefore, there was no need to worry now.

Ralph had had the bicycle only a few days when a kid approached him and explained that the seat was a borrowed one and had not belonged to the boy who sold the bike. Rate had no cause to disbelieve the story, so he relinquished the seat to the kid who claimed it. Now, he not only had a rather battered, used bicycle, he had one with no seat. Oh, well, it was all right to ride a short distance around town although it would never serve for a longer trip. He gave a mirthless chuckle. Guessed he should be like Joe who could sit on the handlebars of his bike and peddle all over town. All the other boys had tried and tried to ride like this, but none had been able to manage. Ralph had tried a couple of times with Bud's bike, but hadn't had very good results. He'd tip over before he any more than peddled once. Yet Joe just zipped right along as if this was the only way to ride. No use to mention the episode about the missing seat to Pa 'cause he'd likely laugh and think the whole situation comical. Guessed he really didn't need a bike anyway 'cause he had plenty else to do.

CHAPTER 3

April was long past and with it the rain, the mud, the sunny-cold days with the damp penetrating winds that always took a person by surprise since the sun made one think it should be warm. Part of thinking it should be warmer was the result of waiting so many days for the ice and snow to be gone, the yearning for the soft, gentle breezes of spring.

Now that a new season for growing was at hand, work was begun to finish the landscaping around the new school. The building had been occupied last fall although there was still some finish work to be done, and so far, only paths led to the doors. Now, sidewalks were laid, a lawn seeded, shrubs and trees planted; at the north side there was a four foot terrace that went down to the playground. It had had to be repaired in spots where small gullies had formed from the spring rains. Now, the workmen were busy sodding the entire sloping area, and all the teachers announced at least once daily that no pupil was to walk on that new sod. In fact, some of the teachers issued this warning before each recess and again before the dinner hour.

Rate meandered along the complete length of the terrace, from the east end of the building to the west end at which point the whole lawn simply sloped gently to meet the playground. He could still see the outline of the freshly placed sod squares, but he realized that when the grass began to grow, it would be just one solid expanse of lovely green lawn. Sure did improve the looks of everything. In fact, the trees in the lawn, the bushes by the building, all this took away the look of not belonging; it seemed that the building had settled down, become a part of the land it set on instead of setting there raw, and new, and looking out of place. He guessed maybe the building looked smaller somehow, but that was all right; since he knew it really was big, the looks didn't matter all that much.

Yesterday, Rate had noticed a different teacher up in the high school. Someone had said that Mr. VanDeventer, the principal, was sick and that Mattie Smith, who was the County School Commissioner, had come to take over his classes for a few days. My, she was a tall, stern-looking, young woman; bet her face would crack if she smiled.

A day or so later, Ralph had been chasing a ball in the furthest corner of the playground when the bell rang for school to resume. Being Ralph, he could not report for class until he had located the ball which had managed to land in a clump of weeds where it wasn't easily seen; the playground was empty of children by the time he headed for the front of the building.

Since no one was around, he headed for the edge of the terrace--it being in line with the most direct route to the schoolhouse entryway--instead of going to the designated place for the pupils to go up the incline. He felt a small twinge of guilt as he started to walk up the new sod; he knew perfectly well he was disobeying the school rules, but he hadn't seen anyone ahead of him, everyone had already gone into the school.. In fact, he knew he was late, so he was already thinking of what plausible excuse he could give his teacher for being tardy.

He slipped to his knees halfway up the bank. Darn. He started to crawl on his hands and knees when someone grabbed his legs. Where had the person come from? He had thought he was alone. Must be they had hidden behind one of the bushes just so's they could spy on him. Thinking it had to be one of the kids teasing him, he rolled over and swung--and hit Mattie Smith right in the face. Ralph was sure his heart stopped completely when he looked into the fury of those dark eyes. Ohmigosh, what had he done now?

"Young man, not only do you flaunt school rules, but you dared to strike me." The voice was like a thunderbolt.

With that declaration, she began to shake him like a dog does a rat. His head flopped, and his teeth rattled. Good heavens, if she didn't stop, he just knew his head was going to fly off and go rolling across the playground. He guessed she was stronger than most women because it wasn't even winding her; she acted as if she could continue forever. She finally stopped and literally dragged him back to the place where he was supposed to have gone up the embankment in the first place.

"Now, young man, don't you ever let me catch you disobeying rules again. If you ever hit another teacher, I'll trounce you to within an inch of your life. Get to your classroom, and I hope you'll be able to give your teacher a satisfactory explanation for being tardy."

"Yessum."

Rate scurried off, adjusting his shirt as he went. Gripes. If she ever got hold of him again, she'd pretty near kill him, that's for certain. His neck hurt from the way his head had bounced from side to side. Still, he guessed he was lucky at that. He wasn't sure how, but he figured his punishment could have been worse. He'd never seen anyone angrier, that's for certain.

At least he still had the ball so maybe he could tell his teacher that it had taken him a while to locate it, and he hadn't wanted to lose it. He'd be darned if he was going to tell her that he'd just had a run-in with the School Commissioner. He'd never meant to hit *her*, only she'd never given him a chance to explain, just started shaking, and he sure couldn't get a word out with his head trying to flop in all four directions at once. How was he to know who'd grabbed him since they had grabbed him from behind? Especially since he was practically certain he was the only one left outside the building. Boy, that woman must have materialized out of thin air just like some haunt from the grave,

He had reached his classroom door; he smoothed a lock of hair back from his forehead, straightened his shoulders, drew a deep breath and entered the room. He was prepared for anything.

After school, Brownie had questioned Ralph about being tardy, but Rate had given him the same story he had told the teacher. He figured he'd been in enough trouble for one day, and he didn't want the story getting back to his folks. Pa would take a dim view of him pasting a teacher one even if it had been a mistake. He was pretty darned sure Pa would give him a licking, and Pa's lickings were nothing to fool around with. He remembered the last one from a summer or two ago. His backsides had been black and blue for days, and that first day he'd been mighty careful how he'd sat down in a chair. Even Ma had felt sorry for him although she hadn't dared voice disapproval to her husband. Not that he'd ever lied to Pa, but what Pa didn't know couldn't hurt none either.

Blanche liked having her folks live in town. She helped her mother in the house, to be certain, and she often helped with the cooking now that she was older. Still, there were many hours which were made much more enjoyable because she could have girlfriends over.

When she had stayed with Grandmother, she had always hesitated to have a friend visit because no one ever knew what Lovina might say. Somehow, Grandmother was just too outspoken and tactless for anyone to like her very much. In fact, Blanche's girlfriends were extremely timid around Lovina and were always ill at ease in her overpowering presence.

Blanche loved her grandmother, but not with the love she had had for Grandma Smith. Thinking of Grandma Smith made her sigh audibly. My, she did miss her an awful lot. Grandma Smith had been so kind and loving, and so soft-spoken; she just never found fault with anyone--could always see something good in everyone, even to the town ne'er-do-well.

Grandmother Setterington was awfully good-hearted at times, always ready to help a needy family or someone who had had a stroke of bad luck, but to balance the ledger, she was also bossy, opinionated, and could be somewhat of a snob; Blanche often felt that Grandmother's liabilities by far outweighed her assets.

Somehow, Blanche always resented having her Grandmother tell her what she should or should not do. Most of all, Blanche had resented the years when her grandmother had taken her to Christian's in Owosso to buy her school dresses. Never had it occurred to Lovina that perhaps Blanche might like to pick out her own dresses. She had simply asserted her authority and chose the dresses she felt were th best suited for school wear. Once Blanche had tried to discourage her grandmother from buying one particular dress because Blanche felt it was about the homeliest thing she had ever laid eyes on, all to no avail. Lovina had scoffed at her granddaughter and said that since she, Lovina, saw Blanche as others saw her, not just a reflection in a mirror, she was certain her judgment was by far the best. Blanche had started to remind her grandmother that since *her* father was paying the bill, it should certainly give her some say so. However, one look at the unbending expression on her grandmother's face made Blanche take a deep breath and accept the inevitable.

Sometimes, Grandmother looked as if she was carved from granite and was just as unmoving. Some day, Blanche vowed, she would not be dictated to by her grandmother, someday.

It was Blanche's turn to be hostess for the Fimbahu Club. After much bickering, the girls had arrived at this strange nomenclature by using the initials of the original members. There was Fern Wooley, Ila Shellenbarger, Bertha Meyers, Blanche, Gracie Albaugh, Hazel Hamilton and Ulah Wooll. At present, they had ten members. They met at some member's house each week, played silly little games, and talked a lot. Some of the girls were beginning to notice boys, so they ofter discussed "boys" to a great extent.

Actually, Blanche wasn't all that interested in boys, but she hesitated to admit this to the other girls, and they never seemed to notice that she contributed very little to the conversation at this time; mostly, she listened to their observations which she often felt were childish. At present, she had no intention of ever marrying, partly, she supposed, because she did not want to have children. Maybe if it could be guaranteed that she would have a girl, but no use to think about that. Like Ma had only wanted her, and yet, Ma had been blessed-..she wasn't at all sure this was the proper word--with a son as well.

Blanche had no idea how a woman got in the family way, she just knew that it only happened to a married woman, and that it was up to God whether the woman had a boy or a girl.

Blanche had tidied up the parlor and put cookies on a plate to serve her guests. Now, she spoke to her mother of the thought which had been uppermost in her mind while she prepared for the meeting.

"Ma, will you keep Ralph out of the parlor while the girls are here?"

"Land sakes, Blanche, what makes you think he'd want to hang around a group of girls?"

"Just to tease, I guess. Last time, he sneaked up to the door and was trying to listen to what we were saying. He only does it because he knows it bothers me. Can't you please keep him out of our hair?"

I'll do my best," she laughed. "Perhaps he will be off playing with the boys until supper time."

"Don't count on it. He knows what today is all right. This morning, right out of the blue, he asked me if I liked frogs. Honest, Ma, he just might stick a dirty, old frog or something like that in the parlor. I don't trust that boy a little bit."

"I think that is why he asked you about frogs--just to make you worry." "I certainly hope so. Brothers can be such a trial," she said with a sigh.

Miney watched as her daughter turned to leave the room. She was certainly becoming a young lady. There was a time when she'd have been angry with Ralph over his teasing, but now she took it all in stride; perhaps she had just learned to accept the inevitable. Not that Blanche let Ralph get away with anything, because she usually thought of something to do to get even. Miney, perhaps, was reluctant to admit it, but Blanche definitely had a streak of vindictiveness in her, another trait of Mother Setterington quite likely. Still, Mina was sure the children cared for each other. Blanche had apparently outgrown the jealousy she had harbored as a small child, and Ralph never acted as though he resented his sister in any way.

Goodness, another year and Blanche would be through school. A lot of girls were married soon after they finished their schooling, but so far, Blanche had not been interested in any special young man. In fact, she seldom mentioned boys at all. Miney did hate to think of Blanche marrying and leaving home.

Well, perhaps her daughter would become a school teacher, and then she'd be independent and not need a husband.

Miney had been past nineteen when she and Millie were married but if she had had any idea of what the intimate side of marriage was like, she'd have waited until she was older. Of course, she wasn't one bit sorry she had married Millie, he was a mighty fine husband and a good provider; it was just that she hadn't known what to expect. Ma had never told her what was expected of a woman except that she was to obey her husband. It had been a traumatic experience, but Millie had been patient and gentle. Now, Mina thought about Blanche under the same circumstances; it made goose bumps rise on her arms, and she felt the cold fingers of fear trace lightly down her spine; her poor, innocent, lovely daughter to be subjected to the indignities of the marriage bed.

Mina knew the girl should be told something, but how and what? How did she find the words to tell her daughter what to expect from marriage? She guessed she had better start asking the Lord for guidance.

Perhaps Miney had been even too embarrassed to present the problem to God because she never did tell her daughter any of the facts of life. Several times in the next few years she tried, could not find the words, so gave up; then, it was Blanche's wedding day, and it was too late. Miney was actually relieved.

Rate had come directly home from school, helped himself to a couple of cookies and some milk, but had left again. He knew his sister was afraid he'd do something to spoil her meeting. Now, he *had* given considerable thought to the idea of catching some frogs or a snake and turning whatever loose in the parlor; then, he had thought about how angry it would make Ma and had decided against any such ploy. Besides, he was afraid Ma might influence his father into taking some action, and Ralph never knowingly antagonized his father.

When Blanche was involved, Pa was darned awful unpredictable; he might think jokes were funny when played on most people, but he took a dim view of teasing if it was likely to anger Blanche, and snakes or frogs would sure upset her plenty; not that Blanche was lilly-livered about anything; she had plenty of spunk, more so than most girls. Naw, guess there would come other times when he could find something to do to his sister. Life sure would be dull without her, he reasoned.

It was an afternoon after school and Rate was headed for Brownie McNall's place. He had gone home right after school, changed his clothes, picked up his bb gun and left. Here came that Joe Oberlin who was a little older and ahead of Ralph in school. He might not be as much of a bully as Boone, but he sure did like to boss the younger kids around.

"Hey, Rate, where ya goin'?"

"None of your business," came the reply.

"Aw, come on, where ya goin'? Hey, let me see that gun," demanded Joe stepping squarely in front of Ralph.

"Just git outta the way. I'm in a hurry."

"I'm in a hurry," mimicked Joe. "And I said let me see that dumb ole gun. Can't you hear?"

"And I said move outta the way."

Joe made a grab for the gun.

"Let go, Joe. If I wanted you to see it, I'd give it to you. But I don't, so let go before I punch ya one."

The boys began to struggle in earnest. Somehow, Ralph's left hand was over the end of the muzzle when Joe's finger accidentally hit the trigger. The gun fired!

"Ow! Ow!" yelled Ralph. "Now, see what you've gone and done."

"Ohmigosh. I didn't mean to shoot you. Lookit, your hand is bleedin'," the lad observed, his eyes large and frightened.

"What did you expect? That bb is in there. Here, gimme my gun. It's all your fault."

"No, it ain't. Don't you go blamin' me. Ifn you tell, I'll get even. It weren't my fault atall," he objected, dropping the gun to the boardwalk.

Joe had started backing away from Ralph as he uttered his protestations. Now, he wheeled and ran.

Rate heaved a sigh, picked up his gun with his right hand from where it had dropped, and headed resignedly for home. He could just hear his mother since Ma had never been in favor of the gun anyhow. Well, he *had* learned one thing for damned sure. It didn't pay to cock a gun unless you intended to shoot it right away. That much had been just plain carelessness on his part. Gosh, that hand was beginning to throb. It wasn't bleeding all that much anymore he noticed as he looked at it disconsolately.

Rate had gone to the back of the house to come in through the woodshed. He prudently stood the gun in the corner before he came in the kitchen door. His mother wasn't there, so he proceeded through the dining room to the living room where she sat with her chair drawn up by the window to catch the best light for the embroidery work she was doing.

"Ma."

"What is it, Ralph?"

She looked up and saw the boy's face somewhat whiter than usual. "Land sakes, what's wrong?"

"There was an accident. I got shot in the hand. See."

He held out the hand, covered with dried blood, the small, round hole in the fleshy part of the palm still oozing blood.

Miney's face whitened. She stared at the outstretched hand a moment in silence as if struggling to regain her composure and decide what they should do next.

"Come, now, we'd best get you to the doctor. That bb will have to be taken out, that much is certain."

Mina was extremely upset although she tried to keep her voice natural. She possessed a nagging fear of firearms and even though this was just a bb gun, she still felt it was a dangerous weapon. Now, this accident had just proven her point. She didn't even berate Ralph for carelessness when he related the full story while she tidied her hair and found her pocketbook. Would that boy ever quit getting into trouble?

She hustled Rate off to Doc Brown's where the good doctor probed and probed and finally extracted the bb. The charge had been fifty cents.

Now, Ralph sat at the kitchen table soaking the hand in hot epsom salts water which the doctor had assured Miney was even better than salt pork. One thing at least, Ralph hadn't made a sound during the probing although his face had blanched, and she had seen the set line to his jaw as he gritted his teeth against the pain; he had watched the doctor's every move with no show of emotion.

The doctor had said he should soak the hand at least twice a day to promote healing. She just knew Ralph would rebel at this after a day or two. Well, if he gave too much trouble, she'd just have Millie speak to him. After all, if Mother and Father Setterington hadn't given Ralph the gun, the accident would never have happened. Believe you me, she'd be sure to tell Mother about the incident and would take great satisfaction in doing so. Not that it would make Mother regret her choice of gift; no, she'd probably think that in some way it was Miney's fault. Mother was not one to admit that she might possibly have made a mistake. Somehow, with Mother Setterington, Miney always felt she came out on the short end, and it was a most uncomfortable feeling.

At least the hand healed well, leaving only a small red scar which would whiten with time.

Millie had not been overly concerned with the incident, figuring Ralph had certainly learned to be more careful. Miney had been satisfied because it had healed properly. Rate had viewed the incident as simply one more rung on the ladder of life.

Some things just happened, so what was a person to do except take things as they came? No use cryin' over spilt milk.

Rate had been giving plenty of thought to a job for the summer. Life on the farm had kept him reasonably busy, but here in town, there was not that much to keep him occupied. School would be out in another month and then what?--a lot more time to while away.

Rate had been talking to Inez Doty, whose father owned Doty's Hotel, the big white building on the main four corners, and she had said she was going to pick strawberries for Tillotsons. Maybe he'd see if he could pick too, even if picking strawberries wasn't much fun. He'd heard Blanche talking to Ma and she'd said she had given it some thought because she'd like to make a little money. Ma hadn't been too keen on the idea because Ma was old-fashioned and didn't think a proper brought up young girl should do work outside the home unless it was housework.

Besides, like as not, her hands and arms would get browned from the sun; a sunbonnet would shield her face, but a body couldn't pick strawberries with gloves on, and how Miney did hate to see a girl get tanned. A girl should have a delicately white complexion if she was to be considered a lady.

Somehow, Rate had the feeling that Blanche did not go along with Ma's ideas even a little bit. One thing sure, Blanche had a mind of her own. Sometimes she even reminded him of Grandmother, but she'd skin him alive if she ever heard him say that. Sure was funny how mad she got when she was expounding her views on something, and Pa would just quietly say, "Grandmother." Sure made Blanche pull in her horses in a hurry. Once he'd dared to laugh, and she'd kicked him under the dinner table. Course it hadn't really hurt, and it had been worth it just to get her goat a little.

Rate had been wandering around the business section of town, looking at the displays in the windows, when he noticed Mr. Downey, of the Wooley and Downey Hardware, putting a lawnmower in the window. It carried a price tag of seven dollars dangling from the handle. Jeepers, that was a lot of money. Bet a person could make money mowing lawns. Maybe he should check into the matter. Say, maybe he could mow the school's lawn. That should bring a good price since it was so large. Tomorrow, after school, he'd ask the superintendent if they had hired anyone for the job.

Rate discovered that the job was still open, and that it would pay a whole dollar for a weekly mowing although he had been cautioned that mowing also included trimming around the newly planted trees. Wow! At that rate, it wouldn't take long to pay for a mower. For some reason though, he didn't quite feel like asking his father for a loan. Pa was mighty hard to figure out at times, and Rate was afraid his father would laugh at his idea. Nope, he'd have to do this for himself.

Ralph wandered past the hardware store. He turned, retraced his steps, then stopped to look in the window. Sure was a nice looking lawnmower, all shiny and new. Finally, he decided to go inside to get a closer look. Up the steps, through the door, to the sound of a tinkling bell. Yup, there it was. It looked even better from a closer view, the reels were painted silver and trimmed in bright green, the handle was varnished wood.

"Well, Rate, going to buy that there lawnmower?" asked Mr. Downey, one of the partners, as he came to stand beside the boy.

"Oh, hello, Mr. Downey. Well, it's a fine looking mower only I don't have seven dollars."

"Are you interested in buying it?" he persisted.

"Sure would like it. If I had a mower, I could get the job of mowing the lawn for the school. I spoke to the superintendent yesterday and they pay a whole dollar. Like as not I could get other jobs around town."

"Sounds like you could have a profitable business."

"Mr. Downey, I've got a dollar. Could you maybe trust me for the rest and each time I mow the schoolyard, I'll bring the money to you until it's paid for?"

The boy watched the older man's face wistfully.

"Well, Ralph, I'd have to give that some consideration. Have to talk financial matters like that over with my partner, you know. We'd have to take a mortgage on the mower. Do you know what a mortgage is?"

Rate nodded his head; his grandfather had explained that bit of terminology to him one day when Horatio had been explaining a little about the operations of a bank.

"Suppose you come back tomorrow after school, and we'll see what we can work out."

The older man's eyes twinkled, and he smiled kindly.· The look of enthusiasm on the youngster's face made it light up like a Roman candle. Mr. Downey knew the family well, so he had no reservations about entering into such a sale, the lad would be as good as his word. He just didn't want the boy to think everything came easily; however, he already knew what the answer would be.

Ralph had dashed home after school long enough to throw his books on the table, grab a cookie, find out what his mother wanted from up town--she wanted at least one thing each night--and then he took off for the hardware store.

He hardly dared hope that Mr. Downey would actually let him have the lawnmower for only the dollar deposit. His steps slowed the nearer he got to the store. Guess he'd go get the pound of beefsteak his mother wanted first. He angled cater-corner across the street to the butcher shop. Ma had given him exactly twelve cents. Ralph always hated that because he knew it was near to impossible to cut a slice of round steak to weigh exactly one pound, but Ma was too tight to understand. She wanted it sliced very thin so it looked like more, he guessed, and he knew she would brown it until it was actually tough, just so's she could have nice, brown gravy.

After purchasing the meat, he sauntered back along the street until exactly opposite the hardware; with an audible sigh, he stepped up onto the dusty street, scuffing his bare feet in the powder-fine dirt, moving slowly, delaying the moment of facing the storekeeper again as long as possible, such was his fear that Mr. Downey and Mr. Wooley would not think him a good financial risk.

While a rather solemn lad entered the hardware, it was a bouncy, happy lad who came out. He had his precious lawnmower, shoving it carefully in front of him. Oh, boy! He'd start lining up customers as soon as he took the beefsteak home. Course the lawns hadn't started to grow much yet so it would be a week or so before he could use his new mower. Wonder what Pa would say?

Rate found several lawns to mow, including the schoolyard. He mowed some of the smaller ones for ten cents, while for one of the largest, he was paid the astronomical figure of thirty-five cents.

As to what his father thought, Ralph never knew. In his usual noncommittal way, Millie had failed to comment except to remind Ralph that he still had to take care of the horses. Poor Ralph. Once again he was disappointed because his father had failed to give him any words of praise or encouragement.

At least Ma had approved and said that he and Blanche could take turns keeping their own lawn mowed. Always before, the lawn had not been cut, and there had only been paths to the outhouse and to the street from both the front and back door. Miney was certain the place would look much nicer with a neatly mowed lawn, especially since it was such a large corner lot.

Rate had mowed the lawn the first time since there were places where the ground was rough because of the old, dried grass, the remnants of last year's growth. It had been a rather difficult task and he had had to rake and mow and mow and rake to get it all finished. Most surprising of all was the fact that his mother gave him a whole dime for his trouble. Guess sometimes Ma did appreciate him. Said that she liked it better because when the grass got long, she just knew snakes often came right up to the house. In fact, one had crossed her path while she was going to the outhouse one day; she had been so startled she had nearly screamed, and this would have mortified her to death because someone might have noticed where she was going.

It was an unusually warm day in mid-June, and after much arguing, it was decided that since Blanche had been visiting almost from the time school was out-- she'd been to South Lyon to visit first Grandmother and Grandfather, and then had gone to stay with Aunt Ruby--it was certainly her turn to mow the lawn. Rate wanted it done today because he only had two lawns to mow on Tuesday, and he had done them as soon as the dew went off. Tomorrow would be a much busier day for him since he picked strawberries every other day.

Tillotsons owned a sizable chunk of ground north of the school which they had planted to row upon row of strawberries. They didn't have any trouble harvesting such a large crop because half the kids in town were willing to pick at least a few quarts. Each picker was assigned a row with the exception of the few who were so undeniably slow that two pickers were forced to work together on the same row.

It was while picking strawberries that Ralph often watched Inez Doty with something akin to envy. Inez's nimble fingers flew as she moved steadily down her row. Every picking day, she finished her row and because Ralph was so far behind, started at the other end of his row and picked to meet him. Try as he would, fifty-five or sixty quarts were all he could pick in a day while Inez turned out one hundred quarts like clockwork. They were paid one cent a quart for each quart picked so that meant each day Inez took home a whole dollar. He just wished he knew how she managed. Inez good-naturedly teased him about how he wouldn't be able to get along without her to finish his row. She was all right--for a girl, that is.

Ralph had been hoarding his money to have more to spend come the Fourth of July. Other years, Ma had always given him a quarter and sometimes Pa had given him one so he'd had a whole half dollar to spend, but just once he'd like to be able to spend as much as he pleased. Course, he was paying Mr. Downey most of what he made from mowing lawns so in a few weeks the lawnmower would belong to him. Then, Ma had made sure that since he was making money of his own, he had to put his own money in the collection plate at Sunday School and again at Church. Course, Ma made Blanche do the same, so at least in the area of Church, she treated both son and daughter alike.

Blanche had finally capitulated with regard to mowing the lawn, realizing her brother had a valid complaint, but secretly enjoying forcing him to argue his point; she had set in with a will to get the lawn mowed before supper. She never was one for dallying around, always jumped right into anything that needed doing, especially if she disliked the job, to get finished as soon as possible. Mowing lawn was not one of her favorite pastimes although she was quite satisfied with the end results.

The grass was taller than usual in some spots, and she found that the lawnmower did not mow as well when the grass was overly long; it sometimes slid over the grass without cutting, or it pushed so hard she could scarcely move it. She found that by pushing it forward a foot or so, then pulling it back and pushing it forward again, it cut much better even if it was hard work. She just bet that Ralph had been too busy between picking strawberries and mowing lawns for money to bother with their lawn for well over a week.

Goodness, she was breathing hard. Didn't seem as though she had exerted herself this much. Blanche mowed another round. She was definitely having difficulty breathing. She left the mower and started for the kitchen door. Her breaths were coming in gasps. Her chest heaved as she labored to breathe. The air rattled from her mouth as her body worked to force the air from her lungs, and then she gulped to fill her lungs anew with the life-sustaining oxygen. Her lips showed a blue tinge as she became cyanotic.

"Ma! Ma!" she managed as she came in the door and dropped into a straight-backed chair standing by the kitchen table.

Miney came from the dining room. "Blanche! What on earth is the matter?"

"I - I - don't - know. I - I - I - can't hardly - breathe," she managed in between gasps.

"Goodness. I'll call Doc Brown and see if he can come immediately."

Miney rushed to the phone on the wall, turned the crank hurriedly, fumed with impatience because it seemed that it took Central forever to answer her ring, and even longer to ring the doctor's office. Thank goodness the doctor was in and would come right over. She returned to Blanche.

"Let me help you to the couch. Perhaps it will help if you lie down."

"All - - - right," wheezed Blanche.

Rate came in at this moment, stared at the scene before him, then asked, "What's wrong with Blanche? She's breathin' awful funny." He observed his sister in wonder, a frown creasing his forehead.

"I don't know, Ralph. I just don't know. Help me get her onto the couch."

Ralph took one arm and Miney the other. They half-lifted Blanche from the chair and propelled her into the sitting room to the couch. When she laid down, the rasping breathing became much worse and Blanche struggled to sit up.

"I - I can't, Ma. I - can't - breathe at - all when - I lie down," she panted.

"Oh, dear, I don't know what to do. Were you mowing lawn?"

Blanche nodded her head.

"I do wish that doctor would hurry."

Miney wrung her hands, anxiety showing on her face and in her every movement. She went to the window, pushed back the curtain and peered up the street. Not a sign of the doctor. She turned back to watch Blanche whose chest was still working like a bellows in a forge, desperately attempting to provide her body with the needed oxygen. It was difficult for Miney to watch her beloved daughter fighting for each gasp of breath. Never had Miney felt quite as helpless. If only Millie was home, not that he could help Blanche, but his presence would have made Miney feel less anxious. She felt certain he would have shown no undue concern even in these circumstances, and it would have been anyone's guess as to what he felt. Millie just seldom showed his emotions.

"Here comes Doc across the back yard," observed Ralph.

"Land sakes. Of course he'd come that way. It's much shorter. Guess I haven't been thinking clearly."

Miney met the portly doctor at the kitchen door, and quickly ushered him into the sitting room. Doc Brown took one look at Blanche, then looked at Miney.

"Asthma."

"Asthma! Whatever brought that on? There's been no indication before. What can you do for it?"

''Not a whole lot, Miney. We don't know enough yet."

While he talked, he looked through his black bag searching for a specific bottle. He finally came to the one for which he was obviously looking.

"Rate, get me a teaspoon. Miney, I'll give her this liquid now and give you some tablets to have her take each day. Hopefully, the liquid will stop this attack, or at least lessen it to some degree."

Rate returned with the spoon and watched as the doctor filled it with the most horrible smelling, thick, greenish medicine.

"Now, Blanche, it's going to be hard for you to swallow, wheezing like you are. You've got to time it just right so you won't choke yourself. Understand?" She nodded. "Perhaps you had better take the spoon yourself. Here." He carefully transferred the spoon with its evil-looking contents to Blanche's outstretched hand. Even though her hand was trembling from the exertion, Blanche dutifully swallowed the medicine in between gasps. "Now, we have to wait."

"How long is it going to take for Heaven's sake?"

"Hopefully, not more than half an hour. At least in that length of time we should notice some improvement; if there's going to be any."

"Oh, my, that long?" Then his words registered on Miney's worried mind. "You-- you mean it may not help?" she asked as though she was afraid she had not heard him right.

"Well, Miney, you can't expect miracles. Her system has to absorb the medicine, In a few cases; it doesn't help, We'll hope Blanche isn't one of those. Now, I'll leave these tablets and she's to take one with each meal. If she's better in a day or two, you can discontinue using them. This liquid is to be taken only when she has an acute attack."

"You mean there will be more?" Miney asked incredulously.

"Quite likely. She may never have one as severe as this. There's no way to tell that I know of."

In about twenty minutes, Blanche's breathing was gradually becoming easier; no longer did her chest heave, nor did she gasp so hurriedly for air, and no longer was there a rasping sound emitted from her throat. While the breathing was far from normal, it was certainly not as labored even to an unpracticed eye.

"Well, Miney, the worst is over." Even the doctor gave an audible sigh of relief. "See, her lips are losing their blue tinge. She'll be all right now. Give her another spoonful of this in another half hour and I think that should do the trick."

Blanche hoped so too. She felt weak and tired. Must be from working so hard to breathe. Seemed like the air came in all right, but it had been such an effort to expel it so she could get some more. Perhaps it wouldn't have been as bad if she had stopped mowing when she first felt wheezy. She bet the next time she would certainly quit whatever she was doing the minute she noticed her breathing was not normal. In no way did she ever want to be like this again.

The first attack was her worst, partly because Blanche recognized the early symptoms and would immediately take some of her medicine to ward off the onslaught. However, while not a debilitating disease, it most assuredly was an aggravating one. It did try Blanche's patience although she realized there was absolutely nothing she could do about it except restrict her activities somewhat. She learned to avoid extremely dusty places, pollen-bearing weeds, and strenuous physical activity was limited to very short periods of time. Oh, yes, she learned to live with it, and it never once occurred to her to indulge in self-pity.

CHAPTER 4

Haying time had come, and since Millie was now employed by Mr. Pierce, he hired the Keenan brothers, Merval and Jim, and Cash Waldron to do the lion's share. There was one field on the south forty and the fields on the north eighty. Charlie Sweet and Ed Clark had been hired to do the mowing. A man and a team got a dollar fifty for a day's work; a man alone received a dollar. This meant they worked from the time the dew went off in the morning until six or later at night--usually a ten hour day.

Since there was no means of providing the men with a hot meal--there was no house on the north eighty and the small one on the forty had no stove or furniture-- Miney fixed the men a cold dinner each day and drove out to the farm so they could eat at exactly noon. She worried a little because there couldn't be much variety for the men--not everything carried well--although as she watched them wolfing down her roast beef sandwiches, made of thinly sliced meat between thick slices of bread, generously spread with butter, washing them down with lemonade, she felt they didn't much care what the food was as long as there was plenty of it. She managed to have a fresh raspberry pie each day and noted with satisfaction they often came back for seconds; no doubt about it, Miney baked a really tasty pie although hers were rather thin because Miney did not use a deep pie tin; however, her crust was always thin and flaky, so one didn't mind that there wasn't a lot of filling.

She half suspected that lemonade, kept cold in a heavy brown crock, tasted better to them on a hot day than a hot cup of coffee. Lemons were rather reasonable this year or they might have had to make do with just plain water since tea was so expensive she seldom bought any for herself even though she did appreciate a good cup of tea now and then.

All of this certainly did add to her work and she, for one, would be glad when the haying was finished. This year, Millie had made arrangements with Mrs. Onstott to feed the baler men. Thank goodness for that. Miney had always dreaded the time when the baler came. She hated seeing it pull into the yard and heaved a big sigh of relief when it left.

There were times when she felt the role of a farmer's wife was a hard lot in life; wouldn't be so bad if a woman only had to look out for the needs of her own family, but there was always the cooking for extra men; summer months often meant a hired hand lived with them, meaning more washing, more cooking, and more dirt tracked into the house.

At least living in town had lessened her burden somewhat. She wondered if poor Mrs. Onstott knew what she was getting into when she had said she'd feed the baler men? Well, perhaps she had done it before. Miney supposed the earning of a little money of her own was quite an incentive for the woman. Miney fervently hoped all went well for her.

Each year, shortly after the haying season was finished, men came with a baler to bale the hay from where it was stored in huge stacks. That meant there were five hungry men to feed for breakfast, dinner, and supper since the men slept in the barn for the three or four nights they had to stay at one place. Millie sold this baled hay directly to Hanken Bros., a feed mill down by the depot; it was his best cash money crop. The cities harbored a multitude of horses, and it took many farmers like Millie to provide the feed for their voracious appetites.

Rate had the astounding sum of a dollar and a half to spend for the Fourth. He'd been awfully quiet about having so much money in hopes that his father, or his mother, or both would give him a little more. Course Blanche had wrecked that at breakfast. She must have sneaked into his room and snooped until she found his little cache because she knew almost to the penny how much he had. She'd looked at him smugly, and then spoke to no one in particular.

"Ralph's got a lot of money saved for today."

At the word "money," Miney pricked up her ears like a hound on a fresh scent just like both Blanche and Ralph knew she would.

"How much do you have, Ralph?"

He kicked his sister under the table, while she gave him a sweet smile, full of innocence.

"Well, I been saving what I could of my strawberry money. What I didn't have to put into the collection at Sunday School and at Church," he said pointedly.

"That didn't say how much."

"He's got a dollar and sixty cents," volunteered Blanche.

"Is that so, Ralph?"

"No. It's only a dollar fifty. I spent a dime. Ma, she's been snoopin'," he accused.

"Blanche, were you going through Ralph's things?"

"I just wondered how much money he had. That was all. I didn't touch nothing else. Besides, I do have to go in his room if I'm to make his bed, don't I?"

"And, young lady, that is all you are supposed to do. Would you want Ralph going through your things?"

"Oh, Ma, you make it sound so awful. I didn't mean any harm," she defended herself.

"Well, Ralph, since you already have much more than you should spend today, I don't think you need for me to give you any change, do you?"

"I guess not," was the disappointed reply. He avoided looking at his mother. However, he glared at his sister. Just wait, one day he'd get even with old Miss Big Mouth.

Millie had not entered into the conversation, but had kept quietly on with his meal. As he left the table, he spoke to his young son.

"Rate, come outside with me."

"All right, Pa."

Ralph hastily finished his glass of milk and followed his father out to the woodshed.

Now what? Was Pa mad 'cause he'd managed to save some money but wasn't telling anyone about it?

"Well, boy, you've done right well hanging onto money, haven't you?"

"I reckon so. I give part to the Church like Ma says, and I've only got one more dollar to pay on the lawnmower."

"'Pears to me your Ma don't understand such things. Well, not that you need it, but here's a half dollar for today."

"Oh golly Pa. Thanks a lot! I've been lookin' at a jackknife," he confided. "'Cause you know how sometimes they have special prices for the Forth, so I thought I might just buy me one. I got my eye on a real fine one with three blades and a brown and white bone handle. Maybe it will be on sale. Did you want anything else Pa?"

"No. Just don't mention it to your ma. She'd think I was spoilin' you, and we know better, don't we?" Millie winked at his surprised son, then headed for the barn.

"We sure do," Rate called heartily after his father's disappearing figure.

Golly, Pa sure was full of surprises. Now, who would have thought his father would be so generous? He wished he dared to tell Blanche, but she'd tattle to Ma right away. Well, maybe Ma hadn't given him any money, but he still had two whole dollars which was an awful lot of money. Why there just wouldn't be anything he couldn't do today.

It had been a wonderful Fourth of July. There had been a band from Greenbush, the usual horse drawing contests, the horse race from the west city limits to the main four corners of town. Each store had a stand on the boardwalk in front of their place of business, gaudily decorated in red, white, and blue. There had been a baseball game in the afternoon between the Elsie Independents and a team from Maple Rapids; Rate liked baseball so he had been one of the noisiest spectators, heckling the opposing team and cheering the home-town boys. The speeches the speakers gave in the morning hadn't interested him particularly although he had listened quietly out of respect for the speakers. The dancing on the stage built just for this occasion didn't interest him either although he enjoyed the music, and he liked hearing the caller sing the square dance calls accompanied by the rhythmic clapping of a happy crowd.

His money? Well, he had spent a goodly amount. First of all, he'd bought himself that knife he'd wanted. They had had cheaper ones, but his had cost seventy five cents; sure was pretty though. Then, he'd bought candy, drunk lemonade, played some games and had even spent some time at the shooting gallery. At first they'd tried to tell him he was too young, but he'd argued good-naturedly and had won out. He wasn't that good a shot yet--a rifle handled a lot different than a little, old bb gun--but there'd come a time when he'd be able to hit those moving targets, and then he'd have the laugh on them.

Anyway, it had been one swell day and he guessed the best part of it was that most of what he had spent, he'd earned himself so he didn't have to feel beholden to anyone, nor did he have to account to anyone as to how he'd spent his money. It was a mighty good feeling, and he was well satisfied with himself and his station in life.

He wondered if Blanche had had half as much fun as he had. She and her friends seemed so old, and he just wondered if they ever enjoyed anything. They walked around sedately, talked with boys, and didn't seem to do much. Course, who could tell about girls since they got pleasure out of the strangest things.

July 5, and Blanche's sixteenth birthday. Goodness, it didn't seem as though she should be that old. One more year and she would be graduating from school. Blanche studied her reflection in the mirror as she pinned her hair back and tied it with a wide, satin ribbon. Just what would she do when she finished school? Some of the girls were already talking about when they got married and most of them intended to sit at home and wait for some man to come along with a proposal. Well, one thing she knew for certain, that was not for her. She supposed she'd get herself a job someplace, but she hadn't the slightest notion as to what she'd like to do. Blanche slipped the chain of a gold watch over her head. She smiled as she looked at it in the mirror. She remembered last year when she'd worn it for the very first time.

It had been on the morning of her birthday when she had come into the kitchen as usual to help her mother with breakfast, and if Ma had absentmindedly noticed that her daughter was in exceptionally high spirits, she said nothing. Blanche chatted away about the festivities of the day before; they had spent nearly the whole day in Elsie since the Fourth of July was a holiday that Millie in particular enjoyed. He liked standing around swapping yarns with men he hadn't seen for months; of course, Miney always fixed a special picnic lunch for the day, and Millie did love to eat.

It wasn't until they were clearing the table that Miney noticed the watch Blanche was wearing on the chain around her neck. She stopped in the middle of picking up a plate.

"Ettie's watch. You're wearing Ettie's watch," accused Miney.

"That's right, Ma," was the rather defiant reply.

"Really, Blanche, you should have asked," admonished Miney.

"But, Ma, have you forgotten what today is? Uncle George said that I could wear Aunt Ettie's watch when I was fifteen. Well, I"m fifteen today," she announced triumphantly.

"So you are. I do remember that was the stipulation. Please be careful of it, Blanche."

"Oh, Ma! When are you going to quit treating me like a child?"

"I'm sorry, dear, I didn't mean to sound that way. It's just that Ettie's watch is an expensive piece of jewelry, and since she valued it so highly, I wouldn't want it to get broken."

"Don't worry. I think it is beautiful, and it is quite the nicest thing I own. Besides, I wouldn't want to let Uncle George down. He is my favorite uncle, you know."

"Yes, you've always made that quite evident just like Mary is your favorite aunt."

"Does it show that much?"

"I'm afraid it does. Not that you aren't polite as behooves a well-brought-up young lady, but it is easy to tell who your favorites are."

All of her girl friends had been properly impressed with her gift. Much as she had only tolerated her Aunt Ettie, she had really been very appreciative of so fine a gift. It was a shame Aunt Ettie had died leaving Uncle George and the boys alone. Blanche smiled at her reflection in the mirror and once again looked admiringly at the watch. She sometimes felt guilty because she hadn't really liked Aunt Ettie, and she supposed there had been times when she could have been nicer to her. Ma was right, there was a world of difference between her aunts; Lorin was peculiar, Ettie had been afraid of her own shadow, but Mary was warm-hearted, kind, and full of fun; she loved having a group of young ones around her.

Yes, thought Blanche, Aunt Mary, who was only Ma's half sister and quite a bit older, was just the grandest person in the whole world, next to her mother that is. She was more like Grandma than any of the girls, so patient and kind.

Ma wasn't any more like Grandma than Aunt Ettie or Aunt Lorin. Except where her in-laws were concerned, Ma was completely sure of herself and somewhat conceited because Ma always thought anything she did, she did better than anyone else. Of course, this was partially true. Blanche knew that her mother's crocheting was beautifully done and not many women were as painstakingly neat. The same could be said about her embroidery. Somehow, Mina's colors always were blended with exquisite taste; she had an artist's eye for color, and her stitches were dainty and carefully made. When it came to piecing quilts, Miney liked the more intricate patterns and here again, they were painstakingly assembled. Blanche never knew why her mother had never knitted, but somehow this had never appealed to Miney. Grandma Smith had kept them in heavy, black, woolen stockings when she and Ralph were real young. When Grandma could no longer make them, Miney had resorted to store bought stockings.

Guess maybe Ma did have reason to think her work was better than most only sometimes Blanche wished she wasn't quite so outspoken about it since on more than one occasion, Blanche had been embarrassed by her mother's frank statements. One thing was certain, if you didn't want an honest answer, you should never ask Mina Setterington what she thought because no matter how tactless, she gave her honest opinion; never did Miney try to spare another person's feelings by carefully wording her remarks, she was blunt and painfully honest.

There, she guessed she was ready to go downstairs. Wonder what she'd get for her birthday from Ma and Pa. One never quite knew what to expect because the gift often hinged on whether her mother was on one of her austerity binges. Mina had never recovered from her frugal childhood and never could quite believe that times were now better, or that her husband was essentially a good provider. Well, she'd best hurry if she was to be of any help with breakfast.

Blanche had had to wait until the evening meal for her gift. Miney had baked and frosted a cake for the occasion. She had then given Blanche a new apron--a sure indication Miney was being very frugal since the apron was something she had made. However, later in the evening, Pa had managed to slip her five shiny new silver dollars. Since Blanche knew better than to let her mother know about Pa's gift, she'd just bide her time and then buy something she wanted. Pa sure was mighty generous, but then, the Setteringtons had never had to live as frugally as the Smiths.

Along with the hay Millie had already put up, he had a field of wheat on the south forty to harvest. Ralph had gone with Millie to the forty when his father had decided the wheat was ripe enough to cut; it was a little late this year due to a colder than usual summer. Millie hired Jim Keenan and Cash Waldron to work shocking the grain since Ralph was still too small to handle the bundles.

Rate liked the looks of the shocks in the field. After Millie made a few rounds with the binder, which cut the grain, tied it into bundles, dropped them off to the side so the bundles would not be in the way for the next round around the field, the men followed to pick up the sheaves. One man grabbed a bundle in each hand and set them together with the heads braced against each other, then the other man set his two bundles up to form a cross; next the spaces were filled in for a total of eight bundles in a circle; the last step was to lay two bundles on the top, split so that the heads hung down, to cap it which enabled the shock to shed rain instead of letting the water soak into the dry heads.

Rate liked the looks of wheat shocks better than oat shocks since with oats, they simply placed two bundles on each side of an imaginary line, leaned the heads together and made a long, low shock standing north and south to take advantage of the drying sun on both sides. Besides, oats were easily knocked down in a high wind where the wheat shocks stood much more solidly.

Ralph had driven Gyp to the forty. She had been his horse to drive ever since he had been big enough to harness a horse by himself. She was good and steady, and on occasion he could get her to break into a run for a short distance. He guessed he was right lucky since not every boy his age had his own horse to drive.

From under the shade of an old elm, Rate noticed that Millie had stopped part way around the field, so he meandered over to see what was wrong. Millie was watching Mr. Andrews, who lived across the road, trying to drive a likely looking bay. The animal reared, sashayed from side to side, backed up, and did everything but go quietly ahead.

"Looks like Andrews has bit off more'n he can chew. Way it looks to me, he's never gonna drive that mare," observed Millie. He wrapped the lines around the lever that raised the header and clambered down off the metal seat. "Let's you and me mosey over and see whose horse it is," suggested Millie. "Don't think I've ever seen her here before."

Andrews had given up trying to make the mare do anything. He held the lines limply in one hand a perplexed expression on his face, as if trying to figure out what to do next. The young mare stood quietly, head turned, ears forward, watching his every move. She had an open bridle so no blinders hampered her view. It was as though man and beast were sizing each other up; the mare had won the first encounter and was certainly ready and willing to meet any move the man made with good-natured but determined resistance.

The men greeted each other, and Millie found out that the mare belonged to a man named Beck.

"Think he'd want to trade?" inquired Millie. "I've got a good driving mare I'd swap for this one."

The man didn't know, but he admitted that Beck hadn't had much success with breaking the mare. She was three years old and should have been driving decently now, but look at her. She had proven to be balky and completely unpredictable. He said he'd call Beck and perhaps the man would come talk to Millie.

Millie returned to his work. Rate had a sinking feeling. If the man, Beck, showed up, he just knew Pa was going to trade Gyp. Wouldn't do any good for him to tell Pa he didn't want Gyp traded 'cause Pa would do just as he damned well pleased anyway.

Rate knew his mother would be upset if she knew he was even thinking a swear word. A lot of the boys he chummed around with used profanity regularly, but thus far, Ralph had watched his tongue pretty carefully and seldom swore. He often heard his father rattle off a good string of cuss words when something didn't go right, and yet, Pa was awful careful when he was around Ma.

Rate knew that big as he was, Miney was not above washing his mouth out with soap and water if she ever heard him utter profane words. However, there were times when other words just didn't seem to satisfactorily express how he felt, and this had been one of those times.

When that fellow, Beck, came to see his father, Rate moved closer to listen to what was being said.

"How will you trade?" asked Millie.

"Since your mare's considerably older, I'll take fifteen dollars boot money."

"Hold on a minute. At least mine can be driven, and from all I've seen, you've got yourself a balky mare that isn't even broke properly. Think the boot money should go the other way."

"Can't do it. I just can't pay any extra. I ain't got the money to be honest with you. I bought this mare a couple a weeks ago at a sale, and I spent ever cent I could spare. Didn't know then she'd be wuthless to me. I'll be honest, I ain't never been able to get her to drive. I kin lead her, she's gentle in the stall, but she won't drive. I've whupped her, an' she just stands an' takes it. I'm at my wits end," he said disconsolately.

"Well, I don't normally trade this way, but I've taken a liking to your mare. Don't know why after watchin' her act up so and 'specially after what you've just said. Tell you what. I'll trade even up."

Beck looked discouraged as he shook his head negatively, digesting Millie's offer, then said, "You drive a hard bargain, but all right, even up it is. She ain't no good to me as is."

They unharnessed the mare while Millie went to fetch Gyp. Thus, the swap was made.

"Well, Rate how'd you like the new mare? Pearl's her name." "I don't know why you traded," hedged Rate.

"This time I'm not quite sure either," said Millie with a rueful grin. "Just a hunch, I guess. She's got nice lines and she's just a three-year-old. I checked her teeth myself."

"I wish you wouldn't have traded. I liked Gyp. She was a good horse. Thisun's got a cut on her jaw."

I know. Beck got mad and heaved a rock at her and it cut her. It's nothin' that won't heal."

"I hope it never heals. Would serve you right," muttered Ralph under his breath.

He turned and stalked away, venting his anger on a tin can that he sent spinning away from him with a furious kick that hurt his toe. Dammit all anyhow! Damn, damn, damn. He derived a certain satisfaction by rebelling against his mother's rules regarding swearing. At the moment, it helped to soothe his anger which he wanted to direct at his father, but didn't dare.

What made Pa so damned sure he could drive that mare when the other two men had failed? That was probably the reason she'd been sold by her first owner. What good was a balky mare going to be? Would be sort of funny if Pa couldn't get her to drive to get them back to town. In fact, Rate decided, he just hoped this would happen. Just once he'd like to see Pa get took on his horse trading.

Millie chuckled to himself as he went back to work. Sometimes Ralph amazed him with a sudden show of temper, usually the boy kept his emotions under a tight checkrein. Well, Millie thought, the lad would soon get used to this new horse. She was sound as a dollar although a little thin perhaps, and her performance certainly hadn't been the best, but he just had this feeling. Anyway, he felt he had made a good trade, and only time could prove him wrong.

If he wondered why Ralph let Jim drive them back into Elsie when they quit work for the day, he said nothing. Or if he noticed that Ralph was more quiet than usual, he failed to comment. Strangely enough, they simply hitched Pearl to the buggy, Jim spoke softly to her, and she moved off like she never had a balky streak in her at all. Ralph was truly amazed and decidedly disappointed. He had wondered how Pa would have handled the situation if the mare had taken a notion to balk.

Ralph was coming as close to pouting as he ever had been. He made up his mind he'd give Pearl as little care as possible. Oh, he'd feed and water her all right, wouldn't be humane not to, but he'd be darned if he'd brush her unless Pa specifically said to do so. Now, Gyp had always been curried and brushed each day whether she was driven or not, and on occasion, he gave her a few extra oats. Well, see if this one ever got anything extra. He'd sure laugh if that cut didn't heal like Pa thought it would. Pa always thought he knew so much anyway.

Ralph pretended not to notice when Pearl took to nickering when he came into the barn. He fed her, watered her, cleaned the stables, but other than that, he paid her scant attention. He was still peeved over the trade.

Pearl made him feel guilty the day she rubbed her head against him and nuzzled his neck with her soft, velvety nose. Drat it all! He just wasn't going to learn to like her because there was no tellin' just how long Pa would keep her. Didn't pay to get attached to any horse, not with a gol-durn horse trader in the family.

In spite of himself, Rate's reserve was gradually broken down, and one day he found himself brushing and currying Pearl's glossy, bay coat, talking to her as he did so. He guessed it was hardly the mare's fault she had to live with them. He even noted with satisfaction that his father had been right, and the cut on her jaw had almost healed.

Finally, he decided it was time for him to try driving her. No use to have her stand in the barn all the time except for when Pa wanted to drive her, which wasn't often. Ma always drove Old Mikey if she wanted to go any place. Old Mikey was almost ancient and completely reliable. Anyway, Rate decided he wanted to go out to Watson's farm, which was four miles west of town, to see Hugh. He had asked his father at dinner to hitch up Pearl for him.

Millie had replied, "If you can hitch her up, you can drive her. If not, you can walk."

No use arguing. Pa was not one to change his mind once he had spoken. Ralph gave the matter serious thought. He finally formulated a plan.

Rate went to the Baptist parsonage, which was the house to the west of the barn, to Reverend Thompson's and asked the minister's son, Ralph, who was Rate's own age, to come over and help him. Rate harnessed Pearl with no difficulty, then hitched her up to the buggy with the barn door still closed. Everything went well. Pearl did as she was told and behaved very well. Next, Rate clambered up into the buggy, took a firm grip on the lines and gave a nod to his companion.

The boy hastily opened the barn door, but before Rate could speak to Pearl, she surged forward. Out of the barn they went! The buggy careened up on two wheels, nearly upsetting, as they made the sharp turn into the street. Rate fought to slow her down, but the mare had been inactive for too many days and was enjoying the activity. Finally, before they reached the end of the street, she began to give some response to the lines. The boy could sense that she was now willing to let him be the master. He even stopped her a moment and made her stand just to exert his authority.

He made the mare walk a while, but when he got out of town, around the curves by the cemetery, he let her run. She sure moved well, with a long, smooth stride. Gyp had not been nearly as fast. He slowed Pearl to a trot when she began to sweat. Golly, maybe Pa hadn't made such a bad trade after all. Bet she was faster than that old roan Curly Sherman sometimes drove. Bud Grell had a sleek looking black that his father let him drive, but Ralph was confident Pearl was faster. This just might prove to be interesting, he thought as his spirits soared. He was rapidly forgetting that he had ever objected to the trade in the first place.

As a result of this outing, Ralph began to spend more time with Pearl. Her coat always glistened, and since she had filled out with the amount of hay and grain she had been given since the swap, she was a sharp-looking driving horse. Ralph even brought her an apple or two each day and sometimes he took her a lump of sugar. Pearl knew the instant he stepped into the barn, and her soft nicker was a delight to his ears. Although he might hate to admit it, Ralph was now more than satisfied with the trade. If only Pa didn't decide to swap Pearl, things would be just fine.

CHAPTER 5

The early August day was hot, with the promise of becoming hotter as the sun slowly climbed higher into the heavens. Millie and Ralph had set off early for the farm. Just as Millie had started from the yard, Rate had hollered to his dad to ask if he could go along. He had already filled the woodbox from the stockpile corded in the woodshed. Since Miney only used a fire at meal time, the amount of wood used was minimal compared to winters when the cookstove was also a source of heat for the house. Millie had given his consent. If Rate stayed home, Miney no doubt would have found something for the boy to do, but the lad needed some time around menfolk, seeing how work was done.

Although George Onstott was the renter, Millie had said he'd help with the threshing because he was the one who had planted the wheat last fall. The shocks of wheat had been hauled in from the fields and stacked at the north end of the barn. Men would have to pitch the bundles from the stack onto the table of the separator. In one swift motion, a man cut the bands holding the bundle together which allowed his partner to feed the loose grain by hand into the whirring, flailing mechanism of the machine, separating the grain from the straw. There was also a stack of oats in front of the barn. This would be pitched onto a wagon and transported over to the separator since this was a lot easier than resetting the bulky thresher.

The huge, cumbersome, black, steam engine, with the red canopy, moved slowly into place. It's heavy iron wheels, almost hiding the driver from view, crunched loudly on the gravel, then became silent as they sank into the soft, grassy ground alongside the barn. The chain lengths that went from the steering mechanism to the front wheels groaned loudly with every turn the operator gave the solid, iron, steering wheel as he jockeyed it backward and forward, inching the monster into position.

They had set up with the separator at the end of the barn, beside the wheat stack and would make the straw stack off to the north side of the stable door. This was quite a stretch from the granary, with the shortest distance taking the men through an alleyway in the barn.

Rate watched the coal being shoveled into the hungry, red, mouth of the steam engine until the proper amount of pressure had been reached. With a grinding and squeaking, the long belt started slowly in motion, the wheels and sheaves moving faster and faster. In moments, the separator was purring smoothly, and the men up on the stack started tossing the bundles to Jim who was standing on the small platform waiting for Ezz to cut the bands so he could feed the heads into the gaping hole.

Soon, the dusty straw was being shoved up the wooden rack by a spiral auger to spill over where several men snatched at it with pitchforks and started building their stack.

The men tending strike box, a rectangular wooden box that rolled on a track under the low belly of the machine, began to work in earnest as the dark, golden kernels of grain began to fill the box; it held exactly a half a bushel. Another box was pushed forward shoving the full box out the other side where that man promptly dumped the grain into a bag; the process was repeated until the bag was full.

Now, the men carrying the bags began to work unceasingly. Since it was a long walk from the separator to the granary where they dumped the bags into a bin, it kept them busy. Millie shouldered his bag of wheat with ease; although it weighed over one hundred pounds, it was no great feat for a man of his size; for some of the men, it was a struggle to get the heavy bag balanced on their shoulder.

It was midafternoon when Millie called to Ralph.

"Rate, the men could use a drink. Go to the house and ask Mrs. Onstott to give you a pail of water and a dipper."

"All right, Pa."

When Ralph came back with the pail of water, the first man he met was his father. He stopped, set the pail down, and watched as his father took a dipperful and drank, unmindful of the little that dribbled down his chin.

"Boy, that tasted right good. Didn't realize what a thirst I really had."

He took another dipper of water, started as if to take another drink, then threw the entire contents in Ralph's face. It had taken the boy completely by surprise, but he made no sound as his father shouldered his bag of wheat and moved off chuckling to himself.

With a gleam in his eyes, Ralph watched his father leave; being the nature he was, he had no intention of allowing his father to escape without some sort of retaliation. As he watched the broad shoulders disappear into the alleyway, a plan formulated. He knew the order of the men carrying the bags, and it had never varied. Pa came right after Charlie, so he'd just move to the other end of the alley and wait. He moved off to the side where the men, hand on hip, balancing a bag of grain on one shoulder, passed by without noticing the boy and his pail. The wait seemed long, but Ralph was patient. Finally, Charlie went by so Rate knew the next man coming through the corridor should be his father. He peeked around the corner to make certain; the alleyway was rather dark, but there was no mistaking the form of his father since not many men had Millie's height and breadth; his bulk filled the narrow space.

Rate took only one glimpse, afraid of being seen, picked up the pail of water, and waited. No sooner had Millie cleared the entryway when splash! A full pail of cold water hit him in the face. Millie spluttered, leaned his bag of wheat against the wall, and took off after the disappearing form of his son; the water mingled with the sweat, completely soaking the front of his shirt and running in rivulets to dampen his pants. Even though Rate had a head start, he was no match for Millie's longer stride, and the distance between father and son narrowed quickly and steadily.

Rate had headed out the drive and up the road toward Swarthout's. Millie gave a hearty laugh when he finally caught his young son up by the hickory tree which was almost halfway to the corner; even though he was breathing heavier than usual, Millie picked up the struggling boy, tucked him under his arm, and started back for the barn.

A large stock tank stood in the barnyard; the windmill was turning gently, pumping a small though steady stream of cold water into the tank. Millie carried Ralph over to the tank, held the squirming body out over the water, one hand clutching his shirt and the other firmly grasping him by the seat of his pants.

"Looks a mite cold, don't it, boy? Now, how'd you like a swim on such a hot day?"

Ralph knew better than to voice his opinion, and pride kept him from begging; besides, he knew nothing would deter Millie from his mission. For what seemed an eternity, he hung over the water, knowing full well that sooner or later his father intended to drop him into it, clothes and all. He also realized how cold it would be since the windmill had been running for the better part of the day.

Just drop me and get it over with, thought Ralph. Anything but this infernal waiting.

Splot! One young boy disappeared beneath the surface of the cold, clear water, only to come up sputtering, with teeth chattering. Millie had already started back to his job, his merry laugh floating back to Ralph as the lad climbed hastily out of the tank.

Tarnation! Pa had bested him once again. It didn't seem quite fair that his father always won out. As he climbed out of the tank, he debated about what to do. If he hiked home, Ma would surely holler at him. Besides, it was a three and a half mile jaunt which he was in no mood to take in his present condition. Course if Pa was with him, why then Pa would patch things up with Ma.

Guess he'd just find him a solitary spot and spread his shirt out to dry. The sun was so hot by now, he knew it wouldn't take long. He supposed he'd have to lie out in the sun for a while and see how much his pants would dry off. Guess if he slipped into the tool shed, he could step out of them long enough to wring out as much water as possible. Rate wore no underwear these summer months, so this posed no problem.

Gripes. Even if his pants did get dry, Ma was sure to notice all the wrinkles where he had twisted them to remove the water and wonder what had happened. Ma wasn't likely to view the episode in the same light as he and Pa.

Well, maybe Pa had got the best of him, but that surprised look on Pa's face when caught with that pailful of water had been well worth it. Rate chuckled to himself as he squeezed water from his shirt. One of these days he'd come out on top, and then the laugh would be on Pa.

Rate had been correct in assuming his mother would fail to see the humor of the incident. Miney took life more seriously and had never been one to approve of practical jokes. In fact, she never could see where they were one bit funny. Oftentimes, Millie told her to take life less seriously and realize that some folks just liked joshin' others. Miney just never liked to see someone make fun of someone else, she always felt sorry for the one being teased. She never did understand the side of Millie's nature which somehow always remained a boy, always willing to play a prank, yet able to good-naturedly take any sort of ribbing someone might send his way.

Rate was mowing lawn; in fact, he was attacking that bit of burned, brown grass with a vengeance. It had been so dry and hot these past few weeks that he had figured he was done with lawn mowing until the fall rains. Then today, at the dinner table, Ma had upset all his plans.

"Ralph, yesterday as I walked over to Austin's, I noticed how scraggly the lawn looks. The grass may not be growing, but those pesky weeds surely are. There's chicory stems sticking up all over and there's goldenrod over by the southwest corner, not to mention half a dozen other kinds of weeds. Now, if you'll get out there and mow that this afternoon, it will certainly look a hundred percent better."

"But, Ma, I'd planned on going fishing with Brownie this afternoon."

"You'll have to change your plans. If you get right at it, it won't take long, and then you can go fishing or whatever."

"But, Ma--"

"Boy, don't argue with your mother or you'll not go any place even if you do get your work done."

Ralph looked at the inscrutable face of his father and murmured, "Yessir."

Well, there went his plans all awry. Guess he'd just have to make the best of it.

That was exactly what he was doing. That poor lawnmower really hummed as Rate pushed it over the not too level ground; he was almost running.

"Rate! Rate! C'mon."

Ralph looked up to see Glee Lance from down the street coming toward him on a dead run. He sure looked excited over something. Rate stopped the mower midway across the yard.

"What's going on?"

"C'mon," yelled Glee enthusiastically. "There's an automobile up town."

"How d'ya know?"

"Someone called Ma. C'mon, or we might miss it."

Forgotten was the lawn his mother had said needed mowing. The boys took off together, bare legs flying, the mower abandoned in the middle of a round. Rate even had to grab at his straw hat and shove it down more firmly on his head as he raced along.

They went through the footpath between a couple of houses which brought them out on Main Street. They could see a crowd of people in front of Doty's Hotel.

"See. Didn't I tell ya? Hurry up."

Glee dashed ahead, obviously the better runner of the two. "Can't see nuthin' yet," panted Ralph.

"That hast' be why all those people are there," said an excited Glee. "It just hast' be."

The boys found that on the fringe of the crowd, consisting of mostly men and a few boys, crane their heads as they might, they could see nothing. They began to shove their way forward and then--there it was. An automobile! They stopped and stared.

It looked a little bit like a buggy except it was black, shiny metal with brass trimmings. The wheels were large, the wooden spokes heavy, but instead of being steel-rimmed like wagon or buggy wheels, they were covered with rock-hard, black rubber. The seats were shiny black leather.

The boys gaped in wonderment. Just imagine. Such a thing actually moved with its own power, it didn't need a horse to pull it. The boys edged closer. They couldn't see anything they thought looked like an engine. Must be the engine was a rather small part of the vehicle, and they figured out it was all covered up.

They had finally shoved up close enough where they reached out a tentative hand to touch this mechanical wizard. No one yelled at them not to, so they kept sidling along the side and around the back. When they came to the front, they noticed the nameplate read BRUSH.

Long after the boys had returned home, Ralph thought about the automobile. He guessed he was lucky he hadn't gone fishing with Brownie or he'd have missed the automobile for sure; however, he was of mixed opinions. It was a right fancy looking machine all right, especially when it was all clean, but he bet it would be a sight for sore eyes after traveling through the mud. He knew how badly buggies got caked with mud, and sometimes, the easiest way to wash one was to drive it into the river either below the dam or back of the Page place.

He wished he could have seen that automobile move; he'd heard they made an awful racket. He hadn't known who owned the machine, but he had heard old Mr. Galehouse say that he guessed it was high time he bought one of those contraptions, and Rate supposed there would be others in town who would follow suit.

Trouble was, Rate liked horses. Now, take Pearl for instance. She always nickered a greeting when he came into the barn. She often reached out and softly nuzzled his hand, or his neck, with her velvety nose. Now, no blamed machine was ever gonna do that. Pearl might be a trifle balky at times, he had to admit, but she usually had those sessions when Pa was driving her. Perhaps she did that intentionally because it sometimes became a battle of wills. Mostly, she drove pretty well for him, and she sure was fast. So far Rate hadn't found anyone who could outrun her, and she just loved to run.

At the supper table Ralph asked his father if he had seen the automobile.

"Yes, I saw it. I'd been out east of town, but I got back just before it left."

"What did you think of it?"

"Didn't impress me all that much. They had a hard time starting it. Made so much noise I'd say a man might go deef if he had to listen to all that racket for very long. Give me a good horse any day."

"But, Millie, don't you think they will keep improving them?" asked Miney.

"No doubt they'll try. I can't help but wonder if they will ever really catch on."

Once more, Millie showed his adversity to change. He viewed any new invention with skepticism. He had laughed at the first mechanical sheep shears or clippers as they were called which were run by someone turning a crank, but in the past couple of years, most of the shearers had given up the old type shears for the new mechanical ones. Whether Millie still felt the old hand-operated ones were better or whether he was just too stubborn to admit the change had been for the better, no one ever knew.

Several days after the threshing had been completed, Mina brought up a subject she had had on her mind often of late.

"Millie, aren't you going to have flour ground this year?"

"Can't say as I'd given it much thought."

"Well, you had better start giving it some consideration. I've been using what we had ground last year for over a month now. Don't tell me that I'm going to have to buy flour at the store when I run out."

"Didn't say that, did I?" What would be wrong with buying it at the store?"

"What would be wrong with buying it at the store? I'll tell you what would be wrong with buying it at the store. You know very well their's is never properly aged, and it just does not make good baked goods. At least I'd have thought you'd have learned that much by now. Not to mention how expensive it is."

Miney was indignant, and it showed. Millie could be so provoking at times. Most of the people who grew wheat took their own grain to have it ground into flour. They did this a year in advance because they just knew flour was better after it had aged--of course along with the aging process also came weevil; this meant the flour had reached a "ripeness" whereby it made much better bread, cakes, cookies, and pie crusts; the weevil posed no problem because they were simply sifted out of the flour since they were too large to go through the fine wire mesh of the sifter.

"Since you're sure that's what makes your baking so good," teased Millie, "guess I'll have to see to it next week. You know how I appreciate your good pies, to say nothing of the good bread you bake."

"Now you are just trying to sweet talk me."

"Not at all. Just stating a fact. Don't I always eat seconds?"

"Oh, Millie," she laughed, "that's just because you always have such a whoppin' big appetite. I never felt how good it tasted made all that much difference as long as it was filling."

"Well, maybe so, but you do bake as well as your mother and everyone around knew what a hand she was with baking. In fact, you bake the best of any of the girls."

"I'm glad you think so. Just don't forget about the flour when next week gets here," she cautioned, extremely pleased with her husband's unaccustomed praise.

"I hardly think you'll let me forget," he chuckled, giving her a quick kiss on the forehead before leaving the house.

That woman would surely mention flour at least every other day until he had some ground. Not that Miney ever actually nagged--she wasn't like that--it was just that she'd find some way to bring the word "flour'' into the conversation.

A mighty fine woman, his wife. His house was always neat as a pin, she had his meals on time, but most of all, she was doing a mighty fine job of raising Blanche and Ralph. He knew she had particularly resented the boy. All those months before he was born, she'd been so cranky and had always lashed out at him, blaming him for being in the family way. Well, little by little the lad had won her affections, and Millie felt that Miney did love Ralph. Of course, she would never love Rate with the same intensity she loved Blanche, but perhaps it was just as well for a boy not to be loved with quite so much possessiveness.

This brought to mind how Ma had always been so partial to Ruby. Ma had bossed him and John from the time they were born, but it was Ruby she had spoiled. Now, ever where Ma went, Ruby had to be right close by. The furthest they had been separated was when Ruby and Mac had lived in Big Rapids.

The whole family knew that Pa had taken Mac into the bank with him at South Lyon more to please Ma than anything else. Course Mac *was* a bookkeeper, but he was one who liked to put on airs--always wanted everyone to know how important he was and liked to flaunt his money.

Ma and Pa had always lived rather conservatively even though they had plenty of money. Ma had always bought the best when she bought, but she had certainly not been a spendthrift. Pa had always seen that he and John had been paid a fair wage for whatever they had done, but he'd "given" them very little.

Ruby had been a horse of a different color. Ma had doled out money to Ruby even after she and Mac were married because Mac was not earning enough money to support the daughter of Lovina Setterington in the manner Lovina felt was her just due. Maybe it was because Ruby was the only girl who had lived; Millie knew he had three sisters in the village cemetery; one had died as a baby, another had been only four, and one had lived to be seven; he could not remember the eldest since he had been only two and a half when she died.

Sometimes, Millie felt that his mother only tolerated him and John, and yet, there were times when Ma had gone out of her way to do something 'specially nice for him. She was always generous at Christmas and often, when they still lived in Elsie, and she had had him and his family over for dinner or supper, she was likely to fix a dish that she knew he was partial to. Ma was mighty hard to figure out, and he guessed he'd just never, never understand her. At least Miney bore no resemblance to his mother in any way unless one counted that both women liked girl children best.

True to his word, Millie took several bags of wheat to the gristmill by Maple River to have it ground into flour.

Years before, a dam had been made by felling trees across this neck in the river and filling in behind the barrier with stones, gravel, and clay to hold the water from flowing down the river. The river channel was twelve feet deep for the most part, running to as much as fifteen at some of the meanders. The dam held the water back to flood a large area directly to the southwest of the road where the land was flat; along the north side, the bank rose sharply for as much as twenty feet or more near the west bend, and the millpond stretched up back of Tweedie's.

Below the dam had gradually filled in; most of the year it was shallow enough so people sometimes drove their buggies in there to wash them; however, only a few yards further, it dropped off once again to a much greater depth.

The millrace had been built along the south end of the dam and when the gates were open, the water rushed through a flume under the mill; two large waterwheels reclined horizontally in the water and the rushing current turned the wheels which in turn powered the huge turbines that manned the massive and extensive milling equipment on the floor above. The wheat moved through many operations to become the fine, white flour Miney coveted.

It took sixty pounds (one bushel) of cleaned wheat (wheat blown free of any chaff or weed seed that had not been taken out by the thresher) to make forty-two pounds of flour. The milling process separated the bran and middlings from the white part of the wheat kernel; the bran, at this time thought of as almost a completely useless portion of the grain, simply dribbled out the back of the mill into the river. It had only one use: if a horse or cow was off its feed, a hot bran mash usually restored the animal's appetite; most farmers saved the middlings for hog feed.

Millie was no exception. The bran from his bags of wheat ran into the river and the middlings were bagged to add to the swill when they slopped the hogs; although he had no hogs of his own this year, he knew George would appreciate his thoughtfulness in keeping the middlings. It was the little acts of being considerate that kept a good relationship alive between owner and renter; it never hurt to admit you were human was Millie's way of thinking.

Horatio might not have agreed with this bit of philosophy, nor would his father before him, but when it came to business matters, Millie was never to have the coldhearted, impersonal approach that had typified his father and grandfather.

"You're in trouble now," hissed Blanche as her brother came in the back door to the kitchen.

"Why? I haven't done nothin'."

"Wait until you know who's here. Tillie Lance."

"That old busybody? What's she want?"

"Don't you even know?"

"How would I know? She must of seen someone doin' something and is around spreadin' the good word. She only visits to gossip about what's none of her business in the first place."

"You really don't know, do you?" asked Blanche, giving him a perplexed look.

Rate shook his head. He had gone to the cookie jar while talking, and now he eyed his sister as he munched his cookie.

"Well," Blanche whispered, "I heard her tellin' Ma she saw you coming out of the saloon, and Ralph Setterington, you surely know you aren't supposed to go there. Of all places!"

"Oh, that," he said in an indifferent way.

"Yes, that. Ma kind of smoothed it over because she doesn't like Tillie any better than we do because I've heard her say that Tillie is happiest when she's stirring up a hornet's nest. But you just wait until she leaves and Ma gets hold of you."

"Don't guess I'm any too scared."

"Ralph, you're just getting too big for your britches. Ma maybe thinks you're too big to lick any more, but she can sure make you stay home and in your room. Shouldn't think you'd like that any too much."

"Mostly, she just yells at me lately," he explained.

Blanche was right. Tillie had no sooner left than Miney called for Ralph. When he appeared before her, she asked him if he had been in the saloon.

Ralph looked his mother straight in the eye and emphatically said, "No."

"Ralph Horatio, don't lie to your mother. Tillie Lance said she *saw* you come out of there bold as brass, and she certainly knows you well enough not to have mistaken someone else for you."

"I was not in the saloon," he reiterated with a determined tone to his voice.

"Well then, just where were you?"

"I went into the hotel with Inez. She had been telling me about the open stairway that goes from the lobby to the rooms upstairs. Said it was real mahogany, so I wanted to see it. I'd never seen mahogany before. Gosh, Ma, I never went into the saloon at all. We went into the lobby and I see the dining room to one side, but I didn't even peek into the saloon. Gosh, Ma, that stairway is beautiful. The wood is dark and nicely grained, and it's all shiny. I've never seen anything prettier. What was the harm?"

Millie had come in during this exchange of words.

"Much I care. I'll not have you going any place where someone could mistakenly think you had been in a saloon. You know how I feel about such places and what I think about men who drink."

"I know, Ma, but I didn't see no harm--"

"You just never think. No son of mine is going to frequent a saloon, now or later."

"Miney, leave the boy be," interrupted Millie. "No harm's done. I went to school with Charlie Doty. We were boys when his Pa built that hotel. Why I can even remember that during the winter months Charlie carried a tiny bottle of whiskey to school with him--said it helped him not to catch colds. And there isn't a better man around than Charlie Doty. Anyway, from what Rate says, he only went into the lobby with Inez so there is certainly no fault to find with that. Even ladies go there."

"Well I never! Milford Setterington, I never thought I'd hear you defend Ralph's going into a saloon. Why my father would turn over in his grave if he knew a grandchild of his ever darkened the doorway of a saloon."

Miney looked from father to son, her mouth closed in a firm line. No use to argue. With that set look on Millie's face, he wouldn't change his mind for all the tea in China. She turned to the pantry to get potatoes to start supper. The pans banged louder than usual as she gave vent to some of her frustrations. It wasn't often Millie took the boy's side on any argument, and she couldn't understand his siding against her on this issue. Guess she might as well put the episode behind her although she did wonder if any of her friends had seen Ralph coming out of the hotel. Goodness, she didn't want anyone to think she was letting the boy run wild.

Ralph had been dwelling on memories of Grandmother Smith. She had been dead for four years now, but he found that he still missed her. Sometimes, he just sat and thought of as many things about her that he could remember. One of the ways he recollected her best was just as he would come in the front door, Grandma would be removing her steel-rimmed glasses to fold and put away while she talked; she so often sat by the window where she could watch the front door--the window was high enough so from the outside only her head could be seen--while she knitted. Yessir, Grandma was pretty special, and he sure wished she was still alive. Course Ma had upbraided him when she heard him voice these sentiments one day; she had said we were never to question why God did anything. At least Grandma had liked him even if he was a boy and his mischief-making had only made her laugh.

"Ma, Grandma used to grind her own coffee, didn't she?"

"Yes, Ralph. Don't ever recollect that she ever had any coffee ground at the store. She just bought the beans and ground a little at a time. Guess it seemed as though it lasted longer that way."

"Is that a coffee grinder hanging on the wall by the cellar stairs?"

"You know it is. What a foolish question."

"Whyn't you grind your own then?"

"I did when we were first married up until after Blanche was born. Then, I decided it was just too much bother. I always hated that awful strong smell while grinding coffee beans. Besides, if I ground my own, where would you get lion heads to save?" she asked with a chuckle.

"That's right. I hadn't thought of that. Guess I'm glad you decided to buy it like you do."

For as long as Rate could remember his mother had bought Lion brand coffee, a pound at a time, and had had it ground at the store. The sack had a large picture of a lion's head on the front. Most of the kids in town saved these heads to send in for prizes and Ralph was no exception. Right now he was saving them to get a kaleidoscope. This prize had been more expensive than some of the others so he had canvassed the town to see if he could get any "heads" somewhere else. Aunt Lorin had promised to save hers, along with two or three of the elderly, widowed ladies, so perhaps it wouldn't take too long to save the required number.

Miney was busy baking cookies even if it wasn't Saturday because it was her turn to take some to the Odd Fellows meeting. She had put a quantity of sifted flour into a bowl, added the eggs, a scant cup of lard, the brown sugar, the baking soda, cinnamon and vanilla, and then had begun to mix these ingredients with her hand; she added some sour milk and continued to work flour from the sides of the bowl into the mixture. When the dough reached a certain consistency, she dumped the remainder of the flour back into the bin and began to roll out the finished cookie dough. She cut the cookies with a large, round cutter. Ralph helped himself to some of the scraps of raw dough and left.

Miney hummed as she worked. Then, she remembered her daughter and chuckled to herself. She had been trying to teach Blanche to bake the same as Ma had taught her: nothing was really measured, and a number of ingredients were by the pinchful. Somehow, Blanche just didn't have the knack. For one thing, she steadfastly refused to use her fingers to mix anything, and how was a person to know if the dough felt right using only a mixing spoon? Miney had tried to explain this to her daughter, but Blanche had stood her ground.

To please her daughter, Miney had tried to write down a recipe for some of the cakes and cookies Blanche liked best. It had been a sort of trial and error procedure, and in her own mind, Miney knew that none of those pastries were as good as when she just dumped the ingredients into a bowl with none of that hassle of measuring every single thing. Goodness, wouldn't Ma have had a good laugh watching someone meticulously measuring out the ingredients for a cake? This modern generation just couldn't take the time to learn the old ways. Well, maybe it was for the best. She supposed it would be easier to pass on family recipes if they were written down instead of trusting to a person's memory.

CHAPTER 6

It was time once again to buy the children's school clothes. Mina had made Ralph's his first few years of school, but she had made Blanche's only the very first year. From that time on, Lovina had taken her granddaughter to Owosso to Christian's to see her outfitted for school. When Horatio and Lovina had moved away from Elsie, Lovina had taken her daughter-in-law aside and made it perfectly clear that she expected Miney to continue taking Blanche to Owosso for her clothes; Lovina was certain the Bates store in Elsie did not have suitable apparel for any granddaughter of hers. Miney did not have enough backbone to stand up to her mother-in-law, so she had continued to go to Owosso to Christian's. She also took Ralph since it just seemed the natural thing to do.

Rate always looked forward to these trips even though he detested shopping with his mother. Why he bet she had him try on every single coat in the store that was anywhere near his size before she made a choice; then, she always worried for fear he'd grow out of it before it was worn out. She always wanted dark colors: Navy blue, dark brown, deep wines, or dark green. He never had any real say although he most certainly would have liked some of the brighter, more interesting colors.

Blanche got to pick out what she wanted, but Ma had explained this by saying it was because Blanche was in high school, already a young lady. Of course, he had heard Blanche tell that all those years she had been forced to shop with her grandmother, Blanche had never had a choice either.

Rate liked the train ride even if it was a short one. They had taken the morning train which would allow time for shopping, then dinner at the hotel, and then the afternoon train home.

It was dinner at the hotel dining room that both Ralph and Blanche enjoyed. The tables were covered with snowy white cloths and a waiter came to the table to serve them. They usually had the special of the day which might be steak, roast beef, beef and noodles, or some kind of pork. Today, it was a generous portion of roast beef; to go with the meat, there was plenty of mashed potatoes and gravy, golden yellow squash, thick slices of warm bread with plenty of butter and jelly, some pickle slices, milk for Blanche and Ralph, tea for Miney, and their choice of pie for dessert. Ralph had apple. This meal cost Miney twenty cents apiece, so she made certain they all cleaned their plates--she wasn't about to waste any of the food she had paid such a high price to get.

Ralph had been contentedly full, so on the way home he was content to watch out the window and dream a little. He guessed the trip had been worthwhile even if he hadn't been allowed to pick out his clothes again this year. At least Ma had asked Blanche's opinion on his coat, and Blanche had persuaded Ma to buy the one he liked. Rate guessed there were times when Blanche did come in handy. Course, one was never sure of Blanche; sometimes, she was quick to tattle to Ma if she thought she'd get him in trouble, but other times, like today, she had helped him get what he wanted.

There were times when he resented the fact that both Ma and Pa favored Blanche in every way, but he guessed his sister didn't have much control over that; therefore, he could hardly blame her. At least Ma never splurged and bought Blanche more clothes than was necessary--Ma was too tight to do that. She always dressed him as good as any of the other boys; in fact, his clothes were far nicer than some.

He supposed this was partly because Ma would feel she couldn't hold her head up if her friends and neighbors ever thought she showed partiality between her children. Both Ma and Pa would find it very difficult to be that honest with themselves-- he was sure that they didn't show favoritism as something they had carefully planned, it just happened; therefore, in the obvious ways they had to prove to the world both children were loved equally, so that meant he was always dressed as nicely as his sister.

Anyway, the day hadn't been all bad, and Ma hadn't even yelled at him once. She was usually upset if he forgot his table manners, but today, he'd been extra careful, and Ma had nodded her head in approval.

* * * * * * * * * *

Millie came into the kitchen and lowered the milk pail to the floor by the cabinet; it was partly full of frothy, warm milk.

"Miney," he called. "Here's the milk."

He didn't wait for her answer, but went back into the woodshed to wash up. A pail of water set on a bench beside an enameled washbasin; a towel hung on a nail to the side by the window. This part of the woodshed had flooring of rough-cut boards, worn smooth with use, which were two feet wide. Most of the structure, the part where the wood was neatly corded, had only a dirt floor. It was handy having the woodshed built right onto the house because all summer Miney could do the laundry there, and the back door was close to the clothesline; the well was out the other door. They washed up here as soon as it got warm enough in the spring until it got too cold in the fall when the washdish was moved back into the warmth of the kitchen.

Millie finished splashing water on his face to rinse off the soap, groped for the towel with his eyes shut while the water dripped from his elbows; finally, when he made contact with the towel, he wiped his face and hands, ran a comb through his thinning brown hair, and stepped back into the kitchen for supper.

Miney was just straining the milk through a piece of fine-meshed sugar sack into a large bowl; the milk would be put in the safe in the pantry where the cream would rise over night to be skimmed off in the morning; Miney wouldn't have thought they could have oatmeal without thick, yellow cream to pour on a bowl of the steaming cereal.

Blanche had finished setting table, and in a few moments the family sat down to their evening meal. It was just six o'clock.

"Well, Miney," commenced Millie as he cleaned the gravy from his plate with his knife, the blade bending to fit the contour of the plate, "I won't be workin' for Pierce no more."

"What are you going to do? We don't get enough from the farm to live on, do we?" was the apprehensive question.

"I bought me a business." "A business?"

"That's right. I am now sole owner of Will Hamilton's meat market."

"Well, I declare. When did you decide all this?"

"Oh, I been givin' it some thought ever since we left the farm. Have known for some time that Will was lookin' for a buyer. Is that all you're going to say?"

"I don't know what else to say. Did you have enough money to pay for it?" She knew he had banked the entire amount from the sale of livestock when they moved from the farm.

"Almost. Will took my note for the store inventory and equipment. We won't have no trouble atall paying for it if that's why you've got that worried frown."

"You know best." She paused thoughtfully a moment. "Millie, do you really know *how* to run a meat market?"

"What I don't, I'll learn. Can't be too much to it. Will said he'd show me how to make liverwurst, the bologna and wieners, and how to season the sausage. He's going to work with me a couple of weeks until I get the hang of it. Blanche and Rate, what's your opinion?"

"Sounds just fine, Pa. Now Fern's dad won't be the only one who is a merchant," came from Blanche.

"Swell, Pa. Now I won't have to *buy* wieners, will I?"

Millie burst out laughing.

"I might have known you'd think of wieners, Rate. Don't think I ever knew of a kid before who would spend money to buy wieners instead of candy. Well, boy, you just might have to earn them. I've a notion there is going to be a lot of jobs that you can work into doing."

"Suits me, Pa." A frown drew his eyebrows together as he asked, "But will I have to give up mowing lawns?"

"Not until you're a little older. Though, you likely won't be able to pick strawberries next year."

"He'll be glad of that," put in Blanche. "He picks pretty slow and Inez always ended up helping him finish his row," she teased. "Course I think Inez is a little sweet on him anyway."

"You didn't do much better," Ralph retorted, ignoring her remark about Inez.

Mina had sat quietly, her thoughts racing. She hated owing money, but if Millie felt he could be out of debt in a short time, she supposed it would be all right. She had been so glad when they had finally paid off Father Setterington for what they owed on the farm.

Of course, it would be nice to have Millie a business man, made him sound more important for some reason. Not that she had ever been ashamed of Millie in any way; he was an honest, hard-working man and had always provided well for his family. She rather wished he had talked it over with her before he had made up his mind, but that wasn't Millie's way. She was certain he had given it much thought before making his move, it was just that he didn't value her opinion on business matters, and it did hurt her feelings. After all, she wasn't a complete simpleton, she did understand money matters. Well, she'd long ago given up any idea she might ever have entertained about changing Millie; he was what he was, and would be for as long as he lived.

A butcher shop. Well, people did have to eat, and Elsie was a growing community, so he probably would be able to make a living; only time would tell.

School would start tomorrow. Rate supposed he was glad, mostly he liked school. This year he'd go upstairs since he was in the seventh grade. He wondered just how well he'd get along with Miss Finch. She already knew who he was; there was always something he couldn't quite put a finger on about the way she looked at him--those blue eyes of hers seemed to laugh at him--almost as though she could read his mind. He guessed she could be plenty tough although Blanche had never once complained. He'd heard some of the older boys tell that she took no nonsense from anyone, girl *or* boy, and that the strength in her fingers was unbelievable.

Miss Finch was tall, slender, and completely devoid of the more womanly curves. She wore her brown hair pulled severely back into a bun, but during the course of a day, small tendrils always made their escape and gave her a somewhat disheveled appearance. Her nose was thin and straight, the lips thin, the chin strong, but the eyes were what held a person's attention; they were light blue but with the depth of a deep, clear pool and they seemed to sparkle like sunlight on water; often they shone with merriment although the countenance remained stern.

Kate possessed an understanding of young people and used her God-given talent as a teacher to its full advantage. She feared no student. She demanded obedience and got it. If obedience was not instantaneous in coming, her anger erupted like a volcano, and she settled the matter as expediently as possible to the chagrin of the pupil involved.

Ralph slipped quietly into the classroom and picked a desk which stood in the farthest corner away from the teacher's desk; he carefully put away his books and pencil box. Miss Finch looked up from some papers, smiled pleasantly and said, "Good morning, Ralph. Seems you're one of the early ones."

"Good morning, Miss Finch."

Wonder why she looked like the cat that had just swallowed the canary? Golly, did teachers tell other teachers about what kids did in their classrooms? She didn't seem to mind that he'd chosen a desk in the back of the room. Maybe it was just his imagination playing tricks on him. Well, he'd be rather careful for a while at least. No use to get off on the wrong foot right away; if he got in trouble too soon, it might prove to be a pretty long year.

When the session began shortly after the last bell, Kate laid down a few rules regarding behavior, gave the pupils to understand that she expected lessons to be done neatly and on time; then, she carefully explained that since the desks were still new, she expected them to be carefully taken care of; she mentioned that any boy caught using a jackknife on a desk would suffer dire consequences, and the boys believed her. She ended by telling the pupils that each and every one was to go to the drug store and buy a blotter the size of their desk to protect the top; she gave them the size, but added that the druggist was expecting them and knew what they needed.

She expected everyone to have a blotter by school time tomorrow.

No one questioned her, and the next morning each pupil carried a carefully rolled-up blotter, the size to cover his desk. A hole had to be cut to allow the blotter to fit around the inkwell, but Miss Finch had supervised this, so there were no accidents.

A couple of weeks later, Rate was busily working at drawing on his blotter. He had the scene almost finished. He had meticulously drawn a good-sized tombstone and had very carefully lettered in his name, the date of birth, and a date of death; now, he was working on the epitaph. He was almost finished.

So engrossed was he, he did not notice Miss Finch get up from her desk and slowly head for the back of the room, stopping now and then to observe a pupil's work. He had his geography book held in a standing position in front of him, his head was bent close to the desk, a lock of hair fell across his forehead which he absently brushed aside. He did not realize that Miss Finch had stopped beside his desk and stood peering at the heavy, black, block letters: **DIED OF AN OVERDOSE OF ENGLISH.**

A smile flitted across her thin lips, then her face became stern as she spoke, "Well, Ralph, I can see you are hard at work on your assignment."

Rate looked up, a surprised expression on his face, for a moment at loss for words.

"Oh, that isn't geography, is it?" came the question, feigned surprise in the voice.

"No, Ma'am."

"Looks more like English, wouldn't you say?"

He dropped his eyes a moment, then looked back into her fathomless blue eyes and said, "That's what it is all right. English."

"Now, Ralph, I don't hardly remember giving you an assignment like this."

"I - I guess you didn't. It was just something I thought of all by myself. Just a little something extra."

He knew she was playing with him as a cat toys with a mouse. Golly, what was she going to do? She didn't look mad, but she didn't laugh either. He watched her carefully, wide-eyed and innocent. Should he be ready to duck?

Kate thought, that little scalawag. He's not one bit sorry he's done that drawing, nor is he going to make any excuses. Caught in the act, and he can still look at me with that angelic look like he'd never think of doing anything wrong.

This just might prove to be an interesting year. He'll keep me on my toes, that much is certain. I'll never dare turn my back on him for long.

Silkily, she spoke. "Ralph, I don't want you to think I don't appreciate your work of art because I think you've done a mighty fine job of drawing something." Then her voice hardened to steel, "However, it is highly inappropriate as you well know. Tomorrow morning you will have a clean blotter to replace the one you have so flagrantly defaced. Is that understood?"

She had not raised her voice, but had clipped the words short to emphasize her meaning.

"Yes, Miss Finch."

Was that a look of relief she saw cross his face? She had turned quickly away because she was fighting for control; she would loved to have laughed. He was going to be a challenge; she felt it in her bones; however, she also felt he was not really a bad boy, just one with an active mind. She'd just have to see that she kept him busy so he'd have less time to get into trouble. Maybe some of the stories she had heard were true because Ralph's reputation had reached her ears long before he came into her classroom.

Ralph had been relieved. It was too early in the school year to start getting into trouble. Guess he'd just have to be a little sneakier. Miss Finch, it was said, had eyes in the back of her head; everyone said it was uncanny how she seemed to know everything that went on in her classroom. Well, he'd just be a mite more careful. She sure did present a challenge to a red-blooded, young boy who could always dream up some form of mischief.

He was also relieved that he had enough money of his own to buy the new blotter. He didn't relish the idea of having to ask Ma or Pa for the money and then having to explain what had happened. Pa might view the situation with levity, but since it concerned money, Ma would fail to find anything humorous about it. Of course, he might be in bigger trouble if Miss Finch mentioned the matter, but there was something in the way she looked at him which made him confident she wouldn't squeal.

Ralph had gone up town for his mother at noon hour--she had needed a sack of salt; of course, he had already gone to the store before he went to school in the morning because she had needed some baking soda. Golly, with a little luck, she'd probably send him for something after school. That was one thing he could never figure out about Ma: why couldn't she get all she needed for a day or two all at one time? Sometimes, he felt it was just because his mother hated parting with each and every penny, so she wanted to hang onto it until the last possible moment. He didn't mind once a day, but two or three times? Ridiculous.

Of course, today was different. Since Ma had wanted something from the grocery store, it gave him the perfect opportunity to purchase the new blotter. He only hoped the drug store had some left. He'd be in trouble for certain if he showed up at school without the new blotter. No use to worry about something he had no control over.

Just as he neared the four corners, here came Mr. Gatehouse in his new automobile. The dignified old gentleman had been as good as his word and had bought himself an automobile a few days ago. Since then, he'd been working at learning to drive it. Golly, no faster than he drove, Ralph could keep up with him at a brisk walk. Course he did guess he'd get tired before the machine.

Mr. Gatehouse reached the four corners, swung the auto in an arc to the west; but once he had negotiated the turn, he forgot to turn the steering wheel the opposite way to straighten the vehicle. It headed directly for the front of Bates' store.

"Whoa! Whoa!" yelled Mr. Gatehouse, clearly frightened as he leaned back in the seat pulling back on the steering wheel with all his might. "Whoa there, you gol durn thing. I said, whoa!"

With the last screeched command, the front end of the automobile went under the hitching post, jammed there, and stalled.

By now, several onlookers materialized from nowhere and raucous laughter added to the old man's chagrin.

"Don't drive like no horse, do it, Frank?"

"Guess someone ain't never taught this thing the meanin' o' whoa." "Ain't no horse sense to a machine, is there?"

Ralph laughed to himself because it had looked funny to see that automobile just keep turning and not straighten up to follow the road. Still, he did feel just a little sorry for the old man. He knew the men joshing Mr. Gatehouse didn't mean any harm, and they were already working to extricate the automobile from under the horizontal pipe of the hitching post. Mr. Galehouse seemed frightfully upset and was afraid it had ruined his automobile; he fussed and fumed and looked it over critically; however, the men assured him that except for a little missing paint along the hood, it wasn't harmed.

The plucky old gentleman clambered back into his vehicle while a volunteer cranked it for him; the engine sputtered to life, he put it in reverse and backed out into the middle of the street, quite unmindful of the horse and carriage that had to hurry out of his way; this time, he kept his wits about him and used the brake to halt the automobile, changed into a forward gear, and proceeded, albeit somewhat jerkily, on his way.

Since Millie now had the meat market, as soon as school was dismissed, Ralph hurried home to toss his books on the table, change his clothes, grab a cookie or two, and head up town to visit his father at the market. He did this daily because there were days when his father had some chore for him to do. Of course, some nights what his father wanted him to do had to wait until he had taken home some groceries for his mother.

This particular afternoon, Ralph noticed a wagon loaded with watermelons drawn up to the west of Doty's Hotel, by the large, village watering tank where everyone could water their teams. Rate ambled down to look them over; the biggest ones were simply huge. Ralph decided he had an urgent taste for watermelon. The man assured him they were ripe and sweet; in fact, he put one on the ground, pressed on it, and they both heard the cracking sound--unmistakably ripe. Ralph told him he'd be back, but he had to go see his father to get the necessary money. Rate took off on a run, he could taste that watermelon already.

"Pa," he called as he burst into the market, "can I have money for a watermelon?"

"Who's got watermelon?"

"Some fella up by the watering tank. They sure nuff look good and sound ripe."

"What's he asking?"

"He's got all prices. little ones for a nickel, large ones for eight cents, but the big whoppers are a dime. Think we could get one?"

"Tell you what. Pearl's over to the blacksmith's. He should have her shod by now, so's you go take her home, and I'll give you the money for a watermelon when you get back."

"All right, Pa. It won't take but a jiffy."

The smithy was two stores down from the meat market. Sure enough, Cap Sheldon had finished shoeing Pearl, so Ralph untied her halter rope and started for home. They had almost reached the four corners when one of those newfangled automobiles came chugging noisily from the north. Pearl began to prance; Ralph tried to calm the mare; he spoke soothingly and reassuringly to her and stroked her neck while he tightened his grip on the rope. He stopped, wishing that blamed automobile would hurry on past; however, it seemed that just as it was halfway through the intersection, it chugged an extra loud noise and backfired. Pearl had taken as much of this nonsense as she was going to take; she neighed in terror, reared, came down, danced sideways and reared again. She broke Rate's grasp on the rope and took off on a dead run for the safety of her own stable.

Rate's leg hurt. He looked down at his left leg and saw that the heavy, black, woolen stocking he wore was torn from upper calf to ankle and blood was fast filling the gap. He started limping back to the butcher shop.

"Pa! Pa! Pa, I'm hurt," he yelled.

Immediately, Millie appeared at the door. Even at a distance he could see the blood on his son's leg. Not bothering to take off his apron, he closed and locked the door, swooped his young son up in his arms and strode hurriedly for Doc Seal's office which was just beyond the four corners and the closest doctor's office.

"Boy, what went wrong?" asked Millie, concern in his voice.

"You know how scared Pearl is of automobiles, well, one came along just as we got to the corner to turn for home. I tried to hold her.Pa, but there just wasn't no calming her down. She just acted like she didn't know I was there. She musta caught me with her forefoot. She kept rearin' an' I tried my best to keep outta the way."

Rate was plunked down on the examining table, and between him and his father, they got his shoe off and what was left of the knee-length sock. He had a good ten inch gash on the side of his leg where Pearl had caught him with her newly shod front foot. The doctor brought a washbasin of warm water over to the table to cleanse the wound. Rate looked a little skeptical at the dirty, soap scum around the edge of the basin; Ma never had a washdish that dirty in *her* house. Seemed like a doctor should be one to observe the rules of cleanliness.

"Millie, this has got to be sewed up or it will never stop bleeding. You'll have to help hold the boy's leg. I'll call the missus to help with the stitchin'."

Since Doc's office was a couple of rooms in his house, he called to his wife who came in from the kitchen; her hands were flour-covered as was the apron she wore. When it was explained that her help was needed to hold the wound closed while he put in the stitches, she wiped her hands on her apron and took her place by the examination table as if this was a common occurrence. Ralph looked at her hands and noted that bits of flour and dough still clung around the fingernails; he watched the dirty washdish and thought that Ma had always been so persnickety about being clean when anyone had a cut; she always scrubbed the area and any bandage she used was clean, right out of the rag bag.

Millie held the leg in position, the doctor's wife pressed the sides of the gaping wound together while Dr. Beal took nine catgut stitches. Ralph simply clenched his hands into fists and bit on his lower lip to keep from uttering a sound. The leg had been somewhat numbed at first from the initial shock of getting hit with a flailing front hoof, but by the time they were on the last few stitches, all feeling had returned, and Ralph could feel the needle as it was pushed and prodded to get it through the flesh. It didn't seem to be very sharp, and Rate wondered how many others had been sewn up with that same needle. He could feel the thread slide through; then, once more feel the needle penetrate the opposite side of the wound. He was glad when the whole process was finally finished and a rather bulky bandage put in place.

"Now, Rate, you have got to keep off that leg for the next week or so. I don't want you doing anything so those stitches will pull out. That's a pretty deep cut, right down to the bone. Guess your Ma can see to changing the bandage for the next few days, and then I want you back here in a week so I can take a look at it. Now, when I say keep off it, I mean just that. You are to sit with it elevated on a chair or footstool. You can use crutches to get yourself out to the toilet and to meals--other than that, nothing. No weight on that leg for any reason. Know this isn't going to be easy, but if you don't follow orders, it will only make things much worse."

"How long will I be out of school?"

"Can't rightly tell. All depends on how well this heals. I've seen them when they healed up slick as a whistle, and then again, they are nothing but trouble. We'll hope it heals good so maybe you'll only miss a couple of weeks."

Geez, two weeks and he could just imagine how far he'd be behind with all the work Miss Finch piled on them each day.

Miney's face went white when Millie carried Ralph into the house. Millie succinctly explained the situation, he was never one for embellishing facts; then, he hurried back to the market. Miney saw to it that Ralph was made as comfortable as possible in her small rocker with his leg straight out in front of him on a kitchen chair which was just the right height.

"Does it hurt much?"

"Well, it hurts some," he admitted.

"Goodness, I'm not sure your father should have sent you to bring Pearl home. Sometimes, it seems as though she isn't very trustworthy."

"She'd have been all right if that automobile hadn't come along. Did she come home all right?"

A worried frown creased his forehead; he sure wouldn't want anything to happen to Pearl. Bruno sat with his head on his master's leg; Ralph patted the silky head and scratched behind the dog's ears in an absent-minded way, waiting for his mother's answer.

"Yes, and your father put her in the stable before he went back to the market. It is time for me to start supper. Didn't you have a book you were reading?"

"Yes, but it's upstairs in my room."

"Well, I'll get it so you'll have something to keep you busy while I'm in the kitchen."

A book would work for now, but Ralph read quite rapidly, and what would he do with himself if he couldn't get around for a week or so? She dreaded to think of just how the time would drag for the youngster. Well, perhaps she could arrange her work so that she could play a game or two of dominoes during the day.

Millie would quite likely be willing to play a game of checkers after supper if Ralph didn't get tired of losing. That always got under Miney's skin, the fact that Millie had to win every time; she felt that just once in a while Ralph should get to win even if it meant that Millie simply "let" him win. She had ventured to suggest this to Millie once and had been told that he'd teach Ralph in his own way; if she wanted to play with her son and let him win even though he played badly, that was her business. Goodness, Millie was so set in his way that at times she felt he only did it to be as cantankerous as he could.

Miney was indeed correct about one thing: time dragged with unmitigating slowness for her son. In fact, just because he had had toilet privileges, she had to put her foot down about how many times a day he could get himself out the kitchen door, across the woodshed, out the door and down the path to the privy; she explained to him that the doctor had meant this only for a necessity and not as a means of exercise. The other alternative was to use the chamberpot, so Ralph heeded his mother's warning.

Some of his friends from school dropped in during their noon hour, or came over to spend some time after school. Sometimes, they even brought a game to play, or they played checkers. Then, one night, he had a rather unexpected visitor. "Ralph, I've known for some time that certain pupils would do anything to get out of my class, but I never figured you'd slice your leg that badly just to be rid of me."

Ralph laughed; he had caught the unmistakable gleam in her dancing blue eyes.

"Well, Miss Finch, I honestly didn't do it on purpose although it might not have been such a bad idea. At least I haven't had anyone harping at me to do my English," he said mischievously, "so it sure has been peaceful."

"Just for that, I shouldn't give you what I brought. But then, maybe you wouldn't want these books anyhow. Guess I'll just have to take them home with me."

Kate had taken three books out of a crocheted bag, but with an eye on Ralph, she had started to put them back in the bag.

"Aw, Miss Finch, have a heart. I was only teasin'."

They were Horatio Alger books; Ralph had become very fond of the books written by Alger and didn't seem to mind that the theme of each book was the same as the one before: a typical rags to riches story. Ralph had already read one of the three books, but he failed to mention this as he spoke to his teacher.

"Wow! Horatio Alger. I really like his books. Gee, Miss Finch, it sure was swell of you to bring these over."

"Whenever you're finished with these, perhaps I can scrounge up a few more books for you to read. Time kind of drag?" she asked sympathetically.

"Sure does. Ma said she didn't like the looks of my leg when she changed the bandage today. Have to go back to Doc tomorrow, but Ma says she bets he won't let me up and around yet. Don't know when I'll be back to school."

"Just you never mind, Ralph. I'll be sure to save all of your work for you.

Wouldn't want you to miss out on anything," she said, her eyes twinkling.

"I'll just bet you will. Don't suppose anyone has been into any trouble this week?" he asked hopefully.

"It has been extremely quiet. Haven't even caught anyone using a pea shooter. Wonder if you'd know why."

"Who, me? Why, Miss Finch, you know I'd never use one of those things 'specially after you gave us that little lecture such a short time ago. Now, would I?" he asked innocently.

"Thought never crossed my mind."

Teacher and pupil looked at each other and laughed; they did understand one another. Kate knew that no threat would deter Rate from anything he set his mind to. She also knew that if he was caught, he would take his medicine without a squawk. He was some boy, and there were times when she wondered just why Blanche had always been the favorite child--not that she didn't like Blanche, because she did--it was just that Ralph was such an interesting child and from what she had heard, he was not unlike his father.

Why everyone in town knew that Rate Setterington's sons had been in on any mischief-making there was. Wasn't that they hadn't been made to toe the line at home either what with a mother like Lovina. She had ruled the roost, but Horatio had sometimes understood that boys will be boys probably because he had been much the same in his younger years. Seemed like Millie would have found having a son like Ralph much to his liking, and she guessed he did, only it was his daughter who was the apple of his eye.

Well, no matter. Ralph would make out all right; he was well thought of by outsiders so she guessed he could get by on that. Actually, she missed having him in the classroom, and she looked forward to the day when he would return. A boy like him presented a continuing challenge--kept a body alert at all times.

Miney had been right. The leg didn't look good. It was suppurating the entire length of the cut, and the doctor was afraid the infection would cause the stitches to pull out of the putrefying flesh. He took off the ill-formed scab and cleansed the raw sore with alcohol; Ralph gritted his teeth and swore under his breath until the sting subsided.

The doctor gave Miney a salve to put on it each day and sent them back home with the same admonitions: toilet privileges only, keep the leg elevated, and come back next week unless it became reddened quite some distance from the wound. A discouraged lad left the doctor's office. Didn't look as though he'd be going back to school very soon. He was amazed at how much he missed the classroom. Of course, part of it could be he missed the daily battle of wits with Miss Finch. She sure was someone special, no doubt about that.

"Ma, some of my club members are going to gather hickory nuts Saturday. I'm not sure who's driving, but if we need transportation, may I drive Old Mikey?" Inquired Blanche.

"I don't know why not. Where are you going?"

"Miss Finch said we could go back in their woods. She says they have hickory nuts, black walnuts, and butternuts. She might even go with us. Said we could bring a lunch if the day was nice, and we could have a bonfire."

"That was very nice of Kate. Blanche, do you recall how frightened you were to go upstairs to her room?"

Blanche laughed.

"I certainly do. Well, it wasn't my fault if I believed all the stories about her. wasn't the only one who was afraid to go into seventh grade. It is really funny now. Ma, she's the nicest teacher I've ever had. Oh, I like some of the others too, but Miss Finch is interesting, and she just makes it easy to learn."

"I'm surprised that Ralph hasn't complained about her. Of course, he wasn't there long enough to try her patience too much, I guess. Goodness, but I'll be glad when he can go back to school."

"How long do you think it will be?"

"Only the good Lord knows. Last week, Doc said the upper part of the cut looked better, and he did think it had started to heal. Down by his ankle, it looks terrible. Have to take him back on Friday, but I don't think he will let Ralph up yet."

"I suppose I should play a game with him each night. I know it must be awful hard for him to keep so quiet. Course he has had some books to read, and you know Ralph and books."

"Indeed I do. Yes, Blanche, I do think it would be nice if you played some game with him. He likes dominoes, or checkers, or dots, cat's cradle, or even old cat. Right now, anything is a welcome diversion."

How right Miney was. Poor Ralph found that each day of inactivity got worse. On Saturdays, more of his cronies dropped by, and some even showed up on Sundays, but during the week, when they were in school, time moved with excruciating slowness. Course Ma had tried to talk to him more and had played dominoes with him a few times.

There'd been the day when he'd had to hold skeins of yarn for her and Aunt Lorin so they could wind the yarn into balls. The skein came with the yarn wound in a circle, so he had to loop it over each hand; then, just as the strand of yarn was pulled near the right hand, he had to dip the hand just a little so the strand didn't catch and continued to unwind toward the left hand, and then dip that one; if he dipped too far, all the yarn came off his hand, and he got yelled at for not paying attention; so it was arms outstretched and dip, dip, dip with a steady monotony. Oh, well, he guessed he shouldn't complain, especially when Ma had been so good to him, and Aunt Lorin always treated him well. It was just that to his way of thinking, holding yarn was woman's work.

One night he got Pa to reminiscing, and he did like to have his father tell stories. Sometimes, when he looked at his father, it was hard to imagine Millie had ever been a boy, getting into mischief or shirking his work.

"Uncle Vest was always getting himself into trouble of one kind or another," Millie began. "Not anything serious, mind you, just some sort of deviltry. He was only about twelve years older than me, so we did get on, and I guess it never really seemed like he was an uncle--more like he was an older brother.

"There were times when he sure did vex Pa plenty. Uncle Vest used to tell me that Pa just didn't want to recollect the things he'd done as a boy. Anyway, this one night in particular, I recall how mad Pa got."

Millie paused to laugh, and Ralph waited expectantly. No use to try to hurry Pa, 'cause when Pa was story-tellin' he took his own sweet time.

"It must have been well after midnight when there came a banging on the front door. We still lived in the house south of the main four corners, the one that burned a short time later. Anyway, there came this banging, and I heard Pa go to the door only I couldn't hear what was bein' said. I just knowed it was a man's voice, and he sounded angry.

'"Bout that time I came to that I had someone in bed with me. It was Uncle Vest. He lay there smotherin' his laughter with a pillow. He'd sneaked into the house unbeknownst to anybody, and had just crawled in bed with me, not bothering to wake me up.

"It seems that the Sheriff wanted to question Uncle Vest about something and had come to our place lookin' for him. Pa didn't have the slightest idee that Uncle Vest was there, so he told the Sheriff he hadn't seen him. Of course, that weren't no lie since Pa hadn't *seen* him. Pa never knowingly lied to anyone in his life.

"Well, next morning when Pa found out his brother had been in bed with me and knew who was lookin' for him, Pa just hit the ceiling. The madder he got, the more Uncle Vest laughed. About the time I figured Pa was going to throw his brother out on his ear, he stopped yellin', looked at Uncle Vest, and then started laughing. Just like that, Pa was all over being mad. The Sheriff never showed up again, and no one would ever tell me why he wanted Uncle Vest in the first place. Wonder to this day what it was all about. Guess it couldn't have been much or he'd have been back since Uncle Vest stayed with us a few days.

"Uncle Vest sure did have a sense of humor. He enjoyed having a good time- living, he called it. He'd work for a while, and then he'd take off for some place. Usually came back broke. Pa always berated him for being irresponsible. Guess it just took him longer to grow up than it did Pa.

"For some reason, Pa always felt he had to make money. I sometimes thought he drove himself just so he could say he was as good a man as his father.

"My grandfather was a mighty smart man, and he knew how to get ahead. His parents died when he was real young, so he was raised by foster parents; he started out with nothing but a keen mind and a willingness to work; he married a school teacher who taught him to read and write. He sure made a heap of money in timber. Perhaps Pa thought he had to do as well. He sometimes said that Grandfather never told him he did well at anything. I guess Pa just kept trying, hoping that one day his father would give him some praise."

Millie's voice trailed off, and he fell silent, obviously lost in thought.

Ralph watched his father, wondering if he would speak again. Ralph figured he knew just how Grandfather had felt because Great Grandfather had never praised him. Sounded just like him and Pa. There were lots of times when it would have been nice to have had Pa recognize that he'd done a good job at something, with just maybe a pat on the back for all the effort he'd put forth. Funny thing about the Setterington men, in many ways they were alike from generation to generation. Ralph vowed he'd be different if he ever had any kids;

he wouldn't be afraid to hand out praise if it was due. No, sir, a little praise sure never hurt anything.

Friday, Ralph went back to the doctor. When the leg was unwrapped, Dr. Beal looked at it carefully, then shook his head.

The upper part of the cut had definitely started to heal, the scab was a healthy one; the portion near the ankle looked terrible. Proud flesh was bulging here and there from the wound; pus escaped from under the sickly looking soft scab that was there, and the stitches had loosened. It was a mess!

"Rate, you've got proud flesh coming here. Now, it can't heal with that growing, so I'm going to have to burn it off."

"How do you do that?" interrupted Miney, her face visibly whitening.

"I'll treat it with blue vitriol. It won't harm the good flesh, but it will eat away any that isn't healthy tissue. Rate, it's gonna hurt," he warned.

"Nothing about this has felt any too good so far," said Rate. "I can take it."

"Sure you can. You're no sissy."

The doctor took a fresh block of blue vitriol out of the medicine chest. It was somewhat the consistency of soft chalk, and as the name implied was a light blue in color. He rubbed it across the shiny, pink flesh protruding from the cut. For a few moments, Ralph felt nothing, but then it started to burn; it felt as if someone had placed a hot iron on his leg. He clenched his fists and rocked his body back and forth while the doctor continued to rub the caustic on the unsound flesh. He tried to think of just anything except the pain. Finally, Doc was finished; he put a loose bandage back on the leg and gave the boy's knee a sympathetic slap. Looking at the grimace on the boy's face, the doctor spoke kindly.

"It'll stop hurtin' shortly, Rate. Just hang in there. Now, Miney, tomorrow I want you to wash that leg off and put the salve on just like you been doin'. I've taken out the top two stitches because that part is all right. He can get around in the house now, but he can't go back to school. I'm not gonna take any chance of him gettin' that leg hurt. Got that Rate? You can use your crutches around the house as much as you like, but not outside. See you next week."

Ralph's face had blanched with pain; however, the pain was either lessening somewhat, or he was becoming accustomed to it. He sure hoped this would take care of the situation because he didn't relish the thought of all this pain again.

As it turned out, Rate spent a rather discouraging fall. Each week he went to the doctor, and while a tiny bit more of the wound was healed at each visit, there was also more of the shiny, pink, unhealthy tissue protruding along the edge, so the process of burning off the proud flesh continued. Rate dreaded the visit to the doctor more and more. Golly darn, it just seemed as though that leg was never going to be completely healed, and all because Pearl was so blamed scared of automobiles.

At least being able to move around the house was a help to keep him occupied. He could go upstairs and prowl around in the attic--as long as he didn't bump his leg- which was a wonderful place for an inquisitive eleven-year-old. He found some medical books which had belonged to Grandfather Smith, Ma's father. Ralph had known that Hervey Smith had been a doctor, and here was the proof; he looked through them, stopping to read a page here and there. He also found a spinning wheel and a clock whose wheels and gears were made of wood, not metal. Guess he'd have to ask Ma if she knew about these things.

When asked, Miney explained that the clock had belonged to her grandfather Barnes and had been one of the household items brought with him and her mother from New York State. The spinning wheel had belonged to her ma.

"Ralph, I remember when I was small that Ma didn't think she could buy yarn in a store. Said it wasn't all that good and much too expensive. She spun her own wool, dyed it herself with weeds and berries for color--dark brown always came from the outer covering of black walnuts--and knitted our socks, shawls and sweaters. For winter, we always had a knitted woolen petticoat. That log cabin we lived in when I was born, wasn't very warm, mind you. Seems some of the chinking between the logs would loosen, and it let in an awful draft. We only had a fireplace then. Of course, ever since Pa built this house, we've had stoves. There was something nice about a fireplace. A stove is certainly a lot easier to cook on, but there was something awfully cheery about a fire in a fireplace. Ma used to sit in her rocking chair nights and knit by firelight. She knitted so often and so fast, I believe she could have done it blindfolded. Those were good days."

Miney's face looked wistful, almost as though she would like to relive that portion of her life. My but she did have pleasant memories.

"Ma, why's the floors upstairs so uneven? Each room is on a different level so there's all that stepping up or down."

Miney laughed heartily.

"I've often wondered that myself. You see, Pa built this house himself, and he added on a room at a time. I've often wondered if he ever measured anything since nothing is the same measurement--the windows are different sizes, the doors are all different, and the ceilings are all a different height. Guess Pa felt symmetry was not all that important."

"What's symmetry?"

"Sameness. Like all the windows should be the same distance from the floor, the doors the same size and height."

"I understand. Maybe Grandpa just liked to be different." Miney laughed again.

"Guess you could be right there. Pa *was* different. He was a good father although he was very strict. I remember the time he started to whip me. I don't even remember what I'd done to displease him, but he hit me once with the buggy whip. My, it did sting, and it scared me half to death. Your Uncle Jim, my half brother, was home at the time. Well, sir, Jim just stepped in front of me and says to Pa real quiet like, 'Pa, don't strike her again.' Pa raised his arm like he was going to hit Jim. Then, he just turned and walked away. I was a lot younger than Jim, and when he knelt down to ask if I was all right, I threw my arms around his neck and hugged him hard, half-crying, I was. He says, 'That's all right, Miney. Pa won't never use that buggy whip on you again.' And Pa never did. Course I probably toed the mark a little better after that because I sure had no hankering for a whipping. I can still feel how scared I was."

One afternoon, Ralph had been particularly restless so Miney had come up with the idea that he should teach Bruno some new tricks. From somewhere she produced frames for glasses that no longer had any lens in them. She said Bruno should be taught to sit up in a chair with the glasses on and read his newspaper. The dog was exceptionally smart, and in a short time all Rate had to say was, "Bruno, read your newspaper." The dog would jump up in a chair, allow the glasses to be draped over his muzzle, then would sit up on his haunches as long as Ralph held a newspaper in front of him. Bruno also became so adept at catching a ball that he and Ralph spent hours with Ralph tossing a rubber ball to the brindle bulldog for him to catch; he then promptly brought the ball to his master and waited expectantly for Ralph to throw it again.

It was finally decided that Ralph would be able to return to school after the beginning of the year. However, Miss Finch had told his parents that there was no way he could make up so much missed work; therefore, he would have to repeat the seventh grade.

The news didn't seem to bother Rate one little bit. School was something he often tolerated as a necessary evil. He loved history, liked reading as long as it wasn't some sissy stuff, and he was good at arithmetic; it was English, spelling and composition that he could do without.

They often chose up sides for spelldowns at school. Two team captains were picked; they each chose a person, then that person picked the next so each member had a chance to pick a team member except for the last one chosen. Guess who was always the last one chosen? Course he couldn't blame anyone since if he got past his first word, it was a minor miracle. He remembered the day he had really studied very hard for a spelling exam. One of the words had been "gas" which he promptly put down as "gass." When he got his paper back, Miss Finch had merely drawn a line through the g. He supposed she was equating him with that lowly animal, and giving him credit for being just as stupid. Well, he guessed he'd always remember how to spell that particular word. Ma had always been such a good speller, she had never understood why a son of hers had to have so much trouble spelling even some of the most simple words.

His inability to spell hampered his compositions. It wasn't that he didn't have ideas, some of which were really pretty good, it was just that he had so many misspelled words, it was a cryin' shame. His papers always came back with red marks over the entire paper. He didn't suppose any teacher wanted to struggle to read what he had written, and they couldn't give him a good grade because of all the mistakes. Well, fat lot he cared. He certainly wasn't going to depend on good English to make a living when he was grown.

Since he was going to take the grade over, it sure wasn't going to matter how much he played hooky come spring. Ma would frown on the idea, but he just bet Pa would be understanding and let him help with all sorts of things. Pa had said it was about time for him to learn to make wieners since he liked to eat 'em so much. He guessed maybe that wouldn't be such a bad idea. Come spring, he knew Pa had some farm work to do, and even though he did hire George Page to work in the butcher (Ralph pronounced it boocher) shop, there'd still be plenty Ralph could do.

Sure would beat goin' to school. School was certainly better than being cooped up in the house day after day, but still, the spring of the year was made for being outside instead of sittin' in a classroom even if he did like Miss Finch better than any teacher he'd had thus far. Course, he wondered whether Miss Finch would take kindly to him being gone from the classroom without a good reason. Oh, well, he'd get around that difficulty somehow.

CHAPTER 7

Christmas had come and gone. Ralph had received seven books as gifts and had had them read before New Year's Day. They had spent Christmas Day at South Lyon with Grandfather and Grandmother just like usual. There was talk that Grandfather might move to Nashville on the Thornapple River. Seems he had an opportunity to sell his bank for a nice tidy profit so was giving much consideration to beginning a bank in Vermontville. From the talk, Ralph guessed Vermontville and Nashville were close to each other. Of course, it would be expected that Aunt Ruby and Uncle Mac would make the transition with them. Where Lovina went, Ruby had to follow and vice versa. Daughter and mother had no intention of being separated; thus, whatever Horatio decided to do to make money, he accepted the fact that Lovina expected he would share his business acumen with his son-in-law.

The best part about Christmas this year had been his gift from Pa--a single shot, Savage rifle. Millie had been as good as his word because Rate was now twelve. Ma had been more than a little upset, but Pa had simply said, "The lad's old enough, Miney, so just keep still." Well, Ma had quit voicing her objections, but that didn't mean her mind had been changed one iota. He guessed he'd have to be extra careful, then maybe she'd quit her worrying when she learned he was old enough to handle an honest-to-goodness gun, not just some toy popgun. Maybe if he brought home some game, Ma would change her mind and decide it wasn't such a bad idea. Ma wouldn't be too awfully opposed to something that would save her money, you could bet on that. Ma might never actually approve of the gun, but if she could save a dime, Rate knew she would quit voicing any opposition.

Ralph had been sitting at the table laboring over a composition which was due the next day. He should have worked on it at school, but he had read ahead in his reading book and had lost track of the time. His forehead was puckered into a frown; his fingers traced the words slowly and carefully, he was a pretty fair penman for a boy; he stopped a moment, looked in his mother's direction, then asked, "Ma, how do you spell separate?"

"I can tell you that," put in Blanche. "It's s-e-p-a-r-a-t-e."

"You sure it's not er?"

"Am I ever sure. I misspelled it once a couple of years ago and got corrected in front of the whole class. I was so embarrassed at the time. Believe me, that's one word I'll *never* forget how to spell."

"Well, if you're sure."

"She's right, Ralph," came from Miney.

"All right, Ma. I'm tryin' not to have any words spelled wrong on this here composition. If I have very many, Miss Finch will circle each one, and I'll have to rewrite my composition besides write each word correctly twenty-five times. Boy, Miss Finch sure is a stickler on spelling."

"That's one of the reasons she's a good teacher, she doesn't let anyone slack off on his work."

"But, Ma, it's hardly fair 'cause spelling comes so much harder for some of us. Why the other day she let that Ruby Spurbeck stand by herself against a team of the best spellers from the high school and Ruby won," he said, his voice betraying that he felt this was an incredulous feat.

Miney laughed.

"Wonder how that made the older ones feel to have a seventh grader outspell them? Ralph, the Lord does not bestow all talent equally so some spell better, some sew better, some boys handle horses better than others, and the list is endless. The important thing is that we make the most of our God-given talents and don't waste what He has given us."

Rate supposed Ma had a point, but he sometimes wondered why God couldn't have been a little more generous and endowed him with the capability to spell just a little better.

It was one of those sunny days that made a person realize spring was just around the corner; the weather was unseasonably warm, and while the ground was still spongy since there had not been enough rain to settle it after the upheaval of frost, the snow was completely gone.

Ralph gazed wistfully out the window. He could think of a hundred things he'd rather be doing than this assignment in arithmetic. He had a whole page to do, only he'd been frogging around and had finished less than half of the problems. He had tried to persuade his father that there was certainly some reason for him to stay home from school today; however, he hadn't made much headway with that idea since Millie was going out into the country calling on farmers to buy a cow or two for the meat market and line up some prospective sellers for the future.

Millie made these trips whenever the market got low on meat. Last week, he had bought several hogs, and they were now penned at the slaughterhouse located west of town to the village limits, and then north to the back side of the athletic field and park. Only a couple of them were big enough for immediate butchering, but they'd feed the others--they needed some way to dispose of the innards (the whole community pronounced it inwards) from the butchered carcasses, and the pigs fought amongst themselves so anxious were they to eat the entrails--and when they were large enough, they'd find their way into the butcher shop cooler, or be sold. If he got too many hogs ahead, Millie would take them to some pens near the depot and finish them off by feeding them corn for ten days or so, then he'd sell them.

Millie had told his son that there would be other days when he could be of much more use. Of course, when Pa spoke, no one dared argue with him, so Ralph had stayed in school.

Sure didn't help any today, but maybe there'd come another time when Pa would let him skip school to do some work. Golly, if he was home, he could be working on his new kite; after all, it was getting close to the time of year when it would be kite-flying weather, and he still didn't have a kite to fly. The one he'd used last year had taken a nose dive just before the best of the season was over and had been so badly mangled, he'd thrown it away. A boy certainly had to have a kite to fly. Now, he'd have to work on it come Saturday because Pa usually kept him busy after school.

Ralph was bored, restless, and disgusted. He put his hand in his desk to bring out his pencil box because he had made a mistake and needed an eraser. His hand touched something else, and his face broke into a smile. His bean shooter. It was a simple little gadget, just a length of elderberry bush with the pith pushed out to make a hollow tube. It worked right well unless one tried to shoot a bean that was a little oversize; however, Ralph was very selective when choosing his ammunition so this seldom happened. Wasn't it just lucky that he had a few of the small, white beans stashed in his pencil box?

He cautiously slipped a bean into the end of the elderberry pipe, waited until Miss Finch had her back turned to the room to write on the blackboard, and then pow! Harry grabbed the back of his neck. When Harry sneaked a glance behind him, Ralph was busily doing his school work. A few moments later, Leon rubbed the side of his neck, then it was Sam's turn. This had gone on for several minutes. Then, came the summons.

"Ralph Setterington, come with me."

Miss Finch glared at her pupil while he slid out of his desk, and then she stalked out of the door in front of him; prominently displayed behind her back was a razor strap which she was notorious for having used on many disobedient or disrespectful pupils. She headed down the two flights of stairs to the basement room where she always took her pupils to chastise them. She had no reservations about leaving the classroom; she knew as surely as night follows day, they would be silent while she was gone--they dared not be otherwise because she was also noted for walking softly, a trait, she often told them, learned from the Indians.

He'd gone and done it now. Just like the stories said, she must have eyes in the back of her head because he was certain he'd been careful to shoot only while her back was turned. Golly, she usually only took the shooter away from the culprit, but perhaps the fact that she'd issued a sort of ultimatum only a couple of days ago might have something to do with it. If she whipped him, that meant he'd get one from Pa too. That had been the only thing Pa had said to him before he started school was that if a teacher found it necessary to give him a licking, he'd get another when he got home.

Pa's lickings were something decidedly unpleasant to tolerate although it had been two or three years since he'd got one. He wouldn't dare *not* tell his father because sooner or later in this small community someone would tell him. Rate knew he would really be in trouble then, and would get a doubly hard licking to make up for his lack of honesty.

They had reached the basement and entered the room where the country boys usually ate lunch.

"Well, Ralph, let's have it." Miss Finch held out her hand.

"Have what?" was the wide-eyed, innocent reply.

"That bean shooter you have stuck down the front of your shirt."

"Oh," came the deflated reply.

Was that a suppressed grin on her face? Ralph reached down his shirt front, pulled out the article in question, and handed it to Kate as he watched her warily. She took it in her strong hands and broke it in half, the sides splintering as she did so.

"Now, Rate, I thought you had a pretty good memory. We both know it didn't take you any time at all to learn that poem last week, did it?" she asked pleasantly enough.

"Learned it the night before by reading it over two or three times," he stated proudly.

"Well, then, it seems that you should be able to remember a few simple rules, doesn't it?" she purred.

"Yes, Ma'am," he agreed with a sigh.

Darn! He realized almost at once that she had tricked him. So much for this encounter; he'd learn not to volunteer so much, just say a monosyllabic yes or no after this and see how far that got her.

"Then you *do* remember what I said about bean shooters?"

"Yessum," came the resigned reply.

"I should use this strap on you to kind of make it stick in your mind, but I'll let you off easy this once!'

For an instant, relief flashed across his face, and Miss Finch wanted to laugh at the sight.

"Tell you what, Ralph," she confided, "your shirt front makes a poor hiding place unless you get shirts that don't fit quite as well."

The shirts the boys wore had four buttons for a neck opening, and the body of the shirt fit rather closely under the suspenders. Belts had not come into vogue as a means of holding up a boy's pants as yet; the pantleg fastened on a band just below the knee where it fitted snugly over heavy stockings; wide suspenders buttoned to the underside of the waistband.

With that piece of information, Kate held the door open for Ralph to go back upstairs. Well, so much for that. At least he didn't have to tell Pa anything tonight. Wonder if Miss Finch had intended to lick him when they left the room, and if she had, why had she changed her mind?

This was his first trip to the basement, but certainly not his last. He was to have Miss Finch for two more years, and they made countless trips to the basement, always with her in the lead, and always, always with that razor strap held prominently behind her back for him to watch and wonder if on this particular trip she might actually use it. She never did.

When Ralph was grown, and Kate had long since retired from teaching, he had once asked, "Kate, how come you never used that razor strap on me?"

Her eyes had twinkled, and she had laughed as she said, "Guess I always thought that watching it all the way down to the basement was punishment enough. After all, you were never completely certain I wasn't going to use it."

"Aw, Kate, I had it figured out that you were all bluff."

She chuckled at that.

"I'm not saying I shouldn't have used it. In fact, there were times when you undoubtedly did deserve to be whipped, but you always looked so blamed innocent-- not sorry--just like you'd never misbehaved in the first place. We did get along, didn't we, Ralph?" she had asked, a nostalgic note creeping into her voice.

"That's for certain. You taught me a lot--like be sneaky enough not to get caught."

"You rascal. You'll never change." "Would you want me to?"

"Heavens, no. I can't visualize you being anything but what you are," she had replied with a laugh.

Yes, they had had a good relationship, equally rewarding to both.

* * * * * * * * * * * *

Rate had decided he'd better get busy on that kite he intended to build if he was to have it done in time to use this spring. Early Saturday morning, he went to the lumber yard down by the tracks. He stopped in the office long enough to ask if he could have a piece of white pine about four feet long. He was told to go look for himself and pick out any piece he wanted since they had quite a pile of scraps. Some would be shorter, but if he looked long enough, he would undoubtedly find what he wanted.

Rate wanted a knot-free piece with the grain running straight and true. Of course, white pine came mostly in unblemished boards with seldom a knot anywhere. He looked and sorted, and looked some more until he finally found the piece he wanted. The grain was even and fine and straight; with the narrow board tucked under his arm, he headed for home.

Once in the woodshed, he hauled out his trusty jackknife; he held the board firmly and placed the large blade of the knife about a quarter of an inch in from the outside of the board; he knew it would split true the whole length of the board because the split would follow the grain. He shoved the blade into the soft wood almost the full width of the blade, then carefully gave a slight twist, and the small splinter came away from the larger part of the board. He repeated this two more times, then set his board aside as he began to smooth off the rough edges of his pieces.

He took two of the pieces he had splintered off, held them to form a broadened X and fastened them securely together with a stout piece of cord. Then, he ran the next piece through the midsection to extend slightly above the two side pieces and fastened that in place. He notched the end of each piece, being careful not to split them. Now, he took the extra cord, fitted it into each notch and pulled it gently until it formed a supple framework from one wooden strut to the next. He couldn't hold it in place tightly and tie it, but he heard his mother in the kitchen, and when asked, she came to his aid by holding her finger on the crossed string until he could form a serviceable square knot--it had to be a knot which would hold and not slip. He surveyed his handiwork, well pleased with its appearance.

He was now ready to cover the framework. Usually he had to use newspapers, but this year he had some tissue paper that Grandmother had given him at Christmas. Come to think of it, Grandmother wasn't all that bad; she sometimes did very nice things for him at the most unexpected times. He'd been kind of scared to ask for the bright red, tissue paper, but she had been more than happy to give it to him and had been very generous in the amount; he had more than was needed for one kite. He borrowed his mother's scissors and cut the paper to the proper size and shape; next, he took a little flour and water and made a paste. With this concoction, he pasted the red tissue paper in place, folding about an inch of it over the string framework. He had cut enough to put a double thickness on what would be the front of his kite; now, he set it aside to dry.

He went up to his room and found last year's kite string--well, it was really carpet warp, but it sure worked well; he had it rolled around a length of broom handle that was long enough so he could grab it on each side of the bulging roll of cord. He guessed he'd better ask Ma about some rags for a tail; one never knew just how much would be needed, if the wind was light, a kite couldn't be tail heavy and get off the ground.

Miney gave him a couple of worn-out shirts of Millie's and an old petticoat; Rate tore them into four three-inch strips and tied a couple of lengths together. The rest of the job would have to wait until the paste was thoroughly dry. He had barely notched the framework where the heavy cord was to be fitted; a length coming from each brace to meet just above the cross of the X.

This much done, all he needed was kite-flying weather. Hopefully, he wouldn't have too long to wait.

March had come in like the proverbial lion, but had definitely gone out like a lamb--warm, balmy days with the sun already coaxing new life into growing things; the fields had started to green, and even the buds on some of the trees were outdoing themselves getting fat and pudgy, nearly to the bursting point.

With all of this frenzied activity of the spring season, surely in a matter of days must come the winds that were just meant to snatch a young boy's kite and carry it aloft, going ever higher and higher like some huge bird in the sky, impatiently tugging for more string to be doled out by the lad in command. Yup, it sure was getting to be that time of year.

Ralph had only a few days to wait. It had rained a warm April shower the day before, but then, the southwesterly wind had risen to dry off the land and half the boys in school had itchy pants all afternoon just waiting to be dismissed so they could dash home to fly their kites. Ralph was thankful Pa had gone out to buy livestock, so he wasn't expected to check in at the meat market.

Rate had gone with Brownie McNall to get his kite, then the two boys had stopped at Ralph's and were now trudging to a large open field at the west end of the street.

"That's a pretty good wind today, Rate."

"Should make it easy gettin' a kite up. How'd you like mine?"

"Sure looks keen. Where'd you get the red paper?" asked Brownie enviously, his newspaper looking drab by comparison.

"My grandmother. Ma don't never wrap Christmas presents, but Grandmother started doing it a couple of years ago, so she has all kinds of this tissue paper. She had some plain white and some green, but I liked the red best."

"Sure is pretty. How much tail you gonna try?"

"Don't know. That wind is awful strong. I think it will take a really long one."

"Maybe I don't have enough."

"I've got some extra pieces," offered Ralph.

The boys attached the tails; Rate looked undecidedly at his, then added a substantially longer piece. He knew that without the proper weight and balance of a tail, the kite was more than likely to go up a short distance, then take a nose dive to the ground no matter how fast he ran.

"I dunno, Rate. You got an awful lot of tail there. Think if I was you, I'd take off that last piece," suggested Brownie.

"Nope. I'm gonna try it as is. My kite is a little bigger than yours, so I figger it can handle more. You wanna go first?"

Brownie arranged his kite to suit, then started running into the wind; it came off the ground, started its climb into the air, faltered, wobbled, and quick as a wink, turned bottom side up and came crashing back to the ground. The boys gave it a cursory examination and found that, luckily, it hadn't broken.

"See, you need more tail," said Ralph. "Here. You can have what I had left over. I'll try to get mine up while you're fixin' yours."

Rate positioned his kite with the tail outstretched behind so it would not get tangled. He started running. At first, the kite hovered a foot or two off the ground, seemingly determined to go no higher; maybe that much tail was too much drag. Rate increased his speed, *very* cautiously meted out a little more string; then, he felt the unmistakable tug, the wild spirit of a thing alive, tugging and pulling and fighting for freedom. He doled out more string and up, up, forever up, soared his kite, truly a thing of beauty. He had stopped running now, his sides puffing, and concentrated on slowly paying out more line--just enough at a time for the kite to move ever higher. Wow! He didn't remember having flown one this high before. Sure beat last year's model. He looked at his roll of string and noticed he had used nearly all of it. Darn. He wished he had put on more. What a proud feeling engulfed him as he watched his kite sailing high in a beautiful azure sky; now outlined against the background of a scudding gray-white cloud, now etched against the deep, April blue.

Brownie had finally been able to get his kite to fly, but it had not risen to such a majestic height. Others joined them, so there were now several kites in the air; this took more concentration because no one wanted to risk having a midair collision. Ralph noticed that one boy was flying a box kite. Now, that was something Ralph had not yet tried to build. Sure was different looking, and while it did not fly as high as the more conventional ones and perhaps looked a little awkward, it was flying. Guess maybe that would be a project for another year.

Millie came home for dinner each day, and today, the nineteenth of April was no exception. It took only a glance at his face for Miney to see he had something of importance to say.

As he slid into his chair, he spoke. "Ed Hawes stopped by this morning after he had made his usual run to the depot. Said there was all kinds of reports coming in on the key. Seems that yesterday morning they had a big earthquake out in Californey. San Francisco was the hardest hit. Ed says it nigh leveled the entire city."

"My land, Millie. That's dreadful."

Ralph and Blanche had both stopped eating, watching their father, expecting him to continue. Millie took a few bites of food, then went on with his story.

"Came early in the morning before a lot of city folk get up. Guess they are still havin' tremors, so no one knows if there will be another hard one or not. What's worse than the quake is the fires. 'Pears the whole city is built on hills, so in the valleys, the fires are takin' everything. Ed said he couldn't remember how many they figgered is already homeless."

"Pa, what are those poor people ever going to do?" asked Blanche, a worried frown creasing her forehead.

"Don't rightly know. Suppose other parts of the country will try to help. They're gonna need food and clothing, that's for sure. It'll be a wonder if many of them had any type of insurance.

"Oh my, just imagine losing everything you own." Miney spoke softly, almost to herself as she looked about the room.

"Pa, what causes earthquakes?" asked Ralph.

"I don't really know. Something causes the earth to move and shake. They say it causes big cracks in the earth. This isn't the first one they've had in Californey. Makes a man downright glad he's living in a place like Michigan."

"Oh, my, yes," agreed Miney, visibly shaken.

"Was anyone killed?" asked Blanche.

"Reckon so, only Ed says there's no way o' knowin' how many. They won't be able to start lookin' for bodies and such until they get the fires under control. Course with so many fires, there's not enough men or engines to do a proper job. Ed says they are dynamiting buildings in an effort to halt the blaze."

"Makes a person realize how much we have to be thankful for, doesn't it? Those poor people. I wonder if the Church will take a special donation, or perhaps ask for clothes and such?"

"I have no idee, but it seems quite likely."

"Children, you had better hurry, or you will be late for school."

Rate and Blanche finished their meal in silence, then hurried off. Millie had told all he knew about the matter, so he ate in silence. Miney had lost her appetite. All she could think of was the thousands of people who were now homeless. She gazed around her, and while her house was not as nice as some, she was certainly thankful for her home. She found it difficult to imagine what it must be like to have absolutely nothing of life's material things left--not even clothes except whatever one happened to be wearing.

The school was buzzing with the news, and as usual rumors flew fast and furious. Some students were certain the earth had opened up wide enough for entire city blocks to have fallen into the yawning chasm. Rate's common sense prevented him from believing these tall tales.

Once back in the classroom, Rate asked Miss Finch if she knew what caused earthquakes. She drew a circle on the board which she said represented the Earth; she told the class that under this top layer of soil which varied in thickness, there were rocks, and for some reason unknown to her, these rocks sometimes moved. Of course, if they moved, the outermost layer had to move too. She told them the quake sometimes caused fissures ranging from a few inches to several feet in width and sometimes, many, many feet deep.

Students wondered why San Francisco was burning, how had the fires started? She patiently answered their questions obviously believing this was of more importance than their routine classes and assignments. She only regretted she did not understand the phenomenon more fully herself.

That Sunday, in Church, Reverend Thompson offered a prayer for those who had lost their lives, for those who had been injured, and for those hundreds of people who were homeless or had lost loved ones. He announced to the congregation that the Ladies Missionary Society was collecting clothes and bedding as well as monetary donations to be sent to a Church affiliate in San Francisco. He pressed home his point that those of us who are more fortunate should share with our less fortunate brethren because it was the way of the Lord.

Even though Miney seldom had any used clothing to give away, she decided she would donate at least one of her older dresses, and she was certain she could find something of Blanche's and Ralph's as well. Always before, Miney had used the old clothes to make either heavy braided rugs or the tighter crocheted rugs. Whatever was left over from that was stuffed into the rag bag to await the arrival of someone who would give her a few pennies for the rags. Usually, there was a rag man once a year. Well, these homeless people certainty needed the help of everyone, so she would do her best. She supposed there might be one or two old quilts she could part with since she had finished a new one last winter; she had another quilt nearly pieced and would probably have a quilting bee this winter to tie it off. Yes, she was sure the Lord would expect her to give something to those unfortunate people, and Miney honestly tried to do what she felt the Lord expected.

A disaster like the earthquake made everyone stop and think; Rate had given it a lot of thought. He tried to imagine what it would be like to have the house one lived in be shaken down as though it was just a toy, or how a person would feel to be walking along and have a huge crack appear in the street only a few feet away. Michigan sure was a better place to live than California. Sometimes, there were cyclones, but other than that, the elements were kind to Michigan. Rate figured he was pretty well satisfied with his state and decided he'd never go looking for one that was any better.

Blanche had worked for two days cracking and picking out hickory nuts to have for a cake she was to take to a party on Saturday evening. It had been quite a job, but with her usual diligence, Blanche had kept at the job until it was done. She had picked out the nutmeats during the daylight hours to lessen the chance of an errant piece of shell falling in with the nuts. She had stored them in one of her mother's canning jars.

Blanche never quite knew why she took the jar down from the cupboard on Friday evening--just to look at the results of all that time, she guessed. To her astonishment, it was nearly empty! At first she was completely puzzled, but then she began to have mighty strong suspicions. Ralph had made a couple of smart-alecky remarks when she was working at cracking them, for indeed she sometimes did have trouble. On occasion, the nut when hit with the hammer, instead of cracking, would skitter off across the floor. Just seemed that some nuts had a harder shell than others. Once she'd hit her thumb, and Ralph had snickered at that. Well, Mr. Smartypants, she thought, we'll just see what Pa has to say about this.

"Pa."

Millie looked up expectantly from his paper. "What is it, Blanche?"

"You know how I've been working at cracking hickory nuts, don't you?"

"Seems I've seen you working at it a couple of times."

"Well, I put the nutmeats into a jar and set the jar on a shelf in the pantry. Just now I went to look at it, and there's hardly any nuts left--at least not enough for a decent cake."

"Sure you had the right jar?"

"Oh, I'm sure all right. I'll bet Ralph got into them."

"Lessen I'm mistaken, that's him coming in the back door now, so we'll ask. Rate," he raised his voice, "come in here."

"You want me, Pa?"

"Reckon I do. What do you know about some hickory nuts that your sister had cracked and picked out?"

"Took her over two days to do it, and she pounded her thumb more than once," he volunteered, scanning his father's face for some hint as to why the question.

"That all?"

"What else should I know?" he countered.

"Ralph Setterington," interrupted Blanche, "I just know you ate all those nuts I worked so hard to crack."

Ralph grinned and started to give her a flippant retort, looked at his father, and thought better of it.

"Well, Rate, I'm waiting for an answer. Did you eat Blanche's hickory nuts?"

"Guess probably I did," he admitted.

"Oh! I just knew it had to be him. Why this time? Ralph, didn't you know I wanted them to bake a special cake for a party tomorrow night?" she wailed.

"Don't guess I did. I just figured you wanted some on hand. Sure tasted good," he grinned impishly.

"Ralph, I guess you had better get busy cracking hickory nuts. We'll see just how long it takes you to refill Blanche's jar. You do have more nuts to crack, don't you, Blanche?"

"There's lots left from what I picked up in the fall."

"Well, boy, what are you waiting for? You'd best get started."

Ralph glared at his sister, took a pan from the kitchen and went up to the attic to get the hickory nuts. It was still light enough that he sat in the woodshed by the west door and started cracking.

Golly, his stomach hurt. He had sampled the nuts a few nights ago, but he had eaten the lion's share tonight as a sort of dessert. He cracked a few more nuts. His stomach sure felt queasy, he just bet he was going to throw up. A few more whacks with the hammer, and then out the door he flew to the toilet where he proceeded to lose his supper and a considerable quantity of hickory nuts. Oooooh, he felt awful. His stomach churned and rumbled, and he felt a little weak in the knees.

He came back into the woodshed, took up the hammer again, then decided to go ask Pa if he had to finish the job tonight.

Both Millie and Miney looked up as he came shuffling into the living room. "Ralph, whatever is the matter?" asked Miney. "You're white's a sheet."

"I feel awful, Ma. I just threw up my supper."

"Land sakes, what brought that on, I wonder."

"Could likely be too many hickory nuts, couldn't it, boy?" questioned Millie.

"I suppose it might. Pa, I feel terrible. Do I have to finish cracking those nuts tonight?"

"Said so, didn't I?"

"Yes, but--"

"Then, you'd best get busy."

"But, Millie, the boy is sick."

"Miney, keep still. This is betwixt Rate an' me."

"Well," she snorted, "the least you can do is let me give him some ginger tea."

"You're worse than an old hen cluckin' over her brood, but ifn it makes you feel better, go ahead."

Miney swallowed an angry retort. At times, Millie was completely unreasonable. She got up from her rocker and flounced to the kitchen to make Ralph the ginger tea which might warm and settle his stomach. She knew as well as anyone that Ralph had done wrong, but she felt that tomorrow morning he could get enough nuts picked out of the shells to put in a cake. Blanche had had many more than she needed; therefore, he could work on those all day if necessary. Still, Millie had spoken, and she darsent interfere any more than she had by speaking her piece.

She looked at her son as he went listlessly back to his job of hammering hickory nuts on a piece of old anvil to crack them open; he tossed them into a pan where he still had to separate the nuts from the hard shells. My, he did look peaked, but she supposed he'd live through it. Still, there were times when it just seemed that Millie was completely lacking in compassion--the only thing he cared about was that his orders were followed to the letter.

Ralph managed to replace the hickory nuts he had eaten. Even his sister felt just a trifle sorry for him although she had been very angry in the first place. She conceded that maybe he hadn't known she had wanted them for something special. Ralph had said he hadn't known, and her brother was not one to lie. She was willing to bet that from now on, he'd stay out of her baking materials.

She just accepted the fact that her father was always much more strict with Ralph than he ever was with her. Had the shoe been on the other foot, Millie would quite likely have seen the situation as completely humorous.

CHAPTER 8

It was a beautiful, warm, spring day; the sun shone brightly, the crocus, the hyacinths, the daffodils had long ago blossomed and died; the fruit trees had begun to bloom, and in a few more days the lilacs would be a riot of color. Then, the whole village would smell of lilacs; almost every yard boasted a lilac bush or two ranging from scraggly and scrawny to the large spreading bushes looking like a cloud of lavender, or white, or purple.

Miney always welcomed this time of year because all too often the smell of the village emanated from the manure piles beside each barn; it was especially bad when folks started to think about gardens because some of them forked a generous amount of barnyard manure onto the spot to be plowed or spaded for this year's vegetables and oh, how that freshly disturbed manure did stink. Then, there were the times when residents hired someone to clean out the manure piles and the refuse from the privies; both activities added a distinct odor to the air which was difficult to disguise. However, at times like today, Miney was especially thankful for the glorious world God had created, unbefouled by man.

Sunday dinner was finished, and Blanche and Miney were just finishing the last of the dishes. Millie sat dozing in his chair, his stomach full, completely contented with his world. He labored diligently for six days a week, much of the time from sunup until sundown, so Sunday was his day of rest and rightly so. That Miney ever felt a twinge of jealousy because even on the Lord's day she still had three meals to get and dishes to do, never entered his mind. He accepted this as simply a woman's share of the load.

Ralph was out on the front porch playing ball with Bruno. His mother frowned on him going to other boys' houses to play on the Sabbath, so he and Bruno had to be content to amuse themselves.

The unmistakable sounds of an automobile came from down the street. Ralph paused with his hand in midair and glanced toward the sound. He was right. Here came one of those new automobiles, the kind where the style sort of looked like the body of a surrey with a little house stuck out in front to hold the engine. Well, my gosh, it was chugging and banging to a stop right in front of their place. Then, Rate recognized the driver.

"Pa! Pa!" He dashed into the house. "Pa, Mr. Sherman's here in an automobile."

Sleepily, Millie asked, "Which Mr. Sherman?"

"Clayt, that's who. Come see."

Millie had just reached the door as Clayt, who had been their neighbor for years when they lived on the farm, stepped up on the front steps.

"Well, Millie, whadaya think? Ain't she a beaut?"

"Don't rightly know. Guess I'd have to give it a closer look."

"Well, what are ya waitin' for? Come on out and see. I just got her last week, so I'm not real used to startin' her yet."

Ralph was already out to the street looking over the automobile, a Buick. Sure looked all nice and new although a fine coat of dust covered most of the vehicle. It had two lamps in the front for night driving; the leather seats were padded, and the leather fastened with buttons giving it a diamond shape across the back as well as the seat; the top was folded down like a buggy top. It had running boards to step on to facilitate getting into the vehicle because it stood high off the ground on rather large, cumbersome wheels.

"Well, Millie, how about going for a spin? Miney, too."

"Guess I'd have to ask her to see if she'd want to."

"Why wouldn't she want to? C'mon. I'll go ask her."

They went up the steps, across the porch, and into the house. Mina had hung up the dishpan and arranged the dishrag on a hanger; Blanche had finished stacking the pans away so both were finished with their chore. They were in the act of removing their aprons when the two men entered the kitchen.

"Clayt. What brings you here?"

"Came just to see you, Miney."

"Find that a little hard to believe," she laughed. "Well, come on back to the living room and set for a spell. Didn't you bring your wife?"

"Nope. Left her home. Told you I came to see you. Come look out the door. There," he said proudly.

"For land sakes. Is that--that automobile yours?"

"Sure nuff is."

"Tell me, Clayt, do you really feel that these contraptions are entirely safe?" she asked conspiratorially.

Clayton laughed outright.

"Of course I do otherwise I wouldn't have got one. They're the coming thing. There will be a day when the only place you'll see a horse is in the fields working."

"Now, Clayt, let's don't be hasty. I'm of a mind that they just may not pan out," stated Millie.

"Time's a wastin'. How about that ride, Miney?"

"1--1 don't know. I've never even been up close to one you know."

"No time like the present. Besides, Blanche wants to go, don't you, Blanche?" "Sure would be nice, Mr. Sherman. I've never ridden in one yet although we see Mr. Galehouse around town with his quite often." "Grab your bonnet then, and let's get goin'"

Both Miney and Blanche carefully pinned on a hat and followed the men outside. Ralph was already sitting in the high back seat and was joined by Blanche and Miney while Millie clambered into the front. Clayt set the spark lever and the gas lever, then walked to the front where he gave the motor a half turn with the crank. Nothing happened. He fitted the crank back in the slot, and this time gave it a quick complete turn; the engine sputtered, then started, and Clayt raced back to the driver's seat to make an adjustment in the levers. The whole machine vibrated in time with the firing of the engine; Clayt put the automobile in gear, released the hand brake, let out the clutch, and with a jerk and a jump, they started forward.

Around the corner they went, then west on Main Street. Why they were whizzing along at fifteen miles an hour. Here and there, they met a buggy, and while some horses ignored them, one reared and plunged so badly they stopped the car and Millie and Clayton did what they could to help the young man get his horse under control. Millie said nothing, but shook his head; it was easy to see his sympathies were with the young man.

Back at the house once more, the family set about to discuss their outing.

"The ride was just wonderful. Pa, when can we get an automobile?" asked a jubilant Blanche. It was obvious that she was much enthralled.

"Don't think I want one, Blanche. 'Pears to me a horse is one whale of a lot easier to use."

"Oh, Pa, how can you say that? You are never for anything new," she accused. "Well, I for one think an automobile is just the thing to have. After all, we can't always stay where we are, we do have to have progress."

"Grandmother," chided Millie.

"I don't care, Pa. I'll bet Grandfather will have one before long. Just you wait and see. He may be older, but he's not afraid to try something new even if it is partly because Grandmother wants to be ahead of everyone else."

With that, she flounced out of the room. "Ailed her good, didn't I?" laughed Millie.

"Yes, Millie, you did. Blanche never goes halfway in her feelings, she is either for something, or she is opposed to it. I would definitely say she was quite impressed with Clayt's machine."

"Rate, how'd you like it?"

Ralph solemnly eyed his father a moment before replying, then said, "Guess I'd rather drive a horse."

"Good for you, lad. I'm glad to see you aren't going hog wild over the gol-durn things. As I've said before, that constant racket is more'n enough to make a man deef. And look at the trouble they cause. Why half the horses on the road are scared to death of them and their infernal noise. Lookit Pearl, she still hasn't got used to those contraptions although she is some better."

Miney had kept quiet because she was certain Millie would only make fun of her thoughts. The fact was, Miney had been a little frightened; she hadn't liked the noise, and she hadn't liked the vibration. Of course, the seats were nice and comfortable, but they weren't any better than the surrey--at least not much. She guessed she felt much the same as her son; Blanche certainly had been taken with it, no doubt about that. Of course, Blanche had a very adventuresome spirit and was always interested in new inventions.

Rate had been glad for the chance to ride in Mr. Sherman's automobile even if he hadn't been all that wildly impressed. At least he could do a little bragging at school now since not many of his friends had been so fortunate. He guessed the reason he wasn't very excited was mostly because he liked horses. Besides, he just bet those things broke down often, and no one ever had to repair a horse, even if a buggy did require upkeep. Besides, he never had liked the smell of a gasoline engine; to him, the pungent odor of horseflesh was definitely more acceptable.

Blanche had gone to her room thinking about what her father had said. It always made her angry when he intimated that she was like her grandmother. Perhaps she did stand by her decisions a little too staunchly, but she certainly hoped she was more considerate of other people's feelings than Grandmother was. Besides, she didn't try to interfere with other people, she simply wanted to be able to make her own decisions, and Blanche felt that she really did try to look at any situation from more than one point of view.

Blanche just felt that automobiles were going to be the coming thing. How much easier to house a machine that didn't have to be fed, watered, and cleaned up after. She had never relished the chore of harnessing a horse either, so that was one more plus on the side of an automobile. Pa was just too blamed stubborn to admit anything modern had any advantage over the old way of doing things. Of course, these automobiles might be difficult for a woman to start, but she just bet that the next few years would see quite an improvement in them.

She wondered if Pa would ever come to admit there might be an advantage in having an automobile instead of having to drive a horse. Sometimes, she felt that Pa was stubborn just for the sake of being contrary; maybe it was because he had never been allowed to have an opinion of his own when he was a lad living with Grandmother. In fact, Grandmother bossed him after he was married, and she still did, Ma included. Sometimes Ma tried to rebel, but she seldom succeeded. Well, one thing was certain: Blanche had no intention of letting Grandmother run *her* life. Someone had to learn to stand up to that woman.

Instead of waiting for Millie to bring the mail home when he came from the market, Miney usually sent Ralph for it as soon as she knew the morning's mail had been sorted. If Rate wasn't around, she sometimes walked the two blocks to the Post Office herself.

Now, Miney angrily waved a letter in the air to show her husband who had just come into the house.

"Milford Setterington, just you guess what we got in the mail today."

"Certainly looks like a letter, but I have no idee from who."

He peered at his wife closely, sighed, and then said, "Well, maybe I do. Bet it's a letter from Ma 'cause I can't think of anything else to put you in such a fine fettle."

"That's right. Oh, that woman! Just you listen to this. 'Since Blanche's graduation is less than a month away, I will be arriving next Wednesday to oversee the making of her dresses. She will need a white one for graduation, of course, and I think perhaps a blue for baccalaureate. On Saturday, Blanche and I will go down to Christian's to pick out the material. I think Nellie Pershing is the one to have make the dresses since my eyesight is no longer quite good enough for such an undertaking.'"

Miney glanced at Millie to see if he was still listening.

"'You will be good enough to meet my train at 4:30 Wednesday afternoon,'" she finished.

Now, she gave her husband a scathing look as though he was somehow at fault.

"What do you think of that?" demanded Miney.

"Sounds like Ma is going to save you a lot of trouble."

"Oh, Millie, there you go finding excuses for your mother. Now, just this once I want you to stand up to her and tell her that we can manage quite well without her."

"I can tell her, but knowing Ma, do you honestly think it will do one bit of good?"

"I suppose not," came the deflated reply. "It never has before. Why does your mother have to be such an interfering soul? I had thought with her at South Lyon we would be able to live our own lives. Now this."

Miney snatched a handkerchief from her apron pocket and dabbed at the tears that sprang to her eyes; Millie moved over to pat her on the shoulder, clearly made uncomfortable by his wife's tears.

"I'm sure Ma means well. You know how much she adores Blanche."

"Humph. Blanche hasn't been all that popular since Lois was born. Of course, any child that your sister had would come first in Mother's affections just because she's always spoiled Ruby so. I'm telling you here and now that Blanche will not take kindly to this, and she is quite likely to be very outspoken on the matter. She is of an age where she definitely has her own way of doing things which is as it should be."

Millie, already tired of the conversation, sat down and displayed the local paper prominently in front of his face. He knew Miney would have to return to the kitchen soon because she always had his meals ready on time, and that meant his supper would be on the table in another fifteen minutes. Mina knew there was absolutely no need to say anything further to Millie; by his actions, he had given her to understand that the subject was closed. However, he had not reckoned with an irate young daughter.

Miney had given her daughter the letter to read after the supper dishes were done. Blanche looked up from the letter, her eyes disclosing the fury she felt.

"And what makes Grandmother think I want her helping with my dresses? I know what that will mean. It will be 'Blanche, we'll get this material for graduation, and this will do fine for baccalaureate. Now, I think this pattern is very appropriate for graduation' and so forth." She had mimicked Lovina's way of speaking. "I won't get a chance to voice my opinion let alone have it count for anything. I honestly don't care what Grandmother thinks. I'm not going to give in like some namby-pamby. I will pick out my own material and patterns or I won't participate in the exercises," she stated defiantly.

"Now, Blanche, I'm just not sure your grandmother will agree to that," cautioned Miney.

"Ma, just because you and Pa never had the backbone to stand up to her doesn't mean I have to be the same way."

"Blanche Lenore, is that any way to speak to your mother?" demanded Miney, her tone of voice clearly showing her surprise at Blanche's accusation.

"I'm sorry, Ma, but Grandmother just brings out the worst in me. If there was time for her to get a letter, I'd write and tell her not to bother to come, that I can manage quite well without her--good intentions or not."

Millie had sat quietly through this exchange; now, he looked steadily at his daughter and said quietly, "Blanche, you would do no such thing. Your Grandmother is doing what she thinks is best for you, and like it or not, you will not do or say anything to hurt her feelings. Is that understood?"

Blanche glared defiantly at her father.

"Why are my feelings never considered? It's about time Grandmother learned that I have feelings and ideas and--"

"Blanche, that will do." The words were softly spoken, but somehow, they had an ominous tone.

Brown eyes bored into brown eyes until Blanche realized further argument was futile and looked away. Pa just always had to jump when his mother snapped her fingers; he was like a well-trained dog or a marionette on a string. Well, she could tell him one thing: once she was out on her own, there was no way she'd ever let Grandmother run her life. She was not going to be half a person just waiting for Grandmother to make all her decisions, and Pa could just like it or lump it, she didn't much care which.

Lovina arrived on Wednesday afternoon as promised. Somehow, when Lovina put in an appearance, she disrupted the entire household; everything had to be done as she saw fit. Of course, one thing about her, she always expected to help with the housework. If she dusted, she usually grumbled about the arrangement of furniture, leaving no doubt in anyone's mind that she knew it would be a much more attractive room if only the arrangement was changed to suit her. Miney had learned over the years to ignore most of what her mother-in-law had to say because it just seemed that everyone was happier that way; Lovina's bark was often worse than her bite, and a great deal of the time she never followed through with her suggestions--perhaps she simply enjoyed the grumbling.

Lovina and Miney drove to Eureka on Friday afternoon to hire Nellie Pershing to sew Blanche's dresses. Nellie was to come the following Monday and stay with the family as long as her services were needed. There was a tiny bedroom off the kitchen; it was only large enough for a single bed and a small dresser. In fact, Millie had been contemplating tearing out the partition to make the kitchen larger, but for now, it would serve very nicely as a place for Nellie to stay.

Blanche dreaded Saturday. Since Pa would not be with them, she had made up her mind she was going to have something to say about what she and her grandmother bought for her dresses. Somehow, she was not going to let her grandmother dictate to her this time; come hell or high water, she would thwart that woman yet. Blanche really hadn't been all that friendly since her grandmother had arrived; she had been polite, but rather cool and reserved because inwardly, she was seething like a covered pot about to boil over.

If Millie noticed his daughter's behavior, he made no mention of it. He often said, "Let sleeping dogs lie." And he probably felt this adage was certainly applicable here. Having both his mother and his daughter in the same house was a little like sitting on a keg of gunpowder waiting for someone to light the fuse. Since Blanche was a grown young lady, there was no way she could be intimidated by her grandmother; she was too spunky to let someone shove her around without rebelling.

Millie realized his daughter had a fine, astute mind, and he secretly rather admired her because she did have the courage to stand by her convictions. It was just that it was so much easier to get along with Ma if one humored her--course the same could be said of Blanche.

Women. Sometimes Millie felt as though he would never understand them. He knew how edgy Miney always was when his mother was around for very long; Miney never really tried to oppose Ma, but she sure found fault to him about everything his mother did. He, for one, would be glad when this whole episode was over and his household could return to normal.

Millie noticed that Ralph managed to be around as little as possible. The boy was learning early. He was prompt at meals, but usually skedaddled off immediately after being excused from the table and didn't return until dark. He came to the market right after school and did whatever few chores Millie assigned, and of course, he always took care of the horses.

As soon as school was out for the summer, Millie guessed he'd have to give Rate something with more responsibility. Millie knew the boy could handle stuffing wieners and perhaps something like drawing chickens – Millie took orders during the week for chickens, and they had to be killed and drawn on Saturday morning so the customers could pick them up Saturday afternoon.

For the first time in her life, Blanche managed a compromise with her grandmother. Blanche picked out a blue China silk for baccalaureate, and she selected a plain pattern, no flounces or ruffles for her; the bodice was fastened with tiny buttons down the front, and the skirt was gathered full. Of course, Grandmother decided the bodice would look better if it had some tiny rosebuds daintily embroidered on it to relieve the plainness.

The graduation dress was a delicate white lawn with tucking and fine lace insertions in the waist and lace insertions at intervals in the gathered skirt. It would necessitate a specially made petticoat since the material was so sheer. It was too fussy for Blanche's rather plain taste, but she knew that it was too much to expect to have her way on both dresses. After all, winning one battle out of two was a pretty good record where Grandmother was concerned.

The next few days were the worst Blanche had spent in a long time. Every single day when she arrived home from school, the first thing she had to do was try on one or both of the dresses for a fitting. It seemed to her that she stood for hours, turning this way or that; it was take the dress in a little here, let it out a smidgen there, the waist was a little too long in front since Blanche was not as generously endowed up front as the pattern allowed. If Grandmother hadn't been there like a fire-breathing dragon, the whole procedure could have been accomplished with much less time and effort.

Blanche felt sorry for poor Nellie. Imagine trying to sew something to suit Grandmother. Ma was mighty persnickety, but always with reason whereas Lovina seemed to find fault just for the sake of finding fault--it usually didn't have rhyme nor reason. However, Nellie took it all in stride and kept her good nature throughout the entire stay.

When it came to the hem of the graduation dress, Lovina decided it would set the dress off extremely well to have a hemstitched ruffle at the bottom, and she carefully explained to Nellie that simply no one could do hemstitching as beautifully as *her* daughter. Nellie shrugged her shoulders and said that if Mrs. Setterington wanted Ruby to do the work, she certainly had no objections. Blanche felt that Nellie was probably secretly very pleased since it would let her escape having to listen to Grandmother's complaints and suggestions.

Ruby came at her mother's command, and it was she who finished Blanche's dress. It was indeed beautiful. Blanche looked at it critically. She supposed it was as nice as any dress the rest of the girls in her class would wear, but somehow she just didn't think it "looked" like her. Maybe if she hadn't had to have all those fittings, she could have felt more enthusiasm.

Anyway, it was finished and soon there would be graduation. What then? There weren't nearly as many decent jobs for young women as there were for boys. Some of the girls were already working on their hope chests even though they didn't have a steady beau.

Well, that was one thing for certain, she wasn't going to get married. Of course, she really didn't like to think of what people would say about her being an old maid; she resented that people would give her condescending looks and speak of her as that "poor" Blanche Setterington as though she had some affliction. Why did everyone think a woman must get married? People never seemed to make fun of a bachelor except to intimate that he had been too smart to let some woman catch him. Well, she certainly didn't want anyone pitying her because she chose to remain a maiden.

Grandmother had been hinting about a boyfriend, but Blanche had carefully ignored the remarks so far. It wasn't that she wouldn't want to keep company with a nice young man because Blanche did feel it would be nice to be taken some places by a gentleman. Trouble was, so far all the boys she'd grown up with didn't seem to interest her. Grandmother hadn't better get pushy in this area or Blanche would tell her grandmother to mind her own business. She heaved a sigh. It probably wouldn't stop Grandmother having her say, but she would soon learn that her granddaughter had finally reached an age where she was no longer afraid of her grandmother.

It was Sunday morning, and as usual, Miney was running late. Milford often told her that one of two things was wrong: she either planned too many things to do, or she took too long to do them. She sent Ralph for a fresh pail of water with the admonition that he better get his clothes changed so he would not make them late for Church and Sunday School. Ralph laughed to himself because he knew it never took him long to change clothes and comb his hair; therefore, he was always ready long before his mother and his sister were done with their primping. Ma always took such a long time combing her long hair, carefully braiding it, and the bun in the back had to be just perfect.

Ralph was returning from the well with a full pail of water. Just as he neared the woodshed door, Blanche stepped to the doorway and tossed the dirty water from the washdish out the door in time to catch Ralph with its full force. Without having to think, he automatically threw the contents of his pail on his sister. Blanche looked at her sodden dress in dismay.

"Just you wail until I tell Ma, Ralph Setterington."

"See if I care. You started it."

"I didn't know you were there. It wasn't intentional," she defended.

"Don't give me that bunch of hogwash. You knew Ma sent me after a pail of water."

"How'd I know you were back already? Ma! Ma!" shouted Blanche. "Just come see what Ralph has done."

Miney appeared at the kitchen door fastening the last buttons on her dress. When she saw the bedraggled appearance of her daughter, she came into the woodshed and asked, "Whatever happened?" She looked directly at Ralph for an answer.

"Ma," he began, "Blanche threw a washdish of dirty water on me. See. I'm wet too."

"Blanche?"

"I didn't mean to, Ma. Honest I didn't. I didn't see him coming until I had already thrown the water."

"Ralph, what did you do?"

"I let her have it with that whole pail of water you sent me to fetch. She had it comin'," he added smugly.

"And her all dressed for Church."

Miney picked up a stout piece of wood about two inches wide, long enough and thick enough to make a good paddle.

"Ralph, come here and take what you've got coming," she said angrily. "When will you ever learn not to abuse your sister?"

With a glowering took at his sister, Ralph moved nearer his mother. It was then that he noticed Bruno. The brindle bulldog sat on his haunches, ears perked forward, looking first at Ralph, then at Miney.

Rate grinned a knowing grin.

"Ma, if I was you, I don't believe I'd hit me," he said impudently.

Miney followed his gaze to the dog. Perhaps Ralph was right. Whenever Millie and the boy scrapped, Bruno was quick to take Ralph's part.

"Just you come into the kitchen. You'll not get out of your punishment just because of that dog."

Rate shrugged his shoulders, smiled in a most irritating fashion and preceded his mother into the kitchen. She raised the stick and struck.

Rouff! Bruno came through the screen on the door in one single bound and stood at his master's side facing a white-faced Miney. A low, throaty growl rumbled from his throat as he watched Miney intently. Since she made no further move toward Ralph, his growling ceased, but he still watched her warily.

"Bruno. It's all right," said Ralph. "Are you done, Ma?" he asked, an impish grin turning up the corners of his mouth ever so slightly, the real humor showing in the depths of his eyes.

"Land sakes. I believe Bruno would bite me," exclaimed Miney, her fear evident in the unnatural tone of her voice. "I'll let you go this time, but I want no more of your shenanigans. Do you understand? Get yourself ready for Church. We're almost late now."

Rate scurried off. His sister had already changed into the only other dress she had that was presentable for Church, so she met him on the stairs. He gave her a dazzling smile, and his eyes shone with the taste of victory. She gave him a haughty look in return, clearly disappointed he had not received a sound licking.

Ralph viewed the whole episode as extremely comical. There was no way anyone could have made him believe Blanche had not deliberately doused him with water. He was just thankful he'd had such a ready means of retaliation. Good old Bruno. Bet Ma would never try to whip him again. Sure was a fun day so far.

Miney had regained her composure by issuing orders. That dog had given her such a fright. She knew the dog felt protective of Ralph, but it was a pretty sad state of affairs when his own mother darsent paddle him. If there ever was a next time, she'd make certain a stout wooden door stood between her and Bruno, and then let him try to come to Ralph's aid.

The circumstances for another whipping never arose; at least nothing of enough importance for Miney to make an issue of it, and she was forever grateful.

CHAPTER 9

Baccalaureate was over and with it the usual dull speech that the graduating class had fidgeted through, wanting only for it to be finished.

Tonight was graduation. Ten students, seven girls and only three boys, would receive diplomas for eleven years of schooling. Blanche felt a small twinge of sorrow, realizing that this was a big step forward in her life.

Pa had come home from the store early, letting George Page close up for tonight. Just before supper he called to Blanche from out on the front steps. She had not seen her father look quite this solemn before and wondered what could possibly be wrong; even his eyes upheld the mood--there was not a hint of merriment there, no telltale crinkles at the corners.

Blanche sat down beside her father and asked, "You wanted to see me, Pa?"

"Reckon I did."

"What about?"

"Well, Blanche, tonight is your graduation from high school. I haven't asked you before, but do you have any idee what you are going to do now?"

"Not really. I've given it a lot of thought. I suppose I'll get a job if I can although I don't know what kind of work I'd like to do. I'm not sure I'd like clerking in a store. You know I worked that little while for Mr. Brandau, and I didn't care too much for that. (Brandau's was the only store in town that served ice cream and sold many kinds of candy.) So I just don't know." She sighed audibly.

Millie nodded his head in understanding.

"Have you given any thought to going on to school? Many young girls do, you know."

118

"I don't know, Pa. I guess I've had enough of school for a while. Besides, what is there but teaching, and I'd hate that, or business school, and I'm not sure I'd want to work in an office. Guess maybe I'll have to try different things and see what I like best."

Again Millie nodded his head in agreement. Her judgment was sound, but then, he expected it to be.

"If you decide you want to go to school, I just wanted you to know that I'd pay your way wherever you want to go. It doesn't have to be right away, so take your time deciding. The money will be waiting for you whenever you need it."

"Thanks, Pa. Even if I don't go to school, I appreciate the offer. Most of the other girls are as undecided as I am. Of course, all some of them want to do is get married. That doesn't appeal to me," she said bluntly. "I guess I just want to earn my own way in the world. Lelah has asked me to come to Chicago for a visit, so maybe I'll go there before I look for a job. That is, if you and Ma would pay my train fare. I've got some saved for spending money."

"If that's what you want to do, I reckon I can come up with enough money to get you there--and back," he laughed. "You always did like your Aunt Mary, even as a little tyke. Well, I can understand that. Mary's a lot like Mother Smith and everyone in town thought a heap of your Grandma Smith. She was the kindest, most mild mannered person I ever knew."

This had been a rather long conversation for Millie, and Blanche sensed that he had said all he had to say on the subject of her post graduation plans. She gave him a quick kiss on the forehead and scurried into the house. She knew that these little displays of affection sometimes embarrassed her father, and it was true that she seldom felt the urge to be demonstrative; this had simply been an impulsive gesture on her part.

Millie gazed fondly at the disappearing figure. A fine looking young lady, his daughter. Blanche had a good head on her shoulders, and he just knew that whatever she decided to do, she would do well. Course Ma felt the only truly respectable vocation for a young lady over twenty was marriage; before that, perhaps, they might teach. But times were changing. Millie was not often one to approve of new fads and new ways of doing things, but he guessed there should be more opportunities open to women than to get married and raise children.

Take Miney, for instance. If it hadn't been that marriage was the only alternative to sponging off her parents and being pitied for being an old maid, she would probably never have married. Millie knew his wife was proud of him, and she sure ran him a proper household, but it was something that had been forced on her by society. Miney had never wanted the intimacy a man felt was his due; she had simply tolerated it because she had promised to love, honor, and obey. She didn't complain, she merely became very adept at avoiding intimate, physical contact.

She had never wanted children, and while she doted on Blanche, she had resented the lad for quite a spell. Rate vexed her often enough even now, but Millie felt certain that Miney did love her son, albeit in her own fashion.

However, Blanche was like Miney in some ways, and he felt that was where she got her aversion to marriage. Women were so different. Both Ma and Mother Smith had enjoyed children although the women themselves were as different as daylight and dark.

Since Blanche was not yet seventeen, she had plenty of time to change her mind about a lot of things. One thing sure, she'd not go off half-cocked to do anything. No sirree, that girl was a sensible one, and she'd make up her own mind with no outside help. He chuckled. Even Ma was finding out that she had at least one granddaughter who had a mind of her own and didn't take too kindly to interference, no matter how kindly it was meant to be.

Shortly after graduation, Horatio closed the deal for the sale of his bank in South Lyon. He had done remarkably well in the transaction since he had doubled his investment. Immediately afterward, he and Lovina moved to Nashville; they had a lovely, large home situated on the banks of the Thornapple River. Horatio now invested his money in opening a private bank in Vermontville so Mac could once more utilize his experience as a bookkeeper.

Millie was quick to comment on the fact that Mac could do nothing on his own, he was completely dependent on his father-in-law. Nor could Millie hide the envy he felt regarding the relationship his brother-in-law had with his father. He admitted Mac was capable as a bookkeeper, but no one else would pay him such outlandish wages.

Oliver McQuistion, as well as his wife, did like to live high on the hog and impress people; therefore, he needed the huge wages his father-in-law paid. It bothered him not at all that it was much more than the position warranted. In fact, to Millie, he strutted like a banty rooster, cocksure of his own worth, forgetting to whom he owed his good fortune and income which allowed him to indulge in some of the luxuries of life.

Blanche had gone to Nashville with her grandparents since Lovina said she could use help in getting the house settled. Lovina did hate this moving all around the country, but she had made it a practice never to interfere in her husband's business interests--that was one area where she gave him free rein since it had been apparent very early in her marriage that her husband had his father's knack for making money. Of course, in her house, Lovina ruled supreme, her authority was absolute, and Horatio had always more or less humored her in this department.

Blanche liked the new home well enough, but to her, the home in Elsie, the one she had grown up with, had been far nicer and she sometimes wondered how her grandmother could have given up such a lovely place to live. It made her wonder if money was worth the sacrifice.

With school out for the summer, Ralph contemplated what he could do to keep busy. Millie settled part of the problem by explaining it was time for Ralph to learn to stuff wieners. Millie made wieners once a week the same as he did bologna; there was not as much call for liverwurst, so he sometimes went two weeks before he made another batch.

The casings to be stuffed were animal intestines, cleaned and salted and tightly packed in a small keg. To be used, they had to be removed from the keg and soaked in a tub of cold water overnight to freshen them by removing most of the salt; the casings came in lengths of three or four feet.

Millie showed Ralph about how many casings to take out for a batch of wieners and impressed upon him that they should be separated and completely covered with cold water.

The next day, he showed Rate the second step in the wiener-making operation. Millie had already finely ground the cooked meat scraps in the grinder that set over in the corner and was powered by a gasoline engine. Now, there was a tub of ground meat just waiting to be put into the sausage stuffer.

The sausage stuffer was a large, round cylinder about eight inches in diameter, with a hand-operated plunger in the cylinder; Rate had a special, long-handled, wooden spoon to dip the meat from the tub and carefully drop it into the chute. A tube, on which to fasten the casing, was on the end of the cylinder; it had fittings of different sizes so there was a small one for wieners and a larger one for bologna or liverwurst. Millie carefully explained the necessity of fastening the casing tightly so it wouldn't fly off the nozzle and let the meat shoot out onto the floor.

They filled the first casing. Now, came the tricky part. Ralph watched as his father tied off the end of the casing, then measured off a length of about six inches between each hand, pinched it tightly between thumb and forefinger to force the meat away from the casing, and then twirled his hands away from the body, the center portion between his hands flew in a circle twisting the casing tightly at each end of the six inch length; he moved his hands down the casing and repeated the process only this time he twirled the length pinched off toward his body. When the length of casing was divided into six inch lengths, he hung it on a nearby rack where it glared creamy white against the darkened wood of the rack.

Now, it was Rate's turn. It had looked easy watching Pa do it. Rate filled the casing without mishap. This wasn't half bad, but he learned that there was definitely a knack to twisting wieners. At first, he didn't get them twisted tightly enough, and when he let go, they came partially untwisted.

Pa just laughed and said, "Practice makes perfect." And walked off.

Ralph was not about to admit that it was much more difficult than he expected, so he worked diligently. Unless he held the stuffed casing with just the right amount of tension, the center part between his hands refused to twirl round and round; it was adjustment by trial and error.

At one time, he felt like tossing the whole blamed mess in with the bones and forgetting about it, but he couldn't give up. It took him much longer than it did his father. Gosh, whoever wanted to buy wieners anyway? Temporarily forgotten was the fact that Ralph preferred a wiener to candy any day. There was just something about hearing the skin pop as he sunk his teeth into the tasty meat; but this was before he realized what a pain they were to make.

When he finally finished the last length of casing, Millie showed him how the rack had to be stored in the smoke house for a short period of time to allow the hickory smoke to color the gut casings to a soft brown and set the meat in the casings. From there, they were put in the cooler and were ready to be sold. Of course, Ralph was not quite big enough to handle the rack, but Millie tossed it around with ease.

Finally, the chore was done. When Rate looked at the clock, he noticed it had taken him all morning for just this one job. Pa hadn't said anything although Ralph had not missed the amused look on Millie's face each time he checked to see how much progress his son had made. Ralph said not one word of complaint. He knew he'd get better at it, and he firmly resolved to get good enough to be able to finish a length of wieners quicker than his father. He might even go so far as to one day issue a challenge.

Blanche had been home from Grandmother's a week when she decided she would go to Chicago to visit her cousin Lelah. It would seem good to see her Aunt Mary as well. When Aunt Mary had lived in Elsie, Blanche had been a frequent visitor, and since Lelah was only six months younger, they had always got on well.

Miney fussed at Blanche's taking such a long trip by herself, but Blanche had been adamant, and what's more, Millie had stood firmly behind his daughter; he felt there was very little Blanche was not capable of doing on her own. Miney finally kept her fears to herself and simply helped Blanche ready her clothes and pack them.

The whole family had taken her to the depot to see her off. Rate felt that Blanche was sure lucky to be going to see Aunt Mary because he liked her too only he hadn't seen her for a long time. No one had suggested that he might like to go visiting too.

Blanche had been somewhat apprehensive over the long train ride by herself, but she had kept up the appearance of complete calm. She certainly hadn't wanted her mother to know she had a few misgivings.

Blanche had known that Uncle Jap had been poorly for the past couple of years, but she had not realized he was no longer able to work at his job on the streetcars. As a result of this, Aunt Mary took in boarders. Her eldest daughter, Hattie, who was seventeen years older than Blanche, worked in a tailor's shop to help her mother with expenses. Now that Lelah was out of school, she would be looking for employment too, at least for the summer.

When Blanche first learned of the situation, her first reaction was to take the first train back to Elsie so she wouldn't be in the way or be a burden on their limited finances. However, the warmth the family showed her soon changed her mind.

Hattie insisted on giving up her room to Blanche, saying she slept equally well on the sofa. Hattie was short in stature, very plain to the point of being homely, with her dark hair combed in such a way as to skillfully cover her large ears; she had an odd laugh, but she also had a heart of gold. After being in her presence only a short time, one forgot her lack of physical beauty because her beauty came from within. She was truly a gem.

It was soon decided that since Blanche and Lelah were having such a delightful time together, Blanche would look for a job so she could pay her share of the load. One morning, she took a streetcar down town to apply for a clerking job at the Carson Perry Department Store. She was scared to death. This was some different from approaching someone she had known all her life as was the case back in Elsie.

Never had Blanche felt so small-townish. Chicago was a large city, and she felt completely alien; however, she was determined. After all, she was a Setterington to the core, and a Setterington would never admit fear over such a trifle as this; therefore, she went resolutely through the doors of the store to ask the first employee she saw to whom should she speak about a job.

Luck was with her, and she was hired on the spot. What a relief! All her worry and fretting had been for naught. It was a mighty happy young girl who went back to her Aunt Mary's to relate the exciting news. No doubt about it, Blanche was a very capable young woman.

When Miney received Blanche's letter with the news that she was now an employee at Carson Perry's, Miney sat down and cried. She missed her daughter terribly. Her greatest fear was that Blanche might stay in Chicago permanently. Why had Mary and Jap gone to Chicago anyway? If he had wanted to work on streetcars, they had streetcars in Detroit which was certainly a lot nearer the family. Miney gained some solace in blaming her sister and brother-in-law for Blanche's defection.

Ralph had been on his way home from the butcher shop when Aunt Lorin called to him from her front porch. He liked Aunt Lorin even though she was a little odd.

Guess maybe he liked her mostly because she was one of the few in the family who actually preferred him to Blanche. She asked him about Blanche and asked if he was going visiting this summer. When he said he guessed not, she nodded her head knowingly. Then, she asked if he'd like to have supper with her and Uncle Norman, carefully adding that they were having johnnycake. From the slight smile, it was evident Lorin knew how much Rate liked johnnycake.

Ralph received permission from his mother and had eagerly showed up in plenty of time for supper. One mouthful of Aunt Lorin's johnnycake made him wish he'd stayed home. Lorin put no sugar in her johnnycake, so it tasted nothing like Miney's. (Miney had a sweet tooth, so she tended to put plenty of sugar in what she made.) Ralph did not want to hurt Aunt Lorin's feelings, so he managed to choke down three rather large pieces much to Lorin's satisfaction. Well, at least he'd learned that should she ever give him another invitation, he'd always be busy.

With the hot, dry days, the fine, manure-laden dirt of Main Street rose in clouds of dust with each passing team to settle on the boardwalks, store fronts, and windows. Rate stood in the doorway of the meat market watching the watering tank pass the store, wetting down the street to keep the dust from rising with every rig that passed. As usual, there was a whole raft of young boys running behind the slow-moving vehicle dashing in and out of the spray that was low enough so they only got their bare legs and feet wet.

The tank was a large wooden cylinder with a hand-operated pump to fill it; the driver drove to the creek north of town, threw a hose into the water and pumped the tank full, then he sprayed the streets as far as the business section went, in four directions from the main four corners. The thorough drenching helped considerably although it had to be done every other day. Of course, if a good enough rain came, it might be three or four days before it was necessary to use the tank again.

Ralph remembered how last year he had been one of those who took advantage of playing in the spray. Now, he looked upon it as child's play because this summer he had been going with the older boys to the river--back of the Cobb place--to a swimming hole, and he had learned to swim. He wasn't real good yet, but he was getting better all the time.

He'd been a little surprised that his mother had offered no objection when he'd first asked permission to go with the group of older boys to the river. She hadn't raised any complaint until the night he had come home and proudly stated that he had learned to swim. Now, Ma was forever warning him to be cautious; he guessed she hadn't realized that he'd been going in the water, but had merely thought he was tagging along just to watch the other boys. Golly, she should have known him better than that. He certainly wasn't about to walk over a mile to the river just to sit idly on the bank and watch everyone else have fun, and then walk a mile back.

He'd not been afraid of the water even at first and could dog paddle in no time; however, some of the other boys showed him how to swim on his side, and he was learning to swim on his back.

There were usually ten or twelve boys who made this nightly trek to the river; of course, none of them had heard of bathing suits, and since the swimming hole was well away from the road beyond a grove of trees, the boys simply stripped to the skin. Only one problem arose: occasionally some prankster in the group would take a boy's clothes and tie them in knots; this wouldn't have been so bad except usually the clothes were thoroughly soaked before tying and this made the knots very difficult to untie.

So far, Ralph had been lucky, perhaps because he was younger and most of the boys only teased those their own age; nevertheless, on more than one occasion he'd seen some kid sitting nude on the river bank working frantically to remove the knots from his pants and shirt while the other boys left for home calling back good natured catcalls on how to expedite the procedure.

Millie interrupted Ralph's reverie. "Rate, guess you can clean up now."

"All right, Pa."

The boy turned away from the door and went to the back of the store. It was Wednesday and Millie's day for changing the sawdust on the floor in back of the counter. A large, square, solidly built, block table stood in the middle of the floor a short distance from the cooler. It was here Millie sawed and cut the meat he sold; in fact, much of what he sold was cut to order. The carcass of a beef was quartered and hung in the cooler to be brought out and cut into steaks and roasts on demand; a hog was hung in halves, and the hams were removed for smoking. The tongue and heart were often taken home to his own family or given away since they were worthless to sell. The floor around the table was covered with a substantial layer of sawdust to catch the blood drippings, or the meat scraps which fell from the saw; if the sawdust wasn't changed each week during the spring, summer, and into the fall, it became rancid.

This was one more chore Ralph had to help with now that school was out for the summer. He didn't really mind. It was better than picking strawberries although the pay wasn't quite as good. He set in with a will shoveling the sawdust into a wheelbarrow to be dumped on a pile in the alley back of the store. Sometimes, Pa gave him a little extra spending money for all the work he did, but it never was on a regular basis, so he never knew what to count on from week to week.

He didn't think Ma knew about the extra money, and he'd been darned awful careful not to let Blanche find out either. Honestly, that Blanche could be one of the biggest tattletales ever born, then again, she'd keep quiet when she knew one word from her was certain to get him into a peck of trouble. Like since Pa had said she could play cards and dance, she'd been going rather frequently to the young people's recreation hall next to Pearce's hardware; the young people danced to the tunes from the player piano, played cards, and there was a pool table for their use. Well, he'd started dropping by because pool fascinated him, and he liked the music. Blanche had never mentioned it to Ma.

Course, it hadn't been long before news of his activities had reached Ma's ears, a tribute to Tillie Lance's long nose and her unswerving loyalty to spread gossip as fast as she could gather it. Nevertheless, when Ma had upbraided him, Blanche had taken his part and had pointed out to Ma that if it was permissible for her, it should be permissible for Ralph. Ma hadn't quite agreed with this rationalization, but she had not wanted to argue with her daughter. Since then, Miney had seldom missed an opportunity to expound her views on the subject although she did not forbid his going there.

Yup, Blanche was a hard one to figure out. Gosh, he even missed her. Since she was spending such a long time in Chicago at Aunt Mary's, his home life had been rather dull with no one to pick on. So far, none of her letters had mentioned coming home. He knew Ma was really lonesome. She'd been extra nice to him lately; he guessed it was because she missed Blanche so much. Of course, since Blanche had got a job, she might stay there forever. He'd sure rather have her home.

The day was hot; heat waves shimmered up from the dry, dusty road; small hordes of gnats flocked around each pile of fresh horse droppings; a begrudging breeze stirred the trees intermittently; insects droned lazily and happily, but the birds found it too hot to sing.

Ralph had been unable to find anyone to go fishing with him today so he trudged along the summer-dry road, his feet and legs covered with a fine coat of gray dust; a makeshift fish pole of stout willow rested over his shoulder. In the other hand, he held a partially open lid of the tin can which held his bait, a mass of incessantly wiggling angleworms; his straw hat was pushed far enough back on his head to allow a lock of dark hair to fall across his forehead; he whistled somewhat tunelessly as he scuffed along. He was headed for the gristmill dam. He would have liked it better if he could have found someone to come with him, but since he'd set his mind on going fishing today, he was not about to set his plans aside for lack of companionship.

He crossed the iron bridge and crawled down the bank to the river, being careful not to spill the can of worms. For a few moments he stared, mesmerized by the crystal clear water flowing over the dam. Must be the mill wasn't running today because there wouldn't have been enough water to flow through the millrace and over the dam, not at this time of year anyway when the water was at such a low level for lack of rain. He walked further along, the grass felt damp and cool on his feet; he watched a kingfisher, on an overhanging limb, alert for a fish in the water below; it peered uncertainly at Ralph.

"Don't worry. There's enough for both of us," laughed the boy softly.

Just then, the bird plummeted down into the water, coming back up to its perch with a fish in its strong bill.

"See, what did I tell you?"

Rate picked himself a spot to sit where his feet could dangle in the water--the bank was too high in most places to allow this. However, Rate had known of this particular place where a huge rock had once been embedded, only it had finally fallen out of its niche and left a sort of seat, just right for a lad to sit in, lean back, and pretend it had been made specially for him. Ralph baited his hook, tossed the line in the water, and waited. While he liked to fish if the fish were biting tolerably well, Ralph had no great patience to sit very long unless he received at least a nibble.

He fished mostly because he liked to eat fish. He knew that whatever he caught today, his mother would fry for him for breakfast tomorrow. Fried fish and fried bread-- he could taste it now. If he was lucky, there'd be enough for everyone to have fish, if not, Ma would have a regular breakfast for the others.

Ma never complained about cooking whatever he brought home. Now that Pa had given him his rifle, he'd managed to get a couple of rabbits during the winter and a woodchuck this spring. He was gettin' to be a pretty fair shot, so this fall he'd bet he'd get any number of squirrels. Pa hadn't let him go coon hunting yet, but in another year or so, Pa'd think he was big enough.

He had been half daydreaming, the end of the pole stuck into the soft earth between his legs, as he watched a puffball cloud move lazily across a morning-glory blue sky.

Suddenly, his pole dipped and was almost jerked from his grasp. He clutched at it hurriedly and felt an unusually heavy tug. Cautiously, he pulled on the line. Something was sure heavy on the other end. He knew that a fish wouldn't have felt like that. He peered into the water, and to his surprise saw a turtle trying to swim in the opposite direction with Rate's line in its mouth.

Ralph knew turtles were good to eat because each year men came with big nets and netted turtles just below the dam; they sold the meat to elite restaurants as far away as Detroit and Chicago, and he knew that turtle meat was an expensive delicacy.

Besides, just last week he'd heard that a big turtle had been caught in the basement of Pearce's hardware (This was later to be Carter and Steere, then Dancer's.) much to the wonder of everyone because no one could understand where it had come from. Well, he guessed he'd try to work the turtle up close to the bank; there was a shallow spot where people drove their buggies into the river to wash them. If he managed to coax the turtle there, he could wade in and grab it, making certain to avoid the claws and head.

Carefully and patiently, Ralph maneuvered the turtle toward the drive; while he relished the battle of wits, he soon found that he had to keep the turtle away from any obstruction because it would latch onto anything it could find and hang on with the tenacity of a bulldog. Finally, he stepped into the water, firmly grasped the turtle on each side of its shell and stepped up onto the bank. He used his jackknife to cut the line that protruded from the ugly mouth fastening the turtle to the pole. He had flopped the turtle on its back for this procedure, but now the long neck came darting out of the shell, and quick as a wink, the turtle flopped onto its belly and started off.

"Oh, no you don't. You're not going to get away from me that easy."

He picked the turtle up by its tail, holding it well away from his body out of range of the sharp claws while the feet churned desperately in the attempt to grasp something, but clawed only air. Golly, it was heavy. He surveyed it critically and estimated the dark green shell was at least twelve inches across. It was a long way home; there had to be some easier way to get it there than to carry it.

He climbed back up the bank to the road, forgetting his pole which laid where he had cut it from the turtle. Back across the bridge, he had a flash of thought, and turned into the drive to the gristmill. Mr. Cooley, the owner, was on the platform arranging some bags he had snaked out of the interior of the mill.

"Mr. Cooley, would you let me have a piece of string 'bout so long?" He measured off as far as he could hold his arms apart and still maintain his tenacious grip on the tail of the turtle.

"Whacha gonna do with that turtle?" the man asked, for the moment ignoring the boy's question.

"Take him home to eat. That's why I need the string. I figger if I tie it to his tail and put him on his back, I can pull him. He's awful heavy to carry," explained the lad.

"Reckon we can arrange that, Rate. Just wait there, and I'll get some twine and help you get it tied. Watch yourself. Those claws will dig pretty good and keep away from his mouth. They say a turtle ain't got no teeth, but I seen a jawbone afore, and they are rough enough to feel like sharp teeth. If he gets holt of you, he won't let go."

"I'm keepin' good watch, Mr. Cooley."

In a few moments they had a stout cord snugly attached to the tail and the turtle safely turned on its back. For the moment, it was quiet, all four feet withdrawn, with only the tip of its pointed nose protruding from its shell.

Full of optimism, Ralph set off; the twine held in his hand was long enough to pass over his shoulder so the brunt of the effort was taken by his shoulder. He had gone about twenty-five feet when whomp! The twine was jerked out of his hand. He turned hastily to pounce on the disappearing end of the string. That blamed turtle had got itself flopped over again and was making tracks back to the river. Rate was surprised at its speed. Must be it had never heard that turtles were supposed to be slow and lethargic.

Once again, Ralph placed the turtle on its back, wrapped a double coil of string around his hand and trudged off. He was to learn that the trip back to town was slow and arduous since about every twenty-five or thirty feet, with maddening regularity, the turtle stuck out its head and flopped over where it immediately dug in with all four feet, and tug as he would, Rate could not budge it.

On the way back to the village, Ralph remembered he had no idea how to go about killing and dressing a turtle. He decided to go to Pearce's and ask them what he should do. Mr. Pearce had laughed when Ralph came into the store still dragging the large turtle; step by step, Mr. Pearce explained to the boy what he must do.

Ralph was to let the turtle bite down on a stick to enable him to pull the neck out far enough from the shell so he could cut the head off with a sharp cleaver, axe, or a large, heavy knife. The next step was to split the breast plate with an axe; remove the entrails and then dip the turtle into scalding water for a few seconds to prevent the muscles from violently contracting while the legs were skinned out; if this wasn't done, it was almost impossible to straighten the legs to enable skinning them; it would then be a rather simple matter to loosen the meat from the back of the shell. Mr. Pearce even told him how to cook it. He suggested boiling it until tender, rolling it in flour, then frying until the flour was a crisp, golden brown.

Rate took the turtle home and followed the instructions for killing and cleaning it to the letter. It all worked very well. His mother cooked it as suggested although she explained to Ralph that some people made a soup of the meat, but Ralph had wanted to try it fried.

It was his first turtle, and he decided he knew why they were considered a delicacy. It might have been one whale of a lot of trouble getting it home, but it had certainly been worth the bother. Bet it wouldn't be his last turtle 'cause he'd sure as heck be on the lookout for others.

Tomorrow was Miney's day to churn butter; she had the pans of milk on the stove to scald so the cream would rise better. With Blanche in Chicago and Ralph doing all sorts of odd jobs for Millie at the market besides mowing lawns, she was fairly certain the job of churning would be entirely hers. She hoped the butter would come easily because she had no more love for the job than did Ralph or Blanche. Sometimes, butter came after only a short period of time while on other days, it seemed as though it took forever; occasionally, the cream just seemed to become more watery and never did turn to butter. Thank heavens those times were few and far between.

Miney had hoped for a letter from Blanche for the past two days, but there had been nothing. It bothered Miney that Blanche seemed to be so content living with Mary. Apparently, she found her job to her liking and since she and Lelah were so close, she just never mentioned a time for coming home. It brought tears to Miney's eyes thinking of her daughter. When she wrote to Blanche--she wrote twice a week-- she never missed an opportunity to hint at how lonesome it was without her daughter around. Thus far, it had produced no effect on Blanche.

Reluctantly, Miney admitted she did not quite understand her daughter. She knew she would never have been able to live so far from her parents, and she could not visualize herself clerking in a store, especially one the size of Carson Perry. Blanche was just a very independent young woman. It was not that Miney found this an undesirable trait--in fact, she found it most admirable--it was simply that she did not understand it.

Miney had never had a very adventuresome spirit; now, she recognized that in many ways, Blanche certainly had much more of Mother Setterington's characteristics than she did her mother's. Regardless of who she took after, Miney loved her dearly and would be extremely happy when Blanche decided to return home.

Millie knew the corn on the north eighty needed one last cultivating, and since Ralph had had a little experience last year under Millie's careful tutelage, Millie felt that it was time for the boy to go it alone.

"Rate, you're to go out to the farm today and tell George you need to use Van and the cultivator. She's used to cultivating and won't be any trouble. It will probably take the better part of a day, so you had best take your dinner with you."

"All right, Pa. Do I come home when I'm finished?"

"There's nothing more that needs doin', so reckon so."

Ralph left immediately after breakfast. It was going to be another hot day; he could tell by the hazy way the sun looked this early in the morning, with not a trace of a cloud in the sky.

Ralph enjoyed the activity of nature's creatures. A meadowlark sang, a bevy of quail crossed the road only a short distance in front of Pearl; a band of raucous crows circled over Sherman's woodlot. Crows were a nuisance. He'd be glad when he had a shotgun of his own so he could shoot some of the marauders; a body wouldn't stand a chance with just a rifle. A woodchuck sat on his haunches in a meadow and fearlessly watched the horse and buggy go by. The world abounded with God's creatures, and Rate enjoyed most of them; he even felt no animosity toward the blue racer that startled Pearl by entering the roadway almost at her side; then it glided in front of her for several feet before it slithered back into the protective grasses lining the sandy road.

Rate stabled Pearl, saw that she had some hay to munch, consulted with Mr. Onstott, then harnessed Van; the cultivator had been left in the field from the last time the corn had been cultivated, so he led Van by the bridle down the road toward the field. He noted how much the corn had grown; the recent hot weather had sure given it a spurt upward.

He turned in at the gate, backed Van up to the five-tooth cultivator, fastened her tugs to the hooks on the whippletree and was ready to go. Van needed no lines to guide her; a simple "gee" for right, and a "haw" for left, and she went where directed. Of course, once she started down between two rows of corn, she had enough sense to travel on her own. Ralph's only worry was that he guide the cultivator in a straight line so the outside shovels didn't grab a stalk or two of corn and uproot it.

It was midmorning when Ralph began to acquire a considerable thirst. He wished he'd brought a jar of cold water with him to set under a bush where it would keep fairly cool for quite a spell--but he hadn't been that thoughtful. Finally, he decided to go across the road to Garrett's and get himself a drink; he knew Van was a trustworthy mare and should stand all right until he returned.

He had gone to the pump by the back door of the house; he looked around for the dipper--everyone kept a dipper somewhere near the pump--found it hanging on a nail driven into the house siding, and proceeded to get his drink. Sure tasted good. He finished the second dipperful, replaced the dipper on the nail, thought of going into the house to speak to Suzie, but decided he had better get back to the field before Van got tired of standing and decided to turn around so she could help herself to a meal of tender corn. It had made it to knee high by the Fourth of July and really looked good.

As he came around the corner of the house, he heard the automobile. Oh, no! Would Van stand while that noisy contraption went by? Rate broke into a run. Just as he reached the road, he saw Van start to diddle and dance around, clearly upset by the approaching automobile. Ralph had just cleared the gate when Van took off cater-cornered across the field, the cultivator bouncing and swaying behind her adding to her fright, now in the ground, now on its side, and the corn--it was taking a swath of corn almost as neatly as if a mowing machine had passed.

Ralph knew better than to holler at the frightened horse; he simply followed as rapidly as he could, hoping that when the mare reached the corner by the ditch, she would have enough sense to stop. Whatever would Pa say about the knocked-down corn? Pa was sorta hard to outguess at times like this. Sometimes an incident might make him angry, but on some occasions Pa could see the comical side to something even though it looked serious to someone else. Rate fervently hoped this was one of the times when Pa's sense of humor was at its best.

As Ralph had hoped, Van stopped when she reached the ditch; she stood there blowing from her run, her sides pumping. The lad spoke softly to her, ran his hand along her trembling rump and moved on up to her head keeping up a soothing chatter. The mare's quivering lessened while the lad rubbed her nose, all the while talking softly; Ralph gently turned her around and righted the cultivator; he looked it over carefully, being thankful he could find nothing broken. With the command "gee," Van moved to the right and started down between two rows of corn as steadily as if nothing had happened.

Ralph hesitantly related the events to Millie at the supper table. Much to Rate's relief, Millie broke out in a hearty chuckle, a row of peas balanced precariously on his knife midway to his mouth.

"See, boy, I've told you those infernal machines do nothing but cause trouble. Van would have stood until the cows came home if she hadn't been scared. You'll just have to be more alert in the future, and if you're any where near the road, don't trust any horse to stand."

Little by little, Millie had been increasing the amount of work Ralph did at the butcher shop. Not that the boy didn't have time to still be a boy, but there were added responsibilities. Millie figured the sooner the lad learned that every individual must pay his own way in this world, the better off he would be. Millie had never felt that having an excess of money was so all-fired important--Ruby and Mac were prime examples of that--neither did he want to live from hand to mouth as John sometimes did; he felt that somewhere there should be a middle of the road way of living with a man doing an honest day's work to make a decent living. Now to Millie, a decent living meant a tidy, well-kept home to live in, an ample amount of good food for the table, well-made clothes, money to go visiting on occasion, with a little money saved for a rainy day. He did not feel he had to have the best of everything, neither did he want the least serviceable or least expensive.

Because of his middle of the road philosophy, he wanted Ralph to enjoy doing a day's work for an honest dollar. He wanted the lad to know the value of a dollar, to spend his money wisely; therefore, he expected the boy to accept his responsibility willingly. Millie was not the penny pincher his wife was, and he'd never quite figured out just why Miney was so gol-darn miserly. Of course, if he was to have a choice, he guessed he'd rather have a wife who was careful with her spending than one who could spend money faster than he could make it. He knew of more than one husband who always complained about the way money slipped through his wife's fingers--like water through a sieve. Millie reckoned he had much with which to be satisfied.

Ralph had often helped his mother dress chickens for Sunday dinner while they were on the farm, but he was to learn there was a difference in the procedure at the butcher shop. On the farm, they had killed a chicken by holding it by the legs, carefully placing its head on a chopping block, then chopping the head off with a blow from a sharp axe; the chicken was tossed aside where it jumped and rolled and thrashed around; by the time it was quiet, it was nearly bled out.

The chickens were then scalded in a pail of hot water, and the feathers plucked from the body.

Now, he found there was more to the task.

Millie usually had orders for anywhere from ten to fifteen chickens which meant a lot more picking than one or two that was certain. These chickens, taken from the large chicken crate outside the back door, were stuck with a slender-bladed, sharply honed knife just back of the head; they were held until the blood completely drained out; the process was repeated until the entire batch of lifeless carcasses laid on the bench.

The next step was to scald them one at a time in near boiling hot water so the feathers could be plucked with ease. A tub of water was kept at the boiling point on a kerosene burner just for this purpose; the final step was to "draw" them. This meant the removal of the intestines which were literally drawn out in a long string from a small hole just under the tail; the heart, lungs, and gizzard were left inside; the head and feet were left on; the feet were tied together, the chicken hung over a pole and placed in the cooler until the patrons called for their order.

Ralph really didn't dislike the job, but he found out that he had to be mighty careful when scalding them--not enough and they picked hard, too much and the skin tore to come off with the feathers. He had tried scalding three or four at a time, but that hadn't worked too well because when the carcass cooled down, it no longer picked well. Millie usually knocked a little off the price for a chicken that wasn't in perfect condition, so Ralph put forth every effort not to overscald them.

Rate never liked to have his father criticize his work.

CHAPTER 10

Ralph stood in front of the drug store reading the poster in the window. The Silver family circus was coming to town next Wednesday; it was an event to which the townspeople and the neighboring countryside looked forward each year. It was only a one ring circus and could hardly be compared with Ringling Bros. or Barnum & Bailey since they boasted three rings; nevertheless, the Silver family circus had some good acts. Once every other year or so, one of the large circuses came to Owosso, but they never bothered with the small villages. The Silver family came from Crystal Lake and all they ever played to were the small towns.

Since the Setteringtons now lived in town, Rate had been allowed to go to these performances. For some reason, Pa and Ma weren't too keen on circuses, and because Blanche had asthma, she didn't like being enclosed in a place that got dusty as the performance wore on because it invariably set her to wheezing. Rate didn't much care if it was only one ring; he'd always wondered just how anyone could watch three rings all at the same time anyhow, and he didn't like the idea of missing out on anything.

Sure looked like this was going to be a good one. They had an animal act for the first time this year--it was only three lions, but he'd never seen a lion perform before. Last year, there'd been a man with trained dogs; however, Ralph hadn't figured it was all that spectacular because Bruno could do some of the tricks the circus dogs had done. Now, this would be something different.

He stared at the picture of the man with the lions and wondered how a person went about teaching a lion to do anything. Wasn't as if a body could grab 'em by the scruff of the neck and shove 'em around; he guessed he'd like to see them for certain. Then, there was the horses--my he did like to see a horse do tricks. He liked watching the tumblers and the trapeze artists; because Rate knew he was anything but nimble himself, he always had a profound respect for anyone who could do anything that required a lot of coordination and agility.

Guess he'd go on over to see if Brownie McNall or Don Besley knew about it yet. Maybe if Pa didn't have any chores for him at the market next Wednesday, he and some of his cronies could wander down and watch the circus set up. Rate knew the circus arrived on its own railroad cars in the middle of the night, and before noon, the bigtop would be all in place just waiting for the afternoon performance. They gave two performances, one in the afternoon and one in early evening. Of course, around midday, there was always a parade with gaudily harnessed horses pulling still gaudier-painted wagons, but best of all was the wagon with the calliope; the music just seemed to go right through a body, and it set the whole town in a festive mood. Boy, he could hardly wait until next week.

The day before the circus was to arrive, Rate had made the wieners for the week and had scurried around doing any odd job he could find before Pa so much as suggested it. Come closing time, he had made up his mind he'd ask Pa the all important question while they walked home together. Walking with Pa was more like trotting because with Pa's long legs, he took an unusually long stride; Ralph always did take short steps, even when he had attained his full growth, but now, he took almost two steps to Millie's one.

Father and son were headed west on Main Street; they would cut through by the Methodist Church and come in the back door at home. Millie was quiet as was so often his way, seemingly lost in thoughts which he felt no compulsion to share with anyone.

Rate hesitated a moment, wondering if he should break into his father's meditation. Finally, he heaved a sigh and spoke.

"Pa, some of the fellas is gonna go watch the circus set up tomorrow morning. Might I go with them?"

Millie looked at his son and laughed.

"So that's why you were hustlin' so all-fired hard all day to get all the work done. Wondered what had given you all that extree ambition today."

"I always do my work, don't I?" countered the lad.

"Didn't say you don't. Merely said there seemed to be some extree special zeal today."

"Well, can I?"

Pa still hadn't answered the all important question.

"Far as I'm concerned, it's all right. Best check with your Ma to see if she has something that needs doing. You goin' to attend one of the performances?"

"Sure am," he responded exuberantly. "I'm goin' with some of the fellas. Guess we're goin' at night since mostly mothers and little kids go in the afternoon-especially little girls."

"Got anything against girls?"

"Nope, not especially, but they *are* a nuisance at times."

"You'll change your tune afore too many more years pass," was the solemn prediction.

By now, they had reached the back door. It was time to get washed up since they knew Mina would be putting the finishing touches on supper just about the time they stepped through the door.

Rate met Don Besley and Brownie McNall early the next morning, and they hurried over to the vacant field where the circus was setting up. The scene that greeted them reminded Ralph of a giant anthill with people scurrying in every which direction. It took only a few moments of observation to discover that there was indeed a purpose to every movement made, each person had a specific job to do at a specific time; this rigid discipline was producing astounding results. Already the huge tent was ready to be raised.

The boys wandered off to the wagons.

"L-l-looky there, R-R-Rate. B-b-bet ya w-w-wouldn't want him t-t-t- step on your foot, w-w-would ya?" stammered Don pointing to the sole elephant the circus boasted. The beast was tied to a stake in the ground by means of a chain around one leg. The huge pachyderm was eating from a pile of hay placed directly in front of it and well within reach of its trunk. The boys watched as the elephant lifted a generous amount of hay and crammed it unceremoniously into its mouth; all the while he swayed back and forth, oblivious to anything but his voracious appetite.

"Guess it would be worse than a horse. Wonder if we'd dare go over by him?"

"You can if you want," put in Brownie. "Me, I can see fine from right here."

They walked over to the cage with the lions; one raised his head and looked sleepily at the three sets of eyes staring at him.

"T-t-they don't l-l-look like m-m-much to me."

"Bet you wouldn't dare go in the ring with them," said Ralph.

"W-w-well, maybe n-n-not. I d-d-don't guess you'd d-d-do it either."

"I'm no dunce. How about you, Brownie? You want to be an animal trainer?"

"Not me. Unless it was horses. Let's go look at the horses."

The three boys wandered over to where the horses were being washed down and curried in preparation to putting on their spangled harnesses with the white bone rings, the bells, and the colored plumes on the bridles.

In less time than the boys had thought possible, the mammoth tent stood ready to receive its crowd of spectators. Now, the roustabouts went to the breakfast tent for their morning meal; soon it would be time to put on their gaudy clothes for the parade. Even the drivers of the wagons had bright-colored uniforms. The steam had to be built up for the calliope; there was no time for anyone to dawdle, performers or crew.

Ralph wondered what it would be like to live constantly with the hustle and bustle of the circus world day after day. It was fun to watch one day a year, but he didn't think it would appeal to him as a steady diet.

The boys were among those lining the streets to watch the parade. The store owners, in the absence of customers, came out to stand with the crowd leaving their stores completely unattended. The parade was coming along East Main Street where it would turn north at the main four corners. The boys had firmly ensconced themselves right on the four corners with the thought in mind that they could now see the parade longer because they could watch it on Main Street, but they could also see it as it turned the corner and headed north on Ovid Street.

First came the calliope, and then the carriage with the barker who shouted to the crowd describing the stupendous acts in language calculated to appeal to the emotions of everyone within the sound of his voice.

The boys enjoyed the clowns most of all. Two clowns came along playing leapfrog with one another looking completely ridiculous with their over-sized shoes, clothes which didn't fit, and silly clown faces; however, it was the third clown the boys appreciated most. He was tall, gawky, and his skinny frame was enclosed in pants ten sizes too large; his face was painted in a perpetual expression of total dejection, and he rode in a little cart that looked more like a child's toy, pulled by what looked to the boys like a miniature donkey. They learned later it was a burro. Of course, the burro was well-trained, and sometimes refused to budge one inch. Finally, the clown projected a pole over the burro's back to dangle a bunch of carrots on a string in front of his face; he kept the carrots just out of the burro's reach, and they proceeded with no more problems.

The evening performance was scintillating. Rate enjoyed all the acts although his preference was still the trained horses. Maybe some day he'd teach Pearl to walk on her hind legs. She was a mighty smart horse, so he bet she could learn.

For quite some time Millie had run a meat route one day a week out east of town. He would go to the meat market at five o'clock and cut meat before the shop opened for the day's business. George Page ran the route for him, and usually did his own loading, knowing just how much ice to pack from the ice house to keep the meat from spoiling.

Millie had gone to the market as usual, cut the meat and then wondered why George hadn't shown up. It was almost eight o'clock when Ralph came into the store.

"Rate, you go on over to Page's and see why George hasn't shown up for work."

"All right, Pa. Bet he was out on a toot last night," volunteered the boy.

"That may all be. You get on over there and find out."

Ralph hurried the few blocks, then rapped on the Page door. George's stepmother answered his knock.

"Missus Page, Pa wants to know whyn't George shown up for work."

"Land sakes, Ralph, I tried to git him up, but he came home dead drunk last night, and I can't no more wake him than I kin raise the dead. You're welcome to go see ifn you kin git him up. He's flopped acrosst the bed fully clothed."

She held open the screen door, and Ralph stepped into the neat dining room. "Go upstairs. It's the door on the right."

Ralph went hesitantly up the steps. Golly, he just bet it wouldn't do a mite of good. Even before he entered the room, he heard the sonorous snores; he shook George's shoulder and shouted his name, but the young man only mumbled, changed positions, and began to snore once more. He reeked of liquor.

Ralph went back downstairs, explained to Mrs. Page that he had had no more luck than she in rousing her stepson. He hastily excused himself and headed back to the butcher shop. Golly, he wondered what Pa would do about the route. He knew his father had the meat all cut and ready to go.

After hearing the crux of the situation, Millie scratched his head and pondered his next move.

"Rate, they way I see it, you'll have to take the route."

"But Pa, I don't know where George goes. All I know is that he leaves town headed east."

"Well, he follows the main road for a time and then turns north. If you ask the places where he stops, they can likely tell you where to go next. Just do the best you can. We'll hurry and get the wagon loaded. I'm not just certain how much ice George puts in, but don't reckon there's any need to waste it."

In short order, they had the delivery wagon loaded. It was a small, covered rig, and the roof projected out to give the driver some protection from the sun or rain as the case might be. With plenty of misgivings, Rate clambered up on the seat and started off. When he came out of the alley, he turned east out of town.

Gripes. How did Pa expect him to know where he was supposed to go? He wasn't even familiar with the people in this direction. Why in heck couldn't Pa have just forgot about the route for this week? Bet anyone else's Pa would have.

The first place he stopped, he sold a pound of beefsteak; there was no one home the next couple of places. The day sure was hot. There wasn't a cloud in the sky; he bet it was past eighty, and it wasn't even noon. He glanced back into the wagon and noted the blocks of ice seemed to be melting darned awful fast. Didn't look as though they'd last the day like Pa had thought.

He had turned north like Pa said, but now it seemed as though he had gone quite a ways and hadn't passed a farmhouse and nary a one was in sight. Well, he'd turn off the first chance he got. The trouble was, Ralph had picked one of the few roads that led to the sandy, sparsely settled north country, with no crossroads for miles and miles. When he was finally able to turn off, the ice was nearly gone, and he had sold just over a dollar's worth of meat. At least he was getting back into civilization again because he saw a farm up ahead. When he got nearer, he recognized it as the home of Ed Blunt--bet Mr. Blunt would buy some meat. He was right. Ed bought ten cents worth of bologna.

Rate made one more sale for the day. The ice was gone long before he got back to the butcher shop, and the lad fully realized the intense heat was spoiling the meat. He dreaded having to admit to his father that he had sold so little. All he'd taken in was a dollar fifty, and not only that, the rest of the meat was not going to be fit to sell to anyone.

With true unpredictability, Millie made no complaint. All he said was, "There's no use cryin' over spilt milk." They took the spoiled meat out and buried it because already it had begun to smell. A day near ninety with no ice had sure made the difference. It was the last time Millie suggested Ralph take the route.

Miney was terribly worried. She had had a call this morning from her sister, Mary, clear from Chicago. Blanche was ailing, and the doctor thought it might be appendicitis, but since she seemed somewhat improved, he felt she was definitely getting over the attack. The problem was, there was no way for him to predict whether she would have another attack which might necessitate an operation. Miney insisted that as soon as the doctor felt it advisable, Blanche was to come home. For once, Mary agreed with her, saying she could understand that it would make Miney feel better to have Blanche home. Course she had said they would certainly miss her, but if a body was to be sick, they always felt better in their own home. Thus, it was decided that as soon as she could travel, Blanche would return to Elsie.

Although she was worried about her daughter's health, Miney felt infinitely relieved that Blanche would be coming home. She had been terribly lonesome without her daughter. Of course, Blanche had always been gone a lot what with visiting Mother Setterington and Ruby, but that had always been only a matter of days, not several weeks. She often wondered if Blanche ever missed her when she was away; it didn't appear likely. Well, Blanche was one who liked modern ways, and Chicago was certainly a heap different than a small village. She guessed maybe Blanche was meant to be a city girl instead of a farm girl. Now, Ralph was definitely cut out for small town life; he enjoyed the work, and he enjoyed the people. He and Blanche were not much alike, that was certain.

Within a week, Blanche arrived home looking as healthy as ever. When Miney started fussing over her, Blanche showed her impatience.

"Ma, don't fuss. I'm all right now. I've never felt better. Next week, I intend to look for a job. I found that it is really nice to have your own money. I know I've never looked for a really decent job before, one that paid well and was permanent. But that has all changed now."

"Goodness, I didn't mean to fuss," said an aggrieved Miney. She didn't know how to cope with this daughter she no longer knew.

"I'm sorry, Ma. I didn't mean to sound ungrateful. It's just that I'm not a child any longer. I don't know what I'm going to do with my life, but I don't intend to sit around home and make Pa support me."

Miney eyed her daughter speculatively. Finally, she said, "You've changed." Her voice sounded sad.

"Not really. I've just grown up. The first day at Carson Perry's, I was scared to death--afraid I'd do something wrong. Well, I soon learned that I was as good as any other clerk. I didn't have to be unsure of myself any longer. It was a mighty good feeling. Whatever I decide to do, I just know I'll be able to do it well."

"You may not like this, but you are getting to be more like your grandmother every day," observed Miney, a slight frown creasing her forehead.

"I suppose in one way I am," she conceded. "I can tell you this much, I'll never be as insensitive to other people's feelings as she is."

Blanche's brown eyes flashed determinedly, and Miney knew she meant exactly what she said. Sometimes, when she was like this, Miney failed completely to understand her daughter. While Miney did not wish to see her beloved daughter coping with marriage at this age, she was not at all certain she approved of her independent attitude. She guessed she'd rather Blanche sat meekly at home, learning to cook, bake, quilt, and crochet; she already knew how to embroider, but she had shown no interest in assembling a hope chest.

* * * * * * * * * * * *

Since Millie had had to foreclose on the mortgage to Slinky Marshall for the south forty, he had been at a loss as to what to do with the property. He'd hated like sin to foreclose. Slinky was Sadie Knight's brother and the Knights were neighbors. Pa had told him to foreclose long before he did, but it just hadn't set well with Millie. Finally, it was Slinky himself who had told Millie there was just no way he'd ever be able to pay for the farm. That had been a few years ago, and Millie had been farming the place since; hay and wheat had been the crops, and the last two years, he had pastured the sheep there. Trouble with the place was, the house was pretty small and needed some repair, the granary wasn't much, and it had no barn. Millie had talked it over with Pa--just to get his opinion, mind you--and had decided the property would sell better if it had a barn.

In a matter of days, Millie had made arrangements for Charlie Turner, who was the best master carpenter around, to erect a 36' x 60' barn with a hip roof. Charlie had a crew of eight, and the only help they needed was the day it took to raise the bents and peg them in place.

All this was decided before Millie spoke to Miney, yet she was expected to feed the nine men each day and an untold number the day of the raising. Millie gave little or no thought to the extra work it made for his wife; it was simply something wives were expected to handle if the occasion arose.

At least Millie was thoughtful enough to have a tent set up where the ladies could have a small cook stove to keep the victuals warm--most of the cooking had been done at home with the women transporting huge pots of food to be finished at the sight. A huge kettle of steeped coffee was drawn off to the side of the stove top to keep hot; raw eggs had been dropped in the kettle to settle the grounds.

Blanche was old enough to help her mother with the baking at night. The day of the raising was the worst when they fed thirty or forty hungry men. Blanche could not believe how quickly the loaves of bread and mounds of boiled potatoes disappeared. She and her mother had worked for several days to bake all that bread; it seemed a crying shame to have it devoured so quickly.

Miney was simply glad she had been well, and the ordeal had not upset her stomach. Sometimes, when her stomach bothered most, she was actually confined to bed for a day or two. Luckily, she had kept her health this time. Naturally, she felt as though she would never feel rested again, but this was to be expected. She told herself she was just lucky it was Charlie Turner who was doing the work because he had a reputation for getting a job done quickly. Nine extra men to feed every day took a heap of doin'.

Rate once more was impressed with how the bents, even though assembled on the ground, fit together like an interlocking puzzle when they were raised. He figured the men who scrambled along the timbers to pound the cylindrical pegs in the pre-drilled holes must be related to a monkey. Rate had never been afraid to climb, but he wanted a solid foundation. The bents were not all that steady until safely pegged together. Still, everyone seemed to know his job, and the work went along without a mishap.

The small barn Rate had seen raised on his grandfather's property in town had been nothing compared to this since that barn had been only about half as big and not nearly as tall. Rate had no desire to be a carpenter, but he sure figured a man had to be pretty smart to build a barn.

It took Charlie and crew four days to complete the barn.

CHAPTER 11

The last few days of August rushed by, and Rate didn't know if he was sorry or glad. Actually, he liked school, but he was kind of sorry he'd have to be in the seventh grade again this year. His friends understood, but he was half-certain someone-- Ralph Boone for one--would make a few disparaging remarks. Well, anyone get too mouthy on the subject, and he'd make them sorry even if Ma did get angry if he fought. After all, he didn't intend to let anyone push him around--less'n they was too big to handle, that is.

The first day of school arrived, and Ralph went to his room early so he could have a good choice of desks. He smiled to himself as he chose the last desk in the outside row, the farthest he could get from Miss Finch's desk.

Miss Finch had smiled and spoken pleasantly when he entered the room, but had gone back to some paper work at her desk. Ralph heaved a sigh of relief as he put his books and pencil box in the desk.

He was ready to go outside to play when Miss Finch looked up and spoke, a benign smile on her face.

"Ralph, haven't you got the wrong seat? Remember, this one is yours. I've been saving it special." She tapped the desk closest to her desk with her ruler.

Ralph gave her a grin which admitted defeat. "Guess your memory is better than mine," he said.

Teacher and pupil eyed each other a moment; both sets of eyes twinkled. Kate could hardly suppress the laughter which bubbled inside as she watched her favorite student. Looks like another fun year, she thought as Ralph began hauling his books from the desk. That boy was always a challenge. Students like Ralph were what made teaching so all-fired interesting.

Since Ralph had already covered the material presented the first part of the year, he was bored with school. Kate realized the boy was having a difficult time, so she encouraged him to do extra reading. This suited Ralph to a T. He could easily become absorbed by a book to the extent that he failed to notice what went on in the world around him. This was especially true if the book had to do with history. The exploits of the early explorers always held his rapt attention; therefore, history was one of his better subjects.

Rate had finished his history test early. Well, he hadn't really finished it, but he had done all he intended to do. The test, like most of Miss Finch's, consisted of ten, long, essay questions. He'd been tired of writing before he had completed the second question, but he knew he had to have seventy-five percent to pass. Well, that meant he had to do seven and a half questions.

Kate noticed that Ralph had shoved the folded test paper to the side of his desk with a completely bored expression. Surely, he could not be finished this soon. This would bear investigating.

Kate rose from her desk and began to walk slowly up and down the aisles between the seventh grade desks. All but Ralph were concentrating on the test. Some of them she knew would not have expressed themselves well, but at least they were trying.

She stopped by Rate's desk, picked up his folded test, opened it, and immediately noted the first seven questions had been answered, but only part of the eighth.

She looked at her pupil. He gave her his wide-eyed, innocent look as if wondering why she behaved as though there was a problem.

"You didn't know the answer to number nine and ten?"

"Oh, sure. They weren't hard."

"Would you mind telling me why you didn't do them?"

"I got tired of writing. Those questions take forever to answer. My fingers were almost numb," he said, flexing the fingers of his right hand.

"You *do* intend to pass the class, don't you?"

"Sure do, but 75 percent is passing. I answered enough to get 75 percent." He gave her a smug look.

"What if you have answered one of the questions wrong?"

"But I haven't. I know what I wrote is right. There was no need to do any more," he explained patiently as though wondering why she found his line of reasoning difficult to follow.

Kate stared at her pupil. Little scamp. Well, she'd not argue with him. If he wanted to settle for just passing, fine. However, she intended to go over his paper with a fine tooth comb. Just maybe she could find a mistake, and then he would be under the passing grade. Bet that would take him by surprise;

No matter how closely Kate graded Ralph's test, he came out with a score slightly above 75. In fact, this began to be the standard for all of his tests in all of his classes--he never completed any of them. Kate gave the problem a lot of serious thought, but never found a way to entice Ralph to complete his tests. There were times when the lad was difficult to outwit. Threats would have solved nothing. Kate felt certain that had he so desired, he could easily have had above ninety in everything except spelling and English. She guessed he felt his studies were not all that important.

Kate did not feel she should take the matter up with his parents. Surely, they knew he was capable of better grades. She seriously doubted if anything they said would improve the situation. Rate was clearly a case of you can lead a horse to water, but you can't make him drink.

August had been unseasonably warm, and September was doing its darndest not to be outdone. Millie had been concerned about the amount of ice it took to keep the cooler functioning at the market. Usually, he only had to pack blocks of ice on top of the cooler once a week; the water from the melting ice kept the meat from spoiling for several days.

Millie tried to judge the amount of meat needed so he didn't get too much butchered ahead. He butchered often and made wieners once a week. Course it took a while to use three hundred pounds of beef, but mostly he never had any meat go bad. However, if this hot spell continued, the ice he had stored in the ice house would never last. The past four weeks he had been forced to pack the cooler two days earlier than the usual week.

Well, no use to worry. If he ran out of ice, he'd have to see about buying from the firm which supplied ice for some of the other businesses and the homes which had ice boxes. It would be an unwelcome expense, but a man couldn't operate a meat market with no refrigeration. Guess he'd just have to hope for a break in the weather.

There was a long, low shed by the gristmill which was filled to capacity each year with huge blocks of ice. Just below the gristmill hill, the road curved north to cross the river, then angled southwest along the river channel by the cemetery, then curved sharply west again. The shed was on the east side of the road, handy to the river. It took several days of steady work to fill it to capacity. It was from here the ice came to fill the ice chests of the more affluent villagers. On ice day, half the kids in town ran after the wagon, snatching a sliver of ice as the ice man broke and picked the large blocks to a size needed by his customers.

The ice was covered with remnants of sawdust, but the children merely wiped it off on a bit of clothing; after all, it was clean sawdust, wasn't it?

Millie had accumulated fat meat from pork in the cooler for the past three weeks; now, it was time to try out the lard. He had a large, fifty gallon iron kettle to hold the fat. He would take a strip of fat meat, run a razor-sharp knife right under the skin, then toss the fat into the kettle. He kept a slow fire under the kettle and kept the meat stirred with a heavy wooden paddle. Wouldn't do to burn a batch and spoil it.

The liquid fat was stored in one- and five-pound pails, left to congeal, and sold to his customers. It was a lot of work for the amount of money earned, but if Millie didn't provide this service, his customers would go elsewhere. His wasn't the only butcher shop in town. When added into the overall picture, Millie reckoned it was all worthwhile.

Halloween came and went, and once more Ralph had not been allowed to go any place except to a party given by the Baptist Church for its young people. Rate knew better than to sneak off to join some of his cronies because Millie was not above giving him a licking if he flaunted his father's authority. Pa wouldn't care that he was too big to be licked. Since Rate knew his grandfather had allowed Pa and Uncle John to go out with the boys, he never understood why his father was so set against him ever joining his friends. Pa was never one to explain his actions, not even to Ma, so there was no use to ask.

Funny thing about Pa, he wasn't old enough to go Halloweenin', but just lately Pa had let him wait on customers at the market unless they needed something cut special. Millie had patiently shown Rate how to operate the till where he kept his cash; all the till was was a cash drawer divided into sections to keep the bills and coins separated by denominations, but it was opened by a series of levers on the bottom which had to be pulled in the correct sequence if the drawer was to open. It hadn't taken Rate but a couple of times to memorize which ones to pull. Millie had nodded with satisfaction and merely cautioned Ralph to be careful when making change. Since Ralph had always been good at his sums, Millie was certain the boy would find nothing difficult about this new responsibility.

Winter put in an early appearance. It seemed only yesterday the leaves had garmented the trees in brightly hued colors; now, they had already fallen, leaving the branches stark against a gray sky which now and then spit forth a few flakes of snow.

It turned cold as well. The pond south of town was frozen solid, and the young people had already dug out their ice skates and trooped there en masse for the first skating of the year--and it had barely turned November.

Millie, often a pessimist, was certain all the signs pointed to an unusually hard winter. He said the huge V-shaped flocks of geese had passed over early, the woolly bear's rings were the width which foretold a severe winter, and everyone said animal's pelts had thickened early and were exceptionally heavy. Mother Nature knew how to care for her own, said the old-timers.

Since a severe winter would necessitate a great amount of wood for the stoves' voracious appetites, Millie was filling the woodshed to the rafters with neatly corded wood. Sure would beat having to haul it in from the outdoors when the weather was really bad. Besides, dry wood burned more readily than wood encrusted with frozen snow.

At breakfast, Millie spoke to his young son.

"Rate, when you get home from school, there will be a load of wood thrown off by the woodshed door. I want you to cord the wood in the woodshed. I'll likely be home afore supper with another load to be thrown off."

"All right, Pa." Rate agreed.

However, Ralph learned at school that his group of friends intended to go skating right after school. Golly, Pa had said he was to cord that load of wood right after school, and Ralph knew that by the time he finished, it would be too late to go skating.

He hurried home. Maybe Pa hadn't got there with the first load. He went in the east door of the woodshed, but noted with a disappointed sigh, that outside the west door there was a huge pile of wood blocks, each a little over a foot long. Drat it all. He went into the house, got a couple of cookies from the crock and went into the sitting room to speak to his mother.

"Ma, can I go skatin' and cord the wood later?"

Miney looked up from her patching, eying the boy intently. She had heard Millie tell Ralph the work was to be done right after school.

"Ralph, I just don't know. You know your father said he wanted it done as soon as you got home from school. I think you had better do as he wants."

"But Ma, I can do it when I get home. Why's it gotta be done now?"

"Because your father will have another load to throw off when he gets here. If this one isn't out of the way, where's he to throw the next?"

"Pa won't likely be here before supper, an' I won't be that long." he explained.

"Well, use your own judgment. If you get into trouble, don't blame me."

"I won't. I'll be back early and get right to work," promised Ralph as he darted from the room.

Skating had been especially good. The ice was glass smooth, the air frosty, but with no wind, it did not feel all that cold.

Rate stayed longer than he had intended. Golly, it must be near six o'clock, the hour for the evening meal. He sure hoped Pa was late, then he could at least have a chance to get started on that big pile of wood. Maybe he could get most of it done before supper.

Since Ralph came in the east door, he failed to notice the wagon, piled high with blocks of wood on the other side of the pile which half-hid the door. It wasn't until he stepped into the kitchen and saw his father sitting at the table that he realized just how late it really was. His heart sank. His father gave him a stony stare.

Miney and Blanche were just finishing putting the evening meal on the table. Rate hurriedly washed his hands, ran a comb through his hair, and was just sliding into his chair when Millie spoke.

"There's wood to be corded and a load to be thrown off. I 'spect you had best get at it. Supper will be here when you're finished, not before."

The brown eyes stared intently at his son who returned the look with eyes completely expressionless.

Ralph knew argument would be futile. Both Miney and Blanche kept as quiet as church mice wondering if Millie would say more.

He didn't.

As Ralph slid out of his chair and left the table, his father began loading his plate with plenty of potatoes and a generous piece of roast beef without giving his son a glance. Rate's stomach growled, reminding him just how hungry he really was.

Rate was tired by the time he had the first load neatly corded in the woodshed. It had taken some doing. The stack of firewood was higher than his head. He had begun like a house afire, but had slowed down to a snail's pace for the last few rows. It had been lifting the heavy blocks of wood over his head which had tired him most.

He sat down a moment as he contemplated the wagon piled high with blocks of varying size--a few were not more than eight inches in diameter. Bet this was an even bigger load than the first one. Well, sitting and thinking about it would get nothing done. With a resigned sigh, Ralph began tossing the blocks off the wagon. He attacked each one as though it was to blame for his predicament.

Rate guessed his stomach had given up the idea of getting any food since it had quit rumbling. He knew Ma would have filled his plate and set it in the warming oven above the stove. While it wouldn't be hot, it would still be edibly warm. Biggest problem now was whether he'd have enough strength to eat it. Golly, he hadn't figured cording wood would be quite so tiring, and it seemed that each block he tossed off the wagon was heavier than the one before. Guess he'd sure learned his lesson. When Pa gave a direct order, it didn't pay to mess around with it none.

Winter finally arrived, and true to Millie's predictions, it was severe. The snow came early, and there was plenty of it to provide an ample cover for the ground. The days were cold, but the sun shone brightly, more than was customary, so spirits remained high, and no one really minded the bone-chilling cold-- especially the young people.

There were numerous skating parties on Friday or Saturday evening with a huge bonfire for warmth and light. There were usually wieners and marshmallows to roast, and sometimes hot chocolate to drink.

Ralph hadn't reached the age to be interested in girls. He viewed them as being silly, often incompetent, and someone whose main purpose in life was to be there for boys to tease in all sorts of ways. Of course, when the young people had sleigh rides, very few were paired off in couples, they were simply a large group of young adults who enjoyed being together, singing songs and telling stories on one another.

Rate had volunteered to drive a team for a group of young people from both churches. Mr. and Mrs. Milo Van Deusen had volunteered to go as chaperones-- they were a soft touch and often chaperoned the young people, so they were mighty popular. Some of the group envied Elizabeth because her parents were always willing to get involved, seemingly enjoying young people, the more, the merrier.

Truman Armstrong, one of the partners in the livery stable, had heard about the proposed sleigh ride; therefore, he made Rate an offer.

"Rate, I got this mare that hardly gets no exercise. I was wondrin' if you'd be willin' t' put her in an' drive her on the sleigh Friday night."

"I druther drive my own team," said Ralph honestly.

"But you'd be doin' me a big favor. Honest, Rate, she really needs some good exercise. You know a horse needs to work to keep in shape. How about it?"

"Well, I suppose I could. I'll pick her up about six-thirty. That'll give me time to get her hitched in with Major. He'll work with anything."

"Fine. I'll have her harnessed. It'll save you time." "Don't know what time I'll have her back."

"Don't matter none. You just put her in her stall an' be sure to close the stable door good."

On Friday night, Ralph led Major over to the livery stable to pick up Truman's mare. Just as he'd promised, Truman had her harnessed. He helped harness her in with Major, chuckling as he did so as though something was exceptionally funny. But Ralph just put this down to Truman's strange ways.

Rate drove the team the short distance to Van Deusen's where Mr. Van Deusen helped him hitch the team to the sleigh. Those going had assembled here from all over town. They laughed and chatted as they clambered onto the sleigh and snuggled down to keep warm. A string of sleigh bells tinkled merrily as they moved off. Mr. Van Deusen sat up front with Ralph while his wife was in the sleigh nestled under a horsehide robe with the group.

Ralph turned north at the main four corners. All was going well. They had gone just a block when all hell exploded. The mare's first kick sent Mr. Van Deusen's high hat flying off his head. Rate could do nothing with her. She completely ignored commands and behaved as though she didn't know what lines were for. She kicked over the traces, but luckily, her next kick put her back where she belonged. Rate was afraid she'd go down, and what a mess of tangled leather and horse that would have made.

Someone screamed, and Ralph was aware of Mrs. Van Deusen's voice attempting to calm the girls. That was all he needed, more screaming to frighten the mare and make her even more difficult to calm down. Luckily, Major stood stock still as if patiently waiting for his partner to get all this funny business out of her system.

One of the boys took the lines while Mr. Van Deusen and Rate got off the sleigh. Mr. Van Deusen attempted to hold the mare's head while Rate gingerly set about to unfasten her tugs, dodging flailing feet as he did so. He slipped the outside tug chain loose from the whippletree and let it hang; the mare seemed to sense what was happening. While Mr. Van Deusen was still having all he could do to hold her, she was quieter than she had been in the beginning when it had seemed as though she could kick with all four feet simultaneously.

Rate spoke soothingly to Major as he stepped behind him to reach the mare's other tug. On his first attempt, the vicious hind foot nearly caught him, but he managed to duck just in time. There. He'd slipped this one free. Now, all he had to do was unfasten her lines from Major and unsnap the buckle to the neckyoke ring, and she'd be free of the sleigh.

As soon as the mare realized she was no longer hitched to anything, she quieted to near normal. Rate warily fastened the tug chains to the harness so their dragging wouldn't alarm her. Although she had stopped kicking, she still seemed skittish; therefore, Ralph was mighty careful to make no quick movement of any kind. Cussed mare anyway.

Rate took her back to the livery stable and led her into her stall. Then, the idea hit him that she could very well kick him or crowd him when he went to leave. He hesitated a moment to consider his plight. Confounded mare, she was capable of 'most anything.

That darned Truman had certainly known this would happen, and it was just his way of teasing. No wonder she needed exercise. Rate bet everyone but him had known what the mare was likely to do. At the moment, Rate's sense of humor was completely lacking. Well, he'd be damned if he was going to make any attempt to pull her harness off and likely get kicked for his pains.

An impish smile crept over Ralph's face. He snapped the rope tied to the manger to a ring on her bridle, slipped carefully into the manger, up the hay chute to the haymow, then down the ladder to the floor below and on out the door, being careful to close it tightly after him. Let Truman unharness his mare when he came to work in the morning. Rate half hoped she'd kick Truman 'cause it would serve him right.

Mr. Van Deusen had picked up Major's mate from the Setterington stable and had him hitched in with Major by the time Ralph returned.

The rest of the evening was without incident, and everyone had a good time. Rate wondered if Mrs. Van Deusen realized how close her husband had come to getting kicked in the head. If she had, she certainly didn't let it show. She was an all right lady.

The next afternoon, Rate ran into Truman and called a greeting as though nothing unusual had happened.

"Rate, how come you didn't unharness that mare?"

"Golly, didn't I?"

"No. She was standin' there harnessed and bridled." His tone was slightly accusatory.

"Guess I musta been too tired and in a hurry to get home." Ralph flashed him a beguiling grin.

Truman nodded and walked off. Rate was certain he had detected a look of disappointment in the older man's eyes. Truman, I'd never admit to you how much trouble you caused, thought Ralph. Sorry to spoil your day.

Christmas was only a few days away, school had let out until after the New Year, and already Ralph was bored.

Only that morning he had heard Ma ask Pa when he intended to get a Christmas tree. Pa had been his usual uncommunicative self and had not really given an answer. While Ma had not pressed the matter--having learned from past experience it would do no good--Ralph could see that she was disappointed. Ma set quite a store in having a tree, and Rate would be the first to admit he thought a tree certainly made it seem more Christmasy.

Pa left for the meat market right after breakfast. He told Ralph there was no need for him to come to the market until after dinner; therefore, as soon as he finished chores, Rate had the morning free.

He said not one word to his mother except that he would return before dinner. Since Miney's mind was elsewhere, she didn't even ask where he was going. Usually, she wanted to know his every movement. Rate gave a sigh of relief since he had no intention of disclosing his plans to anyone. He smuggled a hatchet from out of the woodshed and left, heading for town just in case his mother was watching.

As soon as he neared Main Street, he veered west, headed for the river flats where a nice stand of cedar grew, many of them young trees just the right size for a Christmas tree. He smiled to himself as he thought how pleased his mother would be.

The morning was frosty, and the snow creaked beneath his feet. It was absolutely still, not a breath of air stirring. The sky was cloudless, and the early sun's rays set the snow-covered world aglitter. It was a good morning for a hike, Ralph decided. While the thermometer was undoubtedly down in single digits, the absence of any wind, together with the bright sunshine, made one forget how cold it really was.

Ralph moved from one tree to the next, walking around each prospect with a critical eye. It had to be five or six feet tall with a generous amount of branches. The trees growing by themselves, away from others, were the best since they had grown uniformly and didn't have one skimpy side where they were too close to another tree.

Ralph had finally narrowed it down to two. Well, he'd take the one he had to drag the shortest distance. The hatchet was sharp so it took only a few good whacks, and the tree toppled to the ground.

Ralph had just reached the road with his burden when Bert Wooley drew in his horse and cutter to speak to him.

After the pleasantries had been said, Bert asked, "Where'd you get the tree? Over on the flats?"

"Yup. Pa didn't seem to have time to get a tree, so I thought I'd surprise Ma."

"I suppose there are plenty more good trees there?"

"Oh, sure. There's all kinds and all sizes."

"Tell you what, Rate. I'll give you a quarter if you let me have this one. You can get yourself another without much bother."

"I dunno. What time is it? I gotta be home afore dinner."

Bert reached inside his heavy coat and brought out a gold watch. He flicked open the case, then said, "It's only five minutes past ten. How about it, Rate? We got a bargain?"

"All right, Bert. You've just bought a tree."

Rate pocketed the quarter, helped Bert position the tree in the cutter, then retraced his steps to where the tree which had been his second choice stood. Golly, no one ever *bought* a Christmas tree. He'd made a whole quarter. He guessed he was lucky he had reached the road just when Bert came along. Rate felt pretty satisfied with himself.

When he got home with the tree, Miney had already started dinner. However, at Ralph's insistence, she poked her head out the kitchen door to see what he had in the woodshed that was so all-fired important. She cried out in delight when she saw the tree leaning against the wall.

"Why, Ralph, you got us a tree. My, and such a nice one too." She bent and gave him a resounding kiss on his forehead.

Ralph's eyes opened wide in wonder. Ma was always giving Blanche kisses, but he couldn't remember her kissing him for years. Must be the tree had been more important than he realized. He sure was glad he had thought of it.

"Ralph, if you can get it nailed on its stand, Blanche and I can start trimming it this afternoon. We won't say a thing to your father until it's all done."

They went back into the house with Rate dragging the tree into the parlor. Blanche followed, and was busy with a broom and dustpan cleaning up the snow which had been dislodged from its branches. Blanche was as glad as her mother that Ralph had brought them a tree. It wouldn't seem like Christmas without one. Funny, she'd never thought Ralph had ever given much thought to such things as Christmas trees. My, he *was* growing up. Imagine, dragging that tree clear from the river flats. Well, she supposed he had to wear off his energy somehow. Better on Christmas trees than teasing her.

As the result of a year with below normal rainfall, the river was much lower than usual; the edges of the millpond did not extend their usual distance, and the pilings from the old wooden bridge showed just at the top of the ice. Rate didn't remember being able to see them before. He barely remembered the old wooden bridge; at seven, he had been more concerned with the new iron one which had been its replacement.

That night, he asked Millie how come the pilings had been left in place.

"Guess it was too much bother to try to pull them out. Imagine they go down a considerable way."

"How come I haven't seen 'em before?"

"Don't think the water's been this low in years for one thing. You see, that next winter after they took out the old bridge, old man Spurbeck cut the pilings off even with the ice to use for firewood. Guess the water was nearly as low that year. Don't guess it's been as low since you've been big enough to go there skating."

Everyone said Mr. Spurbeck was as poor as Job's turkey. His wife was dead, but he had two daughters to care for. The eldest was an invalid, always in a wheelchair; the youngest, Ruby, went to school with Ralph. She was the champion speller in the school, a fact which never failed to amaze Ralph since spelling had always been his worst subject.

Ice cutting time came in the dead of winter when the temperature hovered near the zero mark; the splashed water froze quickly before it could wet the pantlegs of the men through to their heavy, winter underwear. The ideal thickness of the ice was about fifteen inches, but sometimes, when there had been an uncommonly long cold snap, the ice was almost two feet thick. Since one man ran the gasoline saw which lacked two inches or so of cutting through the ice, another man followed to cut the strip with a special hand saw; then, another man made the crosscut to form the two feet wide blocks.

Cash Waldron and the Keenan brothers usually hired out to Millie, but when his ice house was filled, they hired out to anyone who needed them. They drove the sleighs out onto the ice. Cash was adept at using his long pole with a hook on the end to catch a block of ice and flip it deftly out of the water where someone with a set of ice tongs could haul it over to load it on the sleigh. The river current brought the cut blocks to where the first cut had been made, so the men simply worked methodically to retrieve the heavy blocks of clear ice.

The cutting season was going well. For some reason, Millie decided to let George Page tend the market while he went to the river to help load ice. It was dreadfully cold. Millie began to wonder if he had made a wise choice since it was certainly going to be even worse on the river. The chill would creep through the heavy shoes and woolen socks right on up his body.

A sleigh was drawn out on the ice, the team standing quietly, but no one seemed to be around.

Millie gave a shout, but heard nothing. Strange. He recognized the team. It belonged to Cash Waldron, but Merval Keenan often drove it while they hauled ice.

"Cash! Mervall"

Millie thought he heard a feeble cry. He crossed the remaining distance with powerfully long sides. He reached the back of the sleigh in time to see Merval heave himself out of the icy water onto the ice where the water cascaded around him.

The man looked nearly frozen. "Merval, what happened?"

"I slipped. Honest, Millie, I never thought I was gonna make it. I'd get halfway out, then slip back, and then start all over again. I was gettin' mighty near wore out."

Merval's teeth were chattering by now.

Millie grabbed an extra horse blanket from the sleigh to wrap around his friend. Just then, others arrived. A warm, horsehide robe appeared to add to the blanket, and Merval was spirited off to Waldron's which was close by.

The incident sobered everyone, and each man was mighty careful the rest of the week when they were finally finished. None of them had wanted the same experience. All fully realized Merval was fortunate he had not slipped under the heavy layer of ice, never to rise again.

When Miney heard of the incident, she quickly thanked God that it was not her husband who had been in such dire straits. Seemed like there was always some danger in the work the men had to do. She hoped that Millie would always be extra careful when it came ice cutting time. She realized the work was a necessity, but it still did not keep her from worrying. At least Merval had no family, but she bet his sister, Frankie, had given him a good lecture about being more careful in the future.

CHAPTER 12

Ralph found the school year more interesting after he got beyond those first few weeks to where he had missed everything because of his leg. However, now that he was once again covering material he had covered once before, he found most of his days completely boring. He had an excellent memory, so he already knew the answers without reading the lessons.

Kate sensed this, so she continued to encourage him to read. He had read all the Horatio Alger stories at least twice and had become interested in books by Henty. He liked books which dealt with history, especially early American history. He often tried to visualize what the continent had looked like before the coming of the white man. It was difficult to imagine the forests as they once had been. Now, although much had been cleared, every farm had its woodlot; some of the larger farms had only forty or fifty acres of cleared land, the rest being huge timber. Rate liked the trees, but knew that little by little the farmers would keep whittling away at them in order to have more acres to plant. Almost seemed a shame.

Blanche had been giving serious thought to a job. She had worked for J.A. Brandau's ice cream parlor on Saturdays, but she wanted something more permanent, something which meant she would go to work every day like she had when she was in Chicago.

When Blanche made up her mind to something, she was never one to dally; thus, she began making the rounds of the local businesses shortly after the first of the year. She met with disappointment and frustration until she called on Mr. Sherman who owned and printed the *Elsie Sun,* a weekly newspaper.

Mr. Sherman was short by Blanche's standard--she compared all men to her father who was six foot three--and clamped between his teeth, he always had a big, black cigar. Today, there was only a stump, and Blanche noted that he carried it without it being lit; then, as if noticing for the first time he could not draw on it, he impatiently tossed it aside and proceeded to stoke up a new one, with great, billowing clouds of smoke wreathing his head.

Blanche watched this process with some hesitation. Neither Pa nor Grandfather smoked, and she hated the smelly, old cigar; however, she wanted a job, and at least Mr. Sherman sounded as though he might have an opening.

"Blanche, I need someone to set type. Now, it is demanding work. You have to be good at spelling 'cause some of the folks who send in news items can't spell for sour apples. It takes a while to learn. The type has to be set from right to left, you know, and that's a little tricky to start. There's always a daub of printer's ink clinging to the letters, so it is kind of a dirty job. That's why I wear these sleeve guards," he said, pointing to the ink-smudged second sleeve which fitted at wrist and elbow with elastic. "The pay is $1.50 a week, but when you get so you can set a column and a half a day, I'll raise that to $2.00. Wanna think it over?"

"No, sir. I'll take it," said Blanche determinedly. "When do I start?"

"How's about tomorrow morning. Best wear an every day dress, and by then, I expect you could have some sleeve guards. Don't expect to get much done the first day. There's a knack to putting them little letters in place, and at first, your fingers are going to feel all thumbs."

How right Mr. Sherman was. The going from right to left didn't bother her, nor did the higher and lower case letters, it was just difficult to slip the tiny piece of metal into its proper niche. Once she had even had one in upside down. But with her usual tenacity, Blanche vowed to steadily improve the number of lines she could do. The prospect of a raise was a great incentive.

The spring of the year was always a busy time for farmers. Millie would have been the last to admit it, but he sometimes felt restless in the butcher shop. He decided there were some things that needed doing on the farm whether he worked it or not. That rail fence, along the road north of the driveway, was getting in bad shape. Made it near impossible to let livestock run in the field. There were other, smaller repairs needed, but a man couldn't be in a butcher shop from six to six, six days a week and do the work himself. Couldn't expect the renter to do it either.

Millie finally decided to hire Ed Clark to put in a woven wire fence, the first on the farm. Ed could get the posts driven while the ground was soft and wet. It wasn't an easy job. A beetle ring was slipped over the post to be struck with a mallet to drive the pointed cedar post a good two feet into the ground. However, this much could be done when it was too wet to work the fields.

When Millie discovered the cost of the material--twenty-five cents a rod for posts and fence--he wondered if it was worth the time and money.

Since Blanche was now working every day for Mr. Sherman, she had been saving her money. Sometimes, the dollar fifty she received each week seemed like a great deal of money, but she kept waiting for the day when she would get two whole dollars. She could set nearly a column and a half of type, and Mr. Sherman had promised her a raise when she reached that mark.

Easter was only ten days away when Blanche made her decision. She was going to spend her money to buy a new Easter outfit. She'd not say a word to Ma about her intentions because she didn't want Ma tagging along. For once, she wanted to buy something entirely on her own.

Blanche went to Netzorg's to browse. Actually, it wasn't just Netzorg's since Mr. Netzorg had taken Andrew Ferguson in with him as a partner just this year. However, old habits are hard to break so everyone still referred to the store as Netzorg's.

She looked at the racks of dresses, but nothing seemed to catch her eye. Next, she moved to a rack which displayed suits; some were long-sleeved and some were short-sleeved. She saw one which caught her eye. It was a lovely soft, dove gray. It was rather early in the year for short sleeves, but after seeing this particular suit, Blanche could see no other. She found a pink blouse and a gray hat with a cluster of pink flowers. She was well satisfied with her purchases.

For once, Miney said little when Blanche modeled her new attire. She admitted the pink looked nice with Blanche's dark hair, and that was about all. Blanche was disappointed because her mother hadn't been more enthusiastic.

Easter arrived: sunny and cold with a stiff breeze making it seem even colder. It was definitely coat weather.

Blanche came downstairs dressed in her new finery. Miney looked up, her face showing disbelief.

"For heaven's sake, Blanche, don't you realize how cold it is this morning? If you think you are going to Church with bare arms, you had better think again."

Blanche looked at her mother, and said stubbornly, "I bought this suit to wear today, and I intend to wear it."

"You'll catch your death of pneumonia," lamented Miney.

"No, I won't. It doesn't take that long to walk to Church. I'll be fine."

But Blanche wasn't fine. They had gone only a few steps when her arms were covered with gooseflesh, the hairs standing up in protest. Blanche shivered, but she said nothing. She simply wished Ma would walk a little faster.

Blanche couldn't concentrate on the sermon because she was so cold, but never did she admit to her mother how uncomfortable she had been. She had too much pride for that.

When baseball season came, Rate was asked to play on the high school team. Not enough older boys were interested, or they were too busy working, so they only had ten players. A team liked to have more than one extra player. Besides, the coach had seen Ralph play and decided he would definitely be an asset to the team.

Rate was more than happy to be on the high school team. After all, they played regular games with other schools. He figured he was a pretty fair outfielder since he had a strong throwing arm. He could hit the ball pretty well too, but he realized he was awful slow on the bases. He liked playing left field best since there were usually more balls hit there than there were to right field. Most batters were right-handed, and they hit more often to center or left.

The team often practiced on the playground after school. They played their games at the athletic field west of town.

Ralph was taking batting practice. He had hit a couple of grounders, popped one up to short, flied to left and once to center. He'd let a couple balls go by as being bad pitches. Now, he stood waiting expectantly for the pitch.

Crack! Ralph had connected well. He could tell by the feel that the ball was well hit and would go far. However, as he stood watching its flight, he held his breath apprehensively. He had swung late, and the ball was fouled off in direct line with the school building. There came a cracking of glass as Ralph watched the ball disappear into the schoolroom. Oh, no. Six inches to the left, and it would have bounced harmlessly off the brick wall.

All the boys looked anxiously at their coach. Since the bottom window had been open, the ball had shattered not one, but two panes of glass. No one else on the team had had such bad luck. Of course, no one else had hit a ball that far. Ralph shrugged his shoulders. As Pa always said, what was done, was done. No use to cry over spilt milk.

Before practice had begun, the team had been told that any broken windows must be shared equally; therefore, the $1.52 it cost to replace the two windows was divided amongst the entire team.

Rate took a lot of good-natured ribbing every time he came to bat after the incident. Golly, why did it always have to be him? Why couldn't it have been one of the other boys? Seemed like things went wrong for him with no effort on his part. He often wondered if it would be this way even when he was grown. At least, he conceded, life was seldom dull.

Rate came directly home from school, changed his clothes, and got out of the house without his mother actually seeing him. He'd taken time to wash his face and hands and comb his hair. He had yelled from the kitchen to ask Ma if she needed anything--he had already been to the store before school and at noon hour--and when she said she didn't, he left immediately for the butcher shop. His right eye hurt, and he just knew that it was going to turn black. If Pa was busy, he'd not be likely to notice, but he was certain his mother's eagle eye would spot it the moment he sat down to supper. He dreaded the scene he knew was to come.

Ralph attempted to keep his head averted when he slid into his chair at the supper table. Miney passed the potatoes; then, when she passed Ralph the platter of meat, she caught the discoloration which was beginning to be quite noticeable.

"Ralph Setterington, have you been fighting again?"

"Guess you could say so," he mumbled.

"Speak up, boy. Your ma asked a question."

"Yes, Ma." His voice was loud and clear.

"What was it over this time? No good reason, that's for certain." She glared at her son.

"Aw, Ma, it really wasn't my fault. There was this kid that was bad mouthing Grandfather."

At the word "grandfather," Millie pricked up his ears. "What about Pa?" he asked, his eyes riveted on his son.

"Well, this kid called him a cheat, an' I said he wasn't. One thing led to another, an' afore I knew it, we was in a fight. I think he's got *two* black eyes," Rate stated proudly.

"Did he say why Pa was a cheat?"

"Had something to do with Mr. Brandau. Said Grandfather made him pay twice for the property. That isn't so, is it Pa?"

"Course not."

"Millie, why don't you explain to Ralph just what the transaction was? You know how I've always felt about the whole thing."

Millie looked at his wife a moment, his face expressionless. Miney realized she had displeased him, but it was high time Ralph learned that Horatio Setterington was not the god his son thought him to be.

"Well, Pa, what was Charlie talking about?"

Millie heaved a sigh before he explained.

"Your grandfather owned the property where Brandau has his ice cream parlor. When Brandau wanted to buy, he asked Pa how much for the building. Mind you, nothing was mentioned about the alley and that ice house out back. Pa gave him a price, and Brandau accepted. Pa drew up the papers--Brandau couldn't pay cash-- and gave them to Jay to read before he signed them. 'Tweren't Pa's fault if the man didn't read what they said--it was all there in black and white. Pa had sold him the building but only a foot of land out the back door. When Brandau found this out, he was pretty hot under the collar. He called Pa everything he could lay his tongue to, but Pa said it was all fair and square, and it was. Finally, he came to Pa and arranged to buy the lot behind the store. Pa didn't do anything illegal--"

"Only unethical," muttered Miney.

"It *wasn't* illegal, and Pa *didn't* lie." Millie gave her a look which dared her to disagree further. "Pa's just a good business man. Makes others envious because he's so successful. You did right, boy. A body can't stand by and let someone slander his grandfather."

"Well, I never! Millie, it is wrong for Ralph to start a fight for any reason. You want him to be a roughneck, and I'll not have it."

"The boy did right, Miney. Defending Pa's name was not wrong."

"But--"

"Miney, just keep still." There was no softness in the brown eyes that stared steadily at her.

There was a lot more Miney would have liked to say, but she did not want to antagonize her husband further. In Millie's eyes, his father was perfect, but Miney was not this generous. She actually believed Horatio had taken advantage of J.A.Brandau. It reminded her of the time Horatio had beaten her father out of a good horse. In her opinion, her father-in-law was certainly no saint. However, Miney did admit Father never lied, it was just that one had to listen carefully when he told the truth.

Elsie was not having school this Friday. Ralph hadn't paid any attention when Miss Finch explained the reason. The reason didn't matter to him one little bit. He was thankful for a day off. After all, the weather was getting to be far too nice for any lad to be cooped up in some stuffy schoolroom doing lessons he didn't want to do in the first place--English for instance.

Friday morning, Ralph left the house much earlier than usual. He had been given permission to spend the day with his best friend, Curly Sherman. Of course, Curly would have to go to school, but Rate decided he'd like seeing all his old friends at Stafford. He knew Agatha Anderson who was the teacher. Yup, it just might be fun.

Somewhere along the way, an idea came to Rate, one which he felt would liven up the day. He went down to the river, which was only a short distance from the schoolhouse; here, he caught a number of frogs and stuffed them in his pockets. They were kind of crowded, but it wasn't as if he intended to keep them there for long.

Miss Anderson looked up as he came into the familiar schoolroom. She learned why he was there, then turned back to writing some assignments on the blackboard. This was what Ralph was waiting for.

Cautiously, he slipped into a desk, reached a questing hand inside until he found what he was searching for: a pencil box. He withdrew the oblong wooden box and quietly opened the lid; then, he carefully took a frog from his pocket and stuffed the poor creature into the box. He gently closed the lid and returned the box to the desk.

So far, so good.

Quietly, Ralph disposed of all his frogs in a similar manner. He was chuckling to himself as he thought about what was going to happen. He was glad no one had come in and caught him. If anyone else knew what he had done, it would spoil all the fun.

The children began to arrive, and Ralph was the center of attention. Everyone thought him lucky not to have school.

At 9:00, the teacher rang the bell, and everyone took his seat. Miss Anderson took roll, they stood and recited the pledge to the flag; then, everyone was ready to begin work. Ralph was sitting with Curly. He could hardly contain a snicker as pencil boxes came out of desks all over the room.

A girl screamed!

Miss Anderson looked up from her desk, an enigmatic look on her face as another girl screamed. For a moment, pandemonium broke loose. The girls were not going to sit quietly while some frog leaped across their desk. The boys realized what was happening, and the remainder of the pencil boxes flew open. Frogs were everywhere. Miss Anderson rapped on the desk for order.

Some of the girls were quietly sobbing, but the boys behaved as though this was the greatest joke they had ever experienced.

"Who is responsible for this?"

No one answered. Miss Anderson's eyes swept the classroom. No one looked guilty. However, all of her students had seemed surprised. Ralph. She was certain he was the culprit.

"Ralph, do you know anything about this?"

"Golly, Miss Anderson, what makes you think I'd know about it?" His eyes stared at her boldly, his look completely innocent.

"That doesn't answer the question. Did you put those frogs in the pencil boxes?"

"Guess maybe I did," he admitted with a grin.

The room was filled with a titter of laughter.

She rapped on her desk for silence. Ralph eyed her warily.

"Well, Ralph, since *you* brought those frogs here, *you* can just get them out of here. The rest of you simply ignore him. How many frogs were there?"

"Blesst if I know. Enough to fill my pockets," he added with a mischievous grin.

"You had better get busy," she ordered, ignoring his remark. "I want every last one of those frogs caught." She glared at him as if to accent her words.

The first few were easy to catch. Ralph tossed them out the door knowing they'd make their own way back to the river. Heck, this wasn't so bad. Sure was worth the effort for all the fracas it had caused. He chuckled quietly to himself.

Ralph was after a frog when it leaped on the pile of wood stacked by the stove and crawled into a crack. Soon, three or four more did the same thing. Drat it all. How was he to get them out?"

"Something wrong, Ralph?"

"Oh, no, Miss Anderson. I've got most of them," he explained.

Rate started repiling the wood. There. He got one of the buggers, but the rest had shifted to the new pile. Twice more he repiled the wood. The last time, he didn't find a single frog, so he thought he must have all of them.

"Ralph, are you finished?"

"I think so."

"Then, take your seat and see if you can behave the rest of the day. I'd hate to have to send you home." She smiled sweetly, but her eyes were stern.

Rate was reading a story from Curly's reading book.

Hruumph! Hruumph!

Gripes. That sounded like a frog. All eyes turned on Ralph.

"Honest, Miss Anderson, I thought I had 'em all."

"Apparently, you missed one. Sounds like he's in the woodpile."

Ralph had to pile and repile the wood twice before he caught the last frog. He hadn't figured on all this work, but things sure had been exciting for a while.

Rate was going to the gristmill to go fishing. He hadn't even asked anyone to go with him today. Once in a while, he liked being by himself. Usually, at these times, he did a lot of thinking about a lot of things. He had heard Pa talking the other night with his mother. Pa was sayin' that durin' the haying season and wheat harvest, he thought it might be easier on Miney if they stayed on the forty. Blanche would have to stay in town since she had a job, and he guessed they could come back for weekends. The house was small, but with only the three, they'd manage quite well. Ma had said she wasn't movin' in no house that had stood empty so long lessen it was cleaned, and she had enough to do without worrying about that. Well, Pa had volunteered to hire some neighbor women to do the cleaning, so Ma had finally said she guessed it would work out.

Pa sure was a hard one to figure out . Had to move into town just so Blanche could have a place to stay while she attended school. Now, Pa didn't seem satisfied with town life and being a merchant.

As far as Rate knew, the butcher shop was doing well. At least he'd never heard his father complain about business being poor. Ralph wondered if his father missed being actively engaged in farming. True, he'd never been completely away from it since there had been crops on the forty and the north eighty. Still, it wasn't like having a herd of cows and a bunch of hogs to tend. During the summer, the sheep practically took care of themselves.

School was no sooner out for the summer when Millie, Miney, and Ralph moved out on the forty. Millie had bought eight cows, about to freshen, from Archie Levey for fifty dollars each. Millie figured it was an extremely good deal and would have paid more, but Archie had set his own price. Millie hadn't even had to dicker.

With the cows on pasture, they weren't much trouble. Millie still did the milking while Rate tended the horses, and as each cow had her calf, Rate took over feeding the calves. This wasn't enough to keep him busy all the time.

Some days he walked over to Shermans so he and Curly could do something. Sometimes, Burl tagged along, but mostly the older boys gave him the slip and went off by themselves. Occasionally, they met some of the other boys their age and went swimming in the river.

One especially hot afternoon, Rollie, Burl, Frankie, Curly and Rate had gone swimming back on Pages. When Rate discovered Curly tying his clothes in knots, Rate grabbed Curly's new straw hat, crammed it firmly on his head, ran out on the old tree which stuck out over the swimming hole and dove in.

When he broke the surface, Rate heard Curly yell.

"Just look what you've gone an' done, Rate Setterington."

The other boys looked his way, and all began to laugh--all except Curly.

Wondering what was so funny, Rate stroked leisurely to bring himself to the bank. It was then he became conscious of something touching his shoulders.

"You ruined my hat. Jes' lookit, you ruined my new hat," shouted Curly. "My ma will have my hide for this," he bemoaned.

The brim of the hat had torn loose from the crown, which was still nestled on Ralph's head, and had settled on Rate's shoulders. He did look funny--to everyone who didn't own the hat.

"Aw, Curly, you started it. I just finished it."

"Leastways I didn't do no harm. Your *clothes* aren't ruined. My hat is."

The boys spent the rest of the time bickering, each blaming the other. Rate had had no idea his actions would ruin Curly's hat, and he did feel sorry--sort of. Still, he figured Curly had asked for it. The boy should have known him well enough to know he'd do something to get even. Rate was not one to simply drop an incident without some form of mischievous retaliation, all done in a good-natured manner.

A few days later, Ralph was going in to Elsie. Ma had given him a ride as far as Huffman's, but he still had two miles to walk. He knew he could hitch a ride home with Pa. When he came to the river, he stopped on the bridge to watch the water. Golly, it looked strange. Seemed as though it was covered with something. Now, his curiosity was up. What was that stuff? It was almost like a scum, but it hadn't been that way a couple of days ago.

Rate carefully let himself down the bank to get near the water. He didn't want to slip and fall in here because the channel was deep and the current strong. Besides, the mill was operating today, and he didn't want to be drawn against the grating where the water rushed through the mill's flume. He'd just be careful. The bank was steep in places, but there were small trees to offer something to grasp.

Ralph made it safely to the water's edge to the narrow ledge where he could stand with ease. He gazed in disbelief at the water. Turtles. Baby turtles. That's what he had seen from the bridge. The water was alive with them, too newly hatched to be able to dive, they just floated and bobbed like a cork. He knew the female turtles used the high sandy bank and even the sandy earth across the road in the cemetery as a place to lay their eggs. Once or twice he'd seen baby turtles crossing the road, headed for water; however, he had never seen a sight such as this. Why, there must be hundreds, no thousands. Sure was something to see. What would happen to them? He was sure they would not all survive. Golly, where would they go from here?

Rate knew his sister was older than some of the girls who were keeping company with a young man. Thus far, Blanche hadn't shown any interest in anyone in particular. She never even talked about wanting to go with anyone; she had her circle of friends and seemed quite content.

Ralph knew Claude Going was sweet on Blanche, and Ralph disapproved. He supposed Claude was all right, but in Rate's opinion, he acted feminine, more like a girl than a man. His prissy ways just didn't set well with red-blooded boys. Rate didn't want the likes of Claude paying court to *his* sister.

The young people of the Baptist Church held a meeting before each Sunday evening service. Ralph usually attended, more to suit his mother than because he enjoyed the meetings. Sometimes, they weren't so bad; it all depended on the topic for discussion.

This particular Sunday, one of the boys had confided to Rate at morning service that Claude Going intended to attend evening service; furthermore, he had said he was going to ask Blanche if he could walk her home. Some nerve that guy had! Ralph knew his sister had never given that sissy any encouragement. Must be some way he could save Blanche from having to refuse. What he was really afraid of was that Blanche would somehow feel obligated to accept Claude's offer.

Claude was already seated when Rate entered the Church's classroom. Rate promptly took a seat directly behind Claude. Blanche and her friends sat over to one side. Ralph could see that Claude was making calf's eyes at Blanche although his sister tried her best to ignore him.

Several of the young people had been giving testimony as to why they followed Christ. Most of them had been raised in the Church, but a few had newly joined. They were the ones who had recently found God. Finally, Claude stood, cleared his throat, and startled everyone by stating clearly, "I am a stranger here and a stranger to God." A slight gasp went through the assembly.

Just as Claude sat, Rate stretched his foot forward and tipped the chair just enough so it slid out from under Claude, and he fell to the floor with a thud. The young people laughed discreetly because this *was* the house of the Lord. Claude got up, his face red with embarrassment. He gave Rate a knowing look, but Ralph returned his gaze with a guileless expression as though he had had no part in the accident.

At least Ralph had accomplished one thing: Claude did not ask to walk Blanche home that night or any other night.

CHAPTER 13

One afternoon, Rate decided he felt hot, his head ached, and his throat was sore. Golly, he'd made plans for tomorrow. If Ma knew he didn't feel well, she'd never let him out of the house. At times like this, Ma could be awful stubborn. Well, he'd not say a word and maybe she wouldn't notice.

He didn't feel like eating supper, but didn't want to cause undue attention by saying he wasn't hungry. He felt awful, but he forced himself to behave normally. No one noticed he went to bed earlier than usual.

The next morning, he felt even worse. When he looked into the mirror to brush his hair, he stared. He looked mighty strange. He leaned closer to peer intently at his image. He had funny red spots all over his face. He lifted his shirt and looked at his belly. The mottled red spots were there too. Something was certainly wrong, he just didn't know what.

He went slowly down the narrow stairs. Pa and Ma slept downstairs. He knew his mother would be in the kitchen, and his father would likely have the milking almost done. He was expected to get Pa's driving horse in from the pasture and harnessed so Pa could leave for the market right after breakfast.

"Ma, I don't feel so good."

"Come a little closer. Land sakes, Ralph, I can see why you don't feel well. You've got the measles," announced Miney.

"Measles. Where'd I get 'em from?"

"I have no idea. You get back into bed and keep covered up well. As soon as your father finishes his breakfast, I'll bring you something to eat."

"I'm not one bit hungry."

"Still, you need nourishment. Perhaps an eggnog would taste best. Hurry along now."

"But who's gonna do my chores?"

"I expect your father will have to do them."

Ralph gave her a skeptical look. He bet Pa wouldn't take kindly to havin' extra chores to do, but he supposed he had better mind his mother. Golly, all those plans he had for today sure went to pot. As he went slowly back upstairs, he wondered how long it would be before his mother would let him out of the house.

Miney came up later with a small bowl of oatmeal and a glass of eggnog. She felt his forehead and decided he was feverish. She made certain he was tucked in under the covers; then, she pulled the shade, saying the light was bad for his eyes.

"But Ma, how can I read when it's so dark?" he objected.

"You can't. You are to sleep as much as you can and use your eyes as little as possible. Do you want to ruin your eyes?"

Rate heaved a sigh. No use to argue. Wouldn't get him anywhere. He guessed maybe he *could* sleep some more.

Ralph had a rather light case of the measles, so was only confined to the house for a week. The time sure did drag. Summer days were a complete waste if a body had to be cooped up in the house. He had more important things to be doing.

Grandmother had written asking that Blanche and Ralph pay them a visit. Ralph figured they only asked him because Ma might not let Blanche go alone. Blanche might be through high school, but Ma still bossed her some of the time. Course, if Blanche was really determined, there wasn't much Ma could do. Well, he reckoned he'd like to go visiting. It meant a long train ride, and Ralph sure did like to ride on trains.

Blanche arranged to have the time off from her job at the *Elsie Sun*. Mr. Sherman had been very congenial, saying a visit to her grandparents would be nice.

Blanche told no one that she had a special reason for wanting to go to Nashville. It seemed that on her last visit, she had become friendly with Dora Gaulke who was near to her in age. Dora had a brother, Otis, who was two or three years older, and Blanche thought he was particularly nice. Of course, as soon as she had voiced her opinion to Grandmother, Lovina had immediately said Otis was no good, not a person with whom she wanted her granddaughter associating. Well, thought Blanche, we'll just see. If Otis asks me to go some place, and I want to go, I'll go in spite of Grandmother. I'm eighteen. Plenty old enough to make up my own mind.

Ralph and Blanche left on the early train to Durand where they had a short wait for the train which took them to Charlotte. Here, they had a layover of three, long, tiring hours.

While the time dragged for Blanche, it proved positively boring for Ralph. Ma had packed them a lunch in a basket, but while he was expected to carry the basket, Blanche wouldn't let him even peek to see what Ma had packed. She told him the lunch was to be eaten at noon, not before. The way she looked at him, he figured he'd better follow her instructions. Before they left home, Ma had impressed upon him that Blanche was in charge.

Ralph sat beside Blanche for a while, the hamper of food on the floor at their feet. For a while, he kept glancing at the large clock on the wall, but it seemed as though the hands never moved. He twiddled his thumbs for a time, but soon tired of that. He'd tried to draw Blanche into a conversation, but that failed. He guessed they weren't interested in the same things.

Rate gave some thought to bringing up the name of Gerd Pershing, then thought better of it. Gerd was employed as a cheesemaker and lived in Ovid. He had come calling two Sundays ago. Rate had no idea how Blanche had met him. She certainly had never mentioned Gerd within his hearing. He would liked to have teased her, but Blanche was kind of unpredictable, and he didn't want to make her angry with him, at least not now.

When he rose from his seat, Blanche demanded, "Where do you think you're going?"

"Over to the water cooler. I'm thirsty."

"All right, but you come right back. Ma said I wasn't to let you out of my sight."

"What did she expect I'd do? Get lost?"

"I don't know, but she cautioned me to keep you out of trouble."

"Golly, don't no one trust me?"

"Do you have to ask? Who's the one who's always into some sort of mischief?"

"Darned if I know." He gave her that wide-eyed innocent look which made Blanche laugh.

"Go get your drink."

As she watched him move off, Blanche gave a chuckle. She guessed Ralph was a good brother. He liked to tease, but she could handle that. His mischief-making was usually harmless although he did vex Ma plenty. Blanche figured her father had been much the same when he was young. Ralph was just a chip off the old block even if Pa would be the last to admit it.

Ralph got his drink, stopped to look out a window which was none too clean, then hurried back.

"Blanche, there's a train comin' in from the north. Can I go watch?"

"No. If I let you go, you'll somehow find a way to get into trouble."

"No, I won't. I promise. What could happen? I just want to watch it come in. At least it would give me something to do."

"Well, all right. But, Ralph, promise not to get into any mischief," she pleaded.

He gave her an innocent grin, and said, "Promise."

Blanche watched him go with misgivings. Ralph's promises were somehow different than the average person's. She could not imagine any trouble Ralph could get into, but he had a way of finding trouble when there was none to be found--for anyone else, that is. She sighed, wondering if she would be sorry she had given in to his request.

It *was* irksome having to wait so long for their train. However, there was no direct route to Nashville. It had been much better when their grandparents had lived in South Lyon. However, Horatio could never turn down a chance to make money and had said the offer he received for the bank in South Lyon was too good to turn down. Of course, Blanche had her own ideas as to why this particular move had been made. She was certain Uncle Mac had something to do with it. Oliver McQuistion had ideas and schemes for making money, but Blanche felt they would all be doomed to failure without Grandfather's expertise to aid him.

Sometimes, Blanche wondered why Grandmother had ever approved of Oliver McQuistion as a beau for Aunt Ruby. Perhaps people were right when they said Lovina was afraid Aunt Ruby would be an old maid. In Lovina's eyes, there was nothing worse than having a female family member who was not wanted by any man. After all, a woman's sole purpose in this life was to be an helpmate to some man and the mother of his children.

Frankly, Blanche thought there should be more to life for a woman than this. What was wrong with a woman being in the business world? Grandmother did not approve of her present job. Lovina had said that a sales clerk in a reputable store was acceptable although she thought teaching was a more prestigious position. That was because Grandmother had taught school before she married Grandfather.

Blanche hadn't yet decided what she was going to do with her life. She had started dating just this summer, and while she enjoyed the company of a man, she certainly had given little thought to marriage. Grandmother kept making sly hints, but thus far, Blanche had ignored them. She hoped Grandmother didn't spoil her visit by bringing up Blanche's future. She really didn't want to argue with her grandmother, but she had made up her mind that it was high time Grandmother minded her own business.

Ralph came back precisely at noon. (Blanche surmised it was his stomach which made him so prompt.) He had a smudge on one cheek and some dirt on his trousers, but aside from that, looked all right. Blanche gave a satisfied sigh. She didn't quite know what she expected because with Ralph, it was difficult to tell what he would do. She sent him to wash his hands before they ate.

Miney had packed roast beef sandwiches, some cheese and crackers; tiny, raw carrots because she had just thinned the row in the garden; a small jar of canned peaches, and two generous pieces of raspberry pie. Ma had even splurged and put in a jar of lemonade. Even Ralph's appetite was satisfied before they were finished. Well, perhaps he'd get hungry on the train, and he could eat his cheese and crackers then.

Both Lovina and Horatio were waiting at the station when the train came chugging in. Lovina gave Blanche a hug and then turned to Ralph. She greatly surprised him by giving him a kiss on the cheek. Golly, he never remembered her doing that before. Grandfather had taken his hand just like he was a man and remarked that he had grown since Christmas. For the first time in his life, his grandparents seemed less formidable, almost human. Ralph decided he was definitely glad he had come.

Blanche renewed her friendship with the Gaulkes. Ralph listened as their grandmother told Blanche that Otis was never going to amount to a picayune. Well, Blanche simply set her jaw stubbornly, looked her grandmother straight in the eye and gave her a tart answer.

"Grandmother, I don't think you know Otis well enough to judge him. Besides, doesn't the Bible say judge not lest ye be judged? Well, I think that applies in this case."

Lovina stared at her granddaughter, hardly able to believe the girl's audacity. Then, without a word, she turned and left the room. Blanche gave Ralph a triumphant look, but she, too, said nothing. This was only a minor battle in the war of wills. Apparently both Lovina and Blanche knew it was only the beginning of their war of wills.

Two days later, Ralph was getting restless. He had done several little chores for Grandmother, but he didn't have enough to keep him busy. It was then his grandfather surprised him by producing a fishing pole.

"Rate, how'd you like to go down to the river fishing? They tell me there's a good fishing hole at the edge of our property."

"Guess I'd like it fine."

"Good. I figure a nice mess of fish would taste mighty good."

Ralph dug some worms and headed for the river. Golly, he sure hoped he had good luck. He'd like to be able to do something nice for Grandfather.

As it turned out, Rate caught some good-sized suckers in the Thornapple River.

When he held up his string of catch, both grandparents exclaimed at his good luck.

The next morning at breakfast, Horatio ate with gusto not minding that he had to pick a lot of small bones.

"Rate, these fish sure do hit the spot. I'm glad you had such good luck. Guess Millie didn't exaggerate when he told me what a good fisherman you had become."

Horatio beamed at his grandson.

Ralph was elated. First of all, he'd never had his grandfather praise him for anything, and from what Grandfather said, Pa must have been telling Grandfather about him and his fishing. Golly, maybe Pa did think he could do something well after all.

Occasionally, Lovina would reminisce since both Blanche and Ralph enjoyed hearing the stories she told.

Lovina had been a school teacher in Leamington, Ontario, Canada. In those days, the schoolmarm boarded at different homes in the community. Of course, in time, she became a boarder at the John Setterington household.

"I was boarding with your great grandparents, John and Lucretia Setterington. Back then, a proper schoolmistress wore a plain dress in dark, serviceable material. We wore a fancy white apron over that, and it did brighten the dress a bit. Guess people thought of this as a sort of uniform for a public servant. Well, one night, when I came home from school, Father Setterington--this was before Rate and I were married--sat at the kitchen table with several stacks of gold coin in front of him. Believe me, I had never seen so much money in all my life. To this day, I have no idea how much money he had, but it was certainly in the thousands. Well, I said to him, "I'll take what you don't want, Mr. Setterington."

He looked up with a glint in his eye and said, "Here, you can have all you can hold."

"I gathered up the bottom of my apron and stepped up to the table. Before I realized what he was doing, he shoved all those stacks of gold right into my apron."

"You had all that gold?" asked Blanche, her eyes wide.

Lovina gave a little laugh.

"No, Blanche, I had not one red cent. The weight of the gold ripped my apron right off the waistband, so all that money went crashing to the floor. Father never said a word, just sort of chuckled to himself."

"What did you say?" asked Ralph.

"I don't remember. Something asinine, I suppose. I felt like a complete fool. I got down on my hands and knees and helped him pick the coins from off the floor. I knew he found the situation comical, but I was so embarrassed. You see, Rate and I had begun to keep company by then, and like most young girls, I wanted to impress my future in-laws. I don't know what possessed me to be so brash. Usually, I felt quite intimidated by your great grandfather. He was a fine looking gentleman, like your grandfather, but his black eyes could look right through a person. Well, Father never forgot that incident, and he never let me forget it either. It was one big joke to him."

"Sounds like something Pa would do," said Blanche as she studied her grandmother. Goodness, she had never supposed the person had been born who could intimidate her grandmother. Guess Grandmother had the same human characteristics as anyone else once one got through that hard exterior.

"Yes, *and* your grandfather. I think the Setterington men have much in common from one generation to the next," she said, nodding her head.

Ralph thought this story was exceptionally funny, but he had only laughed a little, not quite knowing what his grandmother expected of him. She must have looked comical crawling around picking up the gold pieces. Golly, Great Grandfather must have been quite a man to have earned all that money. Guess some of his business sense had rubbed off on Grandfather, but Pa just seemed sort of ordinary, making no great strides in the business world. Well, Pa was sure all right even if he didn't have the knack for making money that his father and grandfather had.

Their last night there, Horatio spoke to his grandson.

"Rate, let's take a little walk. I need to stretch my legs a bit."

"All right, Grandfather."

The two set off down the street towards the edge of town. Horatio's stride was long and steady; his broad shoulders square; no one would have guessed he was sixty-five years old. Ralph was proud to be the grandson of this dignified man.

Near the edge of town, a mill set on the bank of the Thornapple River. It was quiet now, but it had been in operation during the day.

"Rate, did you know this mill belongs to me?"

"No, sir."

"Well, it does. Bought it a few months back. Seems it was estate property. Know what that means?"

"I think so. It means someone must have died leaving the mill to more than one heir, so I guess it had to be sold so's they could all get their share."

"That's it exactly. The administrator asked for sealed bids. I asked around a bit and discovered they might have a hard time disposing of the property since it had to be a cash sale. I took the gamble and turned in a bid which was considerably less than the mill was worth. It is really a sound structure, and the equipment isn't all that old. Anyway, since mine was the only bid made, they had to take what I had offered.

"I know the milling business. Learned it from my father back in Canada. I've been making a profit these past few months, and now I have a buyer who will pay double what I gave for it."

"Let that be a lesson to you, Rate. Whenever there's a chance to make a likely profit, don't be afraid to invest. It was the same with the bank in South Lyon. Doubled my investment. However, I don't think Vine and Ruby like living here. Vine hasn't had much to say, but I think Ruby is giving Mac a hard time. Nothing strains a marriage more than a hen-pecked husband. Maybe we'll have to think about getting back to the east side of the state before long."

"You mean come back to Elsie?"

"I think not, but Detroit would be the logical place. We'd be closer to my family in Canada and closer to your family. It would work out better all the way around."

Ralph and his grandfather talked of other things. Golly, this was the best conversation they had ever had. Somehow, in a situation like this, when Grandfather smiled often, he didn't seem quite as formidable. Ralph decided that maybe this was because he was older, no longer considered a child. Anyway, Grandfather had talked to him like he was an adult, and it sure did seem nice.

Seemed as though the summer was going by in a hurry. Wheat harvest had already passed. Rate guessed it was a good thing they'd soon move back to town. When he had to drive into town or come from town back to the farm, Bruno always went with him, trotting just behind the carriage or wagon. Well, just lately this had caused nothing but problems.

Don Huffman, who was about a year younger, owned a big collie. One day, Don had sicked his dog on Bruno. Bruno held his own for a while, but since Rate hadn't stopped, when his master got a short distance away, Bruno took off to catch up. The collie strutted around as though he was the undisputed winner.

This had happened three or four times--Ralph forgot the actual count--and with each new encounter, Ralph became just a little angrier. Then, two weeks ago Saturday night, Don had joined the group of boys who usually hung around together. Almost immediately, he began telling them how yellow Bruno was and how his collie licked the mutt every time.

Ralph hadn't said a word. Even when the boys ribbed him about his cowardly dog, he said little. He had taken it all good-naturedly, at least to all outward appearances.

The following week, Don once again brought up the subject of bulldogs who were scared to fight. It was then Ralph made a decision.

Ma and Pa had already gone out to the forty, but Rate had stayed in town for the Sunday evening young people's meeting. Instead of driving out to the farm after Church, he waited until Monday morning since he was to pick up some feed from the mill on his way.

It was almost midmorning when he left the mill.

The Huffman farm was over a mile away. As he neared the Huffman property, Rate kept a close watch for Don's collie. At first, he saw nothing. Then, something stirred in the weeds along the side of the road. He glanced over his shoulder to see where Bruno was. The brindle bulldog was trotting a few paces behind the wagon, paying no attention to his surroundings, simply intent on following Ralph and the wagon.

"Sic 'im!"

The shouted words took Rate by surprise. He hadn't seen Don standing in the doorway of the barn, pitchfork in hand.

At the yelled command, the collie burst from his cover, hurtling himself at the bulldog.

While the collie was taller, the bulldog equaled him in weight. Bruno was a compact, well-muscled dog.

"Take him, Bruno," commanded Rate quietly as he pulled in the team and got down from the wagon box.

Bruno did not need the second command. He raced forward to meet his over confident adversary. The collie was taken by surprise as Bruno hit him shoulder to shoulder. The unexpected impact knocked the collie off his feet, and Bruno was quick to seize the advantage.

Both Don and Rate stood nearby, each shouting encouragement to his dog. Bruno, in typical bulldog fashion, was attempting to get a throat hold on the collie; but even though down, the collie was putting up a desperate fight.

Finally, Don realized the bulldog's intentions, and he began to fear for the life of his pet.

"Call 'im off, Rate. He's gonna kill Rover."

"Who yelled sic 'im? Not me."

"Come on. Call Bruno off."

"What for? He's yeller and can't fight. That's how you explained it to the fellas. If he can't fight, why're you so scared?"

"Call 'im off before I punch ya one."

"Go ahead. I'll lick you same's my dog is lickin' yours."

The boys squared off, hands doubled into fists. They glared at each other.

"You ain't gonna call Bruno off?"

"Don't see me doin' it, do ya?"

Don moved in quickly and hit Ralph on the chin. Rate countered with a punch of his own. Soon, the boys were rolling over and over on the ground, each getting in a punch whenever he could.

Their shouts diverted Bruno's attention from the collie who took the opportunity to run behind the house, his tail between his legs. Bruno had more important things on his mind than chasing a frightened collie. He watched for an opportunity to help his master.

When he barked in frustration, Rate realized what Bruno was likely to do. Panting, he managed to speak.

"Don, if we don't quit, Bruno's likely to help me out. He's run off your dog, an' he don't take kindly to anyone fightin' with me."

Don jeered at Rate's statement.

"Just 'cause I'm whippin' ya. Don't you try to wiggle your way out of this, Rate Setterington."

Just then, Don felt a tug on his pantleg. He gave the leg a jerk, but it didn't move. Then, he heard the growl. A hurried glance told him Bruno had hold of his pants.

Now Don was scared. To be sure, Bruno only had his pants, but the way he was growling, Don just knew the dog was likely to change his hold, and the next time, he might get a piece of flesh.

The boys quit as quickly as they had begun. Both were disheveled; Rate had a cut lip and Don a bloody nose. However, Rate still had his sense of humor.

"Guess we know whether or not Bruno can fight. Don't see no collie around, do you? Guess this will make something to tell the fellas come Saturday. C'mon, Bruno. We got work to do."

With that, he swaggered back to where he had left the team and wagon on the road. Gosh, he hoped Ma wouldn't notice his soiled clothes. He was in no mood to explain what had happened. Course, he bet Pa would get a chuckle out of it. In matters like this, Pa was a lot more understanding.

It was a hot August day, and since Millie had given Ralph no extra work for the day before he left for town to open the meat market, Rate had gone over to Shermans. He and the Sherman boys, Curly and Burl, decided it was a good day to go swimming.

They were following the river, headed for the swimming hole on the Page farm. They heard noises which sounded a little like the report of a shotgun; yet, there was a distinct difference. None of the boys could figure out what it was. They seemed to be getting nearer the intermittent sound.

Finally, they could hear men's voices. As they rounded a bend in the river, they heard the explosion. The men were dynamiting fish. This meant they had about an inch of dynamite and a cap to which they attached a three inch fuse. The blast killed the fish, and they floated to the top where the men gathered in any which were pan size. Of course, this procedure was illegal.

The three boys were almost upon the men--there were four of them--before they realized the boys were there. Ralph had never seen them before.

Rate grinned and asked, "Whatcha doin'?" He already knew.

"Fishing," replied the nearest man.

"Don't see no poles. How can ya catch fish without a pole?"

Rate thought the man looked uncomfortable. Obviously, the men had not intended for anyone to know what they were doing.

"Can you boys keep a secret?"

All three lads nodded their heads.

"We just whistle an' the fish jump right outta the water onto our stringers."

"We ain't that dumb, Mister," said Curly, his tone a trifle belligerent.

"Hey, we heard the explosions a long ways back. We know you're dynamiting fish. Bet you didn't get anything but a few suckers," said Ralph.

"You boys won't tell anyone, will you? Some folks wouldn't understand," said the man who was spokesman for the group.

"Ain't none o' our bizness what you do," replied Curly.

"I won't tell if you let me throw one o' them things," Rate bargained.

"No. It can be dangerous. Supposin' you got hurt?"

"I'm not gonna get hurt. You just light the fuse and I'll toss it. Come on. Who's to know?"

The man looked at his companions indecisively. One of them nodded his head slightly.

"All right, kid. Just once. Now, when I get the fuse lit an' tell you t' throw it, you get rid of it fast. Understand?"

"Of course," said Ralph as he gave the men a cocky grin.

The man gave Rate a piece of the dynamite, showing him just how to hold it.

Then, he held a match to the fuse which took a few moments to catch. "Now!" yelled the man.

Rate heaved. The men and boys watched as the length of dynamite arched in the air, then came down to explode with a sharp report. Leaves and dirt flew into the air. Rate had thrown so hard, he had missed the river completely, and the dynamite had landed on the opposite bank several feet from the water.

"Well, kid, I don't guess you got many fish with that throw."

Curly and Burl hooted derisively. Ralph gave the men a sheepish grin as he shrugged his shoulders.

"Guess I don't know my own strength," he said by way of explanation.

The men moved off, laughing as they went. The boys heard no more explosions, so they figured the men had given up "fishing" for this day, or perhaps they were moving to a spot where there would be no nosy kids to observe them.

"Gosh, Rate, weren't ya just a little bit scared?" asked Curly.

"Naw. What for?"

"Well, dynamite ain't nuthin' to' fool with."

"I know. I've seen Pa use it on stones an' stumps. He's always mighty careful. Guess maybe that's why I threw so hard. Sure didn't want it going off too close to us."

The boys moved on to the swimming hole. They had wasted enough of their afternoon.

Ralph never mentioned the incident to his parents. While Pa might have understood, he was certain his mother would have bawled him out. This way, everyone was a lot happier.

Miney was glad the summer was nearly over. Millie never realized how much she had disliked living in two places. Seemed as though it made her work twice as hard. Of course, Blanche did a good job of keeping the town house clean, but there was always something to be carted back and forth between homes.

Saturday was baking day, so Miney had to carry the bread and cookies, or perhaps a pie out to the farm on Sunday evening. For once, she kept her thoughts to herself. Sometimes, she didn't understand Millie at all, and this was one of those times. Well, when school started, if Millie didn't move them back to town of his own accord, she would certainly speak her piece.

Besides, Miney was getting sick and tired of having Tillie Lance for a caller bright and early every Saturday morning as regular as clockwork. Talk about a town gossip. Well, Tillie sure deserved a medal for being the only person in town who knew everyone's business better than her own. It was uncanny the way that woman ferreted out what everyone in town was doing: who was in the family way, who came home drunk, who was keeping company with whom, who was having marital problems, and who skipped church last Sunday.

Tillie lived over a block away, but she managed to keep track of every move Blanche made during the week. Blanche had been keeping company with Gerd Pershing from Ovid, a very nice, well-mannered young man. Gerd often came calling on Wednesday evening. Tillie could tell Miney exactly what time Gerd arrived and what time he left. She also knew if he and Blanche went for a drive, and if so, how long they were gone. She never failed to let Miney know that she didn't think it respectable for a young man to call on a young woman when her parents were not in residence.

Miney hated to admit that she wasn't too keen on the idea either, but since Blanche had just turned eighteen, Miney didn't feel she could voice her objections. Besides, Blanche had assured her that she and Gerd sat on the porch in plain view, so there really was no harm done. It just rankled to have that nosy Tillie voicing her opinion each Saturday morning. Miney wished she knew of some way to put the woman in her place, but Tillie had skin like a cast iron kettle and nothing said discouraged her in any way.

Blanche realized what was happening. Sometimes, if she and Gerd went for a ride, they would drive west, and although Tillie was never in sight, Blanche always waved as they passed her house knowing full well Tillie would be peeking out one of the windows. Other times, Blanche took perverse pleasure in going in the opposite direction where they were soon out of Tillie's range of vision. Blanche sometimes wondered if Tillie aggravated other people this much. Blanche would liked to have told the woman to mind her own business, but Ma would frown on that, and it would do no good anyhow. Tillie was not about to change.

Rate and Miney had gone to Elsie after he had finished what chores he had to do. He and Ma would stay in town, while Pa went back to the farm for evening chores and Pa would do the chores on Sunday morning. Pa would come for dinner, but the three of them would be back on the forty for supper.

Rate hadn't found anyone to spend time with, and after wandering around aimlessly, he decided to walk to Sherman's. Perhaps Curly would go fishing with him.

His luck was not good. Both Curly and Burl had gone with their father. Mrs. Sherman didn't expect them back much before supper.

Rate came back by the gristmill where he stood for a time on the bridge looking out over the gently rippling water. A crane rose from the wetlands to the south, a kingfisher sat on a tree limb which protruded over the water. A pair of swallows swooped near the water gathering a meal of mosquitoes. It was a beautiful day, and Rate hated to waste it, but he didn't feel like fishing alone. There were times when a body just felt the need for companionship.

Ralph headed back home. He was halfway up the gristmill hill when he heard a loud thud, almost like the sound of a sledge hammer striking a block of wood. A few minutes later, the same sound was repeated. Ralph's curiosity got the better of him. The sound came from the fields back of Cobb's barn; this was where the boys went to the river swimming. Guess he'd just meander over and see what was going on.

The sight fascinated Ralph. There was a flock of sheep in the field, but for some reason, there were *two* rams. No one ever kept two adult rams with their ewes. As he watched, the rams stood several yards apart, heads lowered, pawing the ground. As if on cue, they began to run, meeting head to head. It was this sound that Rate had heard. Both backed off, turned, retreated, then turned to face their opponent. Once more came the rush, and once more they hit head to head with a resounding thud. Rate knew they would continue to do this until one admitted defeat, or one of them had his neck broken. Gosh, maybe he should tell someone.

Rate went to the house, but no one was home. Well, at least he had tried. He hoped one of the rams would give up. It would be a crying shame to have one killed.

CHAPTER 14

Much to Miney's satisfaction, the last week in August, the three of them moved back into town. Millie was rather pleased with himself since he had found a buyer for the eight cows. He sold them tor $75 each which was $25 a head more than he had paid for them, and he kept the eight calves. Ralph wasn't so sure he liked this arrangement since he had to take care of the calves.

The only fly in the ointment was that the deal left Millie's friend, Archie Levey, more than a little miffed. Millie tried to explain that he had been plain lucky to find a buyer willing to pay that much; however, Archie seemed to think Millie had taken advantage of him somehow.

"Archie, you set your own price on those bred heifers," Millie reminded.

"I know."

"Then what's amiss?"

"You milked 'em all summer, kept the calves, and got more money than you paid for them. Seems I been cheated."

The man stomped off in anger. Well, he'd simmer down after a bit. Millie wondered how Archie had learned of the transaction so fast. He guessed it was just the way of a small town-- secrets were impossible to keep.

When school started, Rate learned the seventh and eighth grade had been moved downstairs away from the high school. He wasn't certain he liked this arrangement, but he supposed he'd get used to it soon enough.

He and Miss Finch were off to a good start again. Once more, she had reserved the desk closest to hers for him. She sure did make it difficult for a fella to have any fun. Still, he really did like her. She was a mighty good teacher, one who was always interesting. Even though strict, she never punished unjustly which was a point in her favor.

Ralph was headed for the railroad tracks by the depot to meet some of his friends. Millie hadn't had any work for him for a change, so Rate was free until supper.

He passed a couple of the large storage tanks which were full of water to be used in case of fire. Elsie's first fire engine had been a hand pumper, but this had been replaced a couple of years ago by a better one, pulled by a team, and outfitted with a gas engine to operate the pump. When there was a fire, the first man to get to the fire house with a team to pull the engine got $5. Since Ralph could remember, there had been no major fires in Elsie, but the threat was always there.

The boys met behind the depot; then, they edged their way toward the huge, elevated, wooden tanks which would be used to store cider later in the fall. One at a time, the boys climbed the wooden ladder and carefully let themselves down into the tank furthest from the tracks. The wood was permeated with the faint odor of cider. The four boys sat, and someone produced a deck of cards. Just recently, the boys had learned to play pedro. Ralph knew his mother would object to his playing cards, but quite some time ago Pa had said it was all right for Blanche to learn. It was just that he was never certain if these rules also applied to him.

One of the boys pulled a pouch of tobacco out from beneath his shirt. Someone else provided a pipe. Ralph had some matches. As the boys played cards, they passed the lighted pipe from one to another. Ralph knew with a certainty his mother would skin him alive if she knew he was learning to smoke. Still, he didn't figure there was any way for her to find out, and what she didn't know wouldn't hurt her. His friends sure weren't going to squeal because they'd be in as much trouble themselves if their parents knew. No one was likely to crawl up here to see what they were doing even if someone had seen them climb into the tank. Not many concerned themselves with what a small group of boys were doing--especially men. Down here, around the tracks, the only workers were men. Ralph felt perfectly safe from detection.

Ed Randall was a little younger than Rate and just about as mischievous. One afternoon, as soon as school had been dismissed for the day, Ed drew Rate aside.

"Wanna have some fun tonight?"

"Doin' what?"

"Takin' the clapper off the school bell."

"How we gonna do that? The school's locked tighter than a drum at night. You know that."

"Just supposin' it wasn't?"

"You're up to something," accused Ralph with a grin which was his stamp of approval.

"I unlocked the window by the fire escape. I'll bet you no one finds out, at least not for a few days," Ed replied with a satisfied smirk.

Rate gave a chuckle.

"What did you have in mind?"

"Meet me about ten tonight, and we'll climb up the belfry and get that clapper."

The boys met as planned, glad the night was overcast with the crescent moon showing only briefly at infrequent intervals. They stole quickly up the south fire escape and were relieved when, with a little pressure, the large window slid silently open. So far, so good.

Rate had brought a small flashlight which they used once they were inside the building. They looked up at the bell hanging nearly a hundred feet from the floor and contemplated their next move.

It was not difficult for two agile youths to climb up to the bell. A crossbeam on each side afforded them a place to straddle with comparative safety while they began their task. Ed had brought some tools with him which he carefully worked out of his pocket.

"Gosh, Rate, this might not be as easy as I thought. Shine the light a little more to the left. There. Hold it steady."

The bell and clapper was much larger than it had looked to the boys from below. The cast iron was thick, the hook which held the clapper in place showed shiny with use, but it looked, and was, solidly built. Ed inserted the claw of his hammer and tried to spread the heavy metal. Nothing budged.

The boys worked patiently at first, not wanting to admit their mission might be doomed to failure. They pounded, pried, and pulled to no avail. Even a cold chisel made no dent in the casting.

"Ed, I don't think we're gettin' anywhere," said Rate as he stopped pounding.

"Let me try once more. I think it gave a little."

Ed took the hammer and chisel while Rate shone the flashlight on the area.

"Guess maybe you're right, Rate. Bet we've been here 'bout two hours an' we're no nearer gettin' that damned clapper than we were before."

"Well, we've been here quite a spell all right. If I don't get home pretty soon, my ma will want to know where I've been."

"Mine too. Well, it was a good idea anyway. Sure would have been funny if the bell wouldn't have made a sound come tomorrow. Bet it would have caused some commotion."

The boys laughed at the idea as they scrambled back down the bell tower. Neither had been afraid, nor had they considered they might have fallen. Back outside, they went their separate ways.

Rate sneaked quietly up the back stairs, shoes in hand. Ma really didn't like him being out this late although Pa seldom said anything. Rate carefully avoided the third step which he knew always squeaked. He tiptoed into his bedroom, slipped out of his clothes, dropped his nightshirt over his head. He was congratulating himself that for once he had come in without his mother hearing him. As he sat on the bed, the springs gave a soft, telltale squeak.

"That you, Ralph?"

So much for outwitting his mother. "Yes, Ma."

"What time is it?"

"Not yet midnight," he answered. It wasn't. It was a quarter to.

His mother made no reply. He wondered what would happen some night if someone else answered her query of "That you, Ralph?" Bet she'd come wide awake in a hurry if a strange voice answered her. The thought made him chuckle. Wonder why he never heard her call out to Blanche like that. Course Blanche didn't hardly ever stay out past ten. Maybe that was why Ma didn't seem to keep such close track of her.

Ralph never considered that Blanche was over four years older.

Miney was busy gathering catnip to steep. Seems as though there weren't as many plants as she usually found, but she couldn't help that. Every year she steeped the plant, adding sugar to make the liquid more palatable, and used it to help relieve the persistent cough which usually accompanied colds. In the same manner, she gathered wild blackberry root to use for dysentery. These home remedies worked just as well as anything given by the doctor, and they were a whole lot cheaper. Mina did like to save a penny if at all possible.

Fall was passing quickly. Some mornings there was a decided nip in the air. Millie had remarked over two weeks ago that he had heard katydids hollering so we could expect a killing frost in six weeks. Ralph wondered what the katydids had to do with it, but he said nothing. He knew he had seen the large Vs of geese heading south, and some of the songbirds were no longer present. Guess most of nature worked on a special time clock, so maybe the katydids knew what they were doing.

Rate and George Lusk were squirrel hunting. Each boy had three or four gray squirrels hanging on his belt indicating his luck had been good. They were north of town wandering from one woodlot to another. No one cared if two boys wanted to hunt on his property, so they simply climbed any fence which obstructed their progress, not knowing or caring on whose property they trod.

Squirrels were plentiful. The boys would sit quietly for a time, making no movement, their eyes searching the nearly bare branches of the trees. When they were rewarded by seeing a small, furry body come out to peek at them, one of the boys would carefully take aim and fire. If they got one or two squirrels in a location, they moved on to another site where the animals were unlikely to have been frightened by gunfire.

Now, they were tired of tramping through the woods and were headed for home. As they neared some farm buildings at the edge of town, they came to a buzz rig where the owners sawed and split their stove wood. Wood chips covered the ground. The boys sent a few sailing into the air, tried to hit a pigeon in flight, and tossed a few at the large, circular saw to hear the musical sound it emitted.

Ralph had moved off some distance when George bent down and picked up a two inch square piece of wood and held it up between his forefinger and thumb. He stopped a moment, considered the wood chip, then called out to his friend. "Rate, think you can hit this?" he asked as he extended his arm.

Without bothering to answer, Rate took a bead with his .22 rifle, and while George stood immobile, his hand outstretched, gently squeezed the trigger.

The chip went flying.

"That answer your question?"

"Yup. Knew you could do it," said George as he rubbed his fingers. The impact of the bullet with the wood had stung his fingers, but he would have been the last to admit he hurt.

The boys continued on their way, neither giving second thought to the incident. No one considered what could have happened if Ralph had missed his target. George had had complete confidence; therefore, his hand had been steady. This was the way of best friends.

The season changed, the frost coming as Millie had predicted; this was soon followed by single digit temperature during the night which warmed to the high teens during the day. Snow came only at intermittent intervals, but when it came, it came with a fierceness not experienced every year. The strong gale-force winds drove the snow to great depths in some areas while other spots were swept bare. The river was one of the latter.

The river had frozen early, and as usual, the boys were anxious to go there skating. The mill pond, being only three or four feet deep in the deepest places, was safe to go on in a matter of days. However, the river channel was quite another matter. The boys waited impatiently for the ice to get sufficiently thick to allow them to skate up river. They soon became bored with the confines of the pond.

Then, came the day when they had all stood around arguing as to whether the channel was now safe.

"Looks good to me."

"Can't go by looks."

"Who wants to test it?"

"Not me. You're forgetting it takes a long time to get thick where the springs feed the water."

Where the river bank was highest, along the north side halfway up to road level, springs flowed freely in summer and more slowly in the early winter, nearly ceasing during the most frigid weather. However, this cold snap had not been of sufficient length to freeze them, and they still spilled their water down the bank into the river channel.

No one ventured off the pond. They played tag, crack the whip, and even jumped over three logs they had placed side by side. Dusk was settling upon them when they decided it was time to leave for the trek back to town.

Ralph and the others had removed their skates, sitting on a large log at the edge of the ice.

"Help! Help! Someone, help me!"

The cry came from across the pond. The words were full of terror and desperation. At first, Rate could see nothing. Then, he noted the gaping hole in the ice on the river channel. Who was missing? A quick head count revealed it was Joe Oberlin.

"What're we gonna do? If we try to get 'im out, we'll fall in too."

Earl Ferguson had not yet removed his skates, and before anyone realized what he was doing, he grabbed a branch that was part way onto the ice and skated in the direction of the cries.

"Ohmigosh. I hope Earl knows what he's doin'," came from one of the frightened boys.

The group began to follow Earl, knowing they were safe while on the pond. Everyone knew where the invisible line between pond and channel was. They stopped far short of it.

Joe kept trying to climb out of the bone-chilling water, but each time, a hunk of ice broke off sending him under the water for a moment. Each time, the boys held their breath until Joe's head reappeared.

Earl skated out as far as he dared, then lay down on his belly; he inched his way forward shoving the branch in front of him.

"Joe. Soon's you can, grab hold of the branch." He moved a few more inches. The ice groaned ominously. "Got it?"

"Y--y--yes. I got it. But I can't do much. My hands is near frozen."

"Just hang on as best you can. I'm gonna back up now. When I get you on the ice, don't try to crawl. I'll pull you. This ice won't take much movement."

With excruciating slowness, Earl backed up, firmly pulling the branch along with him. Another piece of ice gave way, but then, Joe's shoulders and belly were on the ice. A few more inches, and Joe laid stretched out full length on the ice.

The waiting boys cheered.

However, Rate could hear the dangerous cracking noises the ice was making. He knew a sudden move by either of the boys was likely to plunge them both into the icy water. Now, the group yelled encouraging words to the two boys. Finally, Earl reached the safety of the pond and others helped pull Joe along.

The boys rushed Joe across the pond and across the road to the gristmill where they knew there would be a fire in the stove. It was low since closing time was only minutes away, but they could get Joe out of his clothes which were beginning to freeze. The workers produced horse blankets to wrap around the boy's shivering body, and Mr. Blank said he'd drive him home just as soon as he could get his horse hitched up to the cutter.

Rate had never liked Joe very well. He still remembered the time he had had to have the bb cut out of his hand as a result of Joe attempting to take his bb gun away from him. Still, he was glad Earl had rescued the lad. Rate hoped Joe didn't get pneumonia from his drenching. He'd not wish sickness on anyone.

All the way back to town, the boys talked of the near tragedy and how brave Earl Ferguson had been. Everyone agreed that Joe had done a dumb thing. Rate bet they would all have a lot more respect for the channel after this near disaster.

Realizing his parents were certain to hear of the episode, Rate decided it was better for them to hear his version. He knew someone like Tillie Lance would distort the facts, embellishing parts to fit her own warped imagination.

After listening intently as Ralph told his story at the supper table, Millie spoke. "I hope you boys learned a lesson. You know experience teaches a dear school, but a fool can learn no other. I'll wager the Oberlin boy won't forget this for a long time to come. Boy, see that you use more horse sense than he did."

"I will, Pa. I told 'em you can't tell how thick the ice is by just lookin' at it. The rest of us figgered we hadn't had cold weather long enough for the channel to be safe."

"Haste makes waste. In this case, being overly anxious for a little pleasure nearly cost a life."

Miney was quiet, thinking her own thoughts while Ralph and Millie continued to discuss the accident. She had never really liked having Ralph skate on the river, but Millie had laughed at her fears. Well, today's mishap clearly showed the river was not a safe place to skate, no matter what Millie said. Still, there was not a thing she could do about it. She could hardly forbid Ralph the right to go there when his father had no objection. She guessed she'd just have to trust the Lord to keep her son safe.

Horatio came from Nashville to attend to some business matters. Seems he had some notes due, and one, to Charlie Young, long overdue.

Blanche had finished work early at the *Elsie Sun*. Pa, of course, was still at the butcher shop, Ralph was in school, and her mother was at the Ladies Missionary Society meeting. The group was busy tying off a quilt to be given to a needy family for Christmas.

Since Blanche had come in the back door, she thought herself alone in the house; then, she heard voices from the parlor. The deep tones belonged to her grandfather. Blanche peeked around the corner, not really wanting to eavesdrop, but indecisive as to whether she should make her presence known.

The other man was Charlie Young.

"Honest, Rate, I'd a paid afore now, but I ain't never had the money. Times is hard," he whined.

"Times are better than when I made the loan. You haven't even bothered to pay the interest. I'm giving you until the end of the week to come up with the entire debt-- principle *and* interest."

"Can't do it. I ain't got that kinda money."

"Then, sell something. Borrow from someone else. Just get it."

"Don't have nuthin' I c'n sell."

Now, Horatio lost his temper. He raised his voice and thundered. "If you weren't such a no-good skinflint, you would make good on your just debts. You are a liar and a cheat. You promised regular payments. Don't think I don't know that whenever you do make a few dollars, you nearly break your neck getting to Doty's saloon to spend it. If you weren't so shiftless and lazy, you wouldn't have needed the money in the first place. The end of the week, Charlie, or I'll see you sitting in jail. Is that understood?" His voice was hard, the threat real.

"Yes, but it don't rightly change nuthin'. I ain't no magician, Rate, and I can't make money where there ain't none."

Grandfather had a few more harsh words to say, but Blanche had heard enough. She slipped quietly up the back stairs. Never in her life had she seen her grandfather angry; sometimes, he got slightly irritated, but nothing like this. He certainly hadn't minced his words. She wondered how much Charlie Young owed. If he had been such a bad risk, why had Grandfather loaned him the money in the first place? Usually, he was a good judge of character, and he almost never let sentiment rule his business sense.

Before Horatio returned to Nashville, Charlie came to visit him again. Blanche never knew if the man had the money, part of it, or whether he had made some other arrangement for payment. She only knew her grandfather seemed pleased over something.

Blanche had worked faithfully for Mr. Sherman at the *Elsie Sun,* and for a number of weeks now she had been able to set two columns of type each day. When Mr. Sherman hired her, he had promised her a fifty cent raise as soon as she mastered a column and a half. Blanche had made a few off-handed remarks reminding him she had met his criteria, but Mr. Sherman simply behaved as though he hadn't heard her. Blanche finally realized he had no intention of giving her the promised raise.

Blanche was too proud to ask him to keep his word. She was accustomed to the way her grandfather and father did business--a promise made was a promise kept whether it was in writing or not.

After much consideration, she decided to quit. When Mr. Sherman paid her her wage on Saturday night, she told him she wouldn't be back. She turned and left before the startled man could say a word.

The next week found her clerking at Netzorg's Department Store. It was ever so much more pleasant. Mr. Netzorg expected his clerks to serve the public well, and they had to be good with their sums as he would not tolerate errors on their sales slips. However, it was clean work, and Blanche discovered she enjoyed meeting the public. As Christmas neared, they were kept very busy, but it made time pass quickly. Thus far, her favorite customer was Alice Brewbaker because she had had such a large order: wool yarn, material for undergarments and dresses, material for men's shirts, and a few ready-made garments. Blanche thought her a very sweet lady, soft-spoken and refined.

Millie and his family went to Nashville for Christmas. They drove to Ovid to take the train from there, leaving the horse and cutter at the livery stable. They could make better connections this way and avoid the three hour wait in Charlotte.

Once again, John and his family did not join them. Neither Horatio nor Lovina mentioned them. Millie wondered if John was just being cantankerous or if the reason was that he lacked the money for the train fare. John bounced around from pillar to post and was often sadly lacking in cash. Of course, Millie felt that part of John's life style was to irritate his parents as much as possible.

Shortly after the first of the year, Horatio moved to Stockbridge. Here, he dabbled in real estate. Of course, Mac and Ruby made the move too.

* * * * * * * * * * * *

Ralph had always known Kate Finch was not a teacher one should actually out and out defy. He might provoke her some of the time, but he was careful not to push her patience too far.

Harry Clark did not have this much insight. When Kate chastised him for some misdemeanor, Harry had the audacity, or stupidity, to sass her. The entire room was amazed at how quickly Kate moved. She had hold of Harry before a person could say Jack Robinson; furthermore, she dragged him from his desk and began to shake him like a housewife shakes a dust mop. The kids gasped when Harry boldly struck her. Quicker than a wink, Kate kicked Harry's feet out from under him and the startled youth found himself stretched out on the floor; Kate had a firm grasp on a handful of his hair enabling her to pound his head mercilessly on the floor.

The whole episode took only a few moments.

Kate didn't have much to say as she eyed the classroom except that she hoped Harry had learned his lesson well. Ralph thought Harry looked pretty meek as he sat in his desk with his head down, not meeting the eyes of anyone. He looked as if he wanted to cry.

The room was exceptionally quiet for the rest of the day. No one else wanted to test the waters by misbehaving. Kate had resumed teaching as though nothing unusual had happened, but her eyes were cold as she surveyed the roomful of students.

Rate thought Harry had been pretty dumb to get himself into such a fix. He should have known that Miss Finch would settle the matter herself. Other teachers might send students to the principal for discipline, but Miss Finch never bothered. She might be tall and skinny, but she sure was stronger than most women. Harry had learned that the hard way.

One night, when Millie came home from the meat market, he seemed more taciturn than usual. Miney said nothing since she had learned a long time ago that Millie would do no talking until he was good and ready no matter if she did ask questions.

When she joined him after the supper dishes were done, he looked up from his paper and spoke.

"Heard today that Boyd Doyle is going to tear down the old cheese factory. Why his father owned that building back as far as 1875. Boyd says it has outlived its usefulness. Guess he intends to put up a large, cement block building at Elm and Second. Says a more modern building will benefit production. Know one thing for certain, they won't be able to make a better cheese. Certainly won't seem the same with the old building gone. Expect someone will want to build there since the village *is* growing." It was difficult for Millie to make this admission since he seldom wanted the old ways to be changed.

"I expect Boyd feels his new building is progress. Perhaps it will make the men's work easier."

"Well, whatever he calls it, I hate to see that old building go. Know his father would never have agreed to such a move." He paused a moment, then continued. "We used to have some mighty fine roller skating parties on the second floor, didn't we?" He smiled fondly at his wife.

"I was never one for skating, but you boys seemed to enjoy it well enough." Miney replied with a little laugh of remembrance.

"Miney, do you remember the time they dared me to go down the stairs with my skates still on? Wonder I didn't break my fool neck." Millie laughed as he remembered. "Never did like to admit I was afraid to do something. Was always ready to take a dare."

"I know. In that way, you are just like your father."

Millie nodded absently, his mind lost in thought. He had shared as much as he intended with his wife.

It was early on a Saturday morning. Ralph was the only one to appear this early at the mill pond. He knew that by midmorning he would have plenty of company. He guessed some of his friends didn't have as strict a father as Pa. Saturday or not, Ralph had to get up to take care of the horse before breakfast. He was glad Pa had finally sold those eight calves because they sure had been a pain in the neck on school days.

There was a light sifting of sugar-fine snow covering the ice; however, it wasn't deep enough to cause any problem. Besides, it was so light, it was kind of fun to skate through it.

Ralph raced along, then turned both skates sideways, enjoying the sight of the cloud of snow he caused. He skated some figure eights where the snow lay virgin white and undisturbed. He stopped once to look at the tracks of some animal. He wasn't all that good at recognizing tracks, but he was learning. He thought this might have been a fox.

He wished some of his friends would hurry up; it wasn't half as much fun skating by oneself. He took a big circle out across the channel, then back to the edge of the pond. Suddenly, the ice gave way, and Ralph sank to his knees in mud and water. How could this be? The weather had been warmer lately, but not warm enough to cause this. As he struggled to keep his balance, the thought came to him; there must have been a skating party here last night and this was where they had built their bonfire. He'd have been able to see the remains if there hadn't been the new layer of snow.

He struggled forward and was able to get back onto safe ice. His feet already felt cold from the icy water which had filled his shoes. He skated back to the road as fast as he could because he could hear sleigh bells. If he could hitch a ride, he'd be home much more quickly.

Not stopping to remove his skates, Rate crawled up the incline as fast as he could. Yup, here come a team. He didn't know the driver, but that made no difference.

"Hey mister, how about a ride into town?"

"Hop on the back," the man replied drawing in the team.

Gingerly, Ralph jumped on the back, his legs hanging down. Golly, his feet and legs sure were cold. He wished he had something to cover them with, but the sleigh was bare. He decided he'd be better off if he drew his legs up beside him where they wouldn't feel the cold air go by; the man had let the team have its head, and they were trotting briskly.

At the corner by the Methodist Church, Rate yelled his thanks and dropped to the ground. Just before getting into town, he had tried to unfasten his skates, but the leather thongs, encrusted with mud and slush, had frozen stiff. His clothes were stiff too. Felt as though they were frozen to his skin.

As quickly as possible, Rate hobbled the block to his house. Wisely, he came in the back door.

"Ma! Ma, I need help," he called.

Miney came from the sitting room.

"Land sakes, Ralph, what's all the ruckus?" Then, she saw his mud-encrusted legs. "Whatever happened? You must have fallen through the ice. Get those skates off this instant"

"I can't, Ma. They's froze so bad, they won't come off."

In the warmth of the kitchen, Rate began to realize just how cold he really was.

His teeth began to chatter, and his entire body shook.

"Goodness. What shall I do? I know, you sit here in this chair by the door. I'll get a tub of warm water for you to soak them off. Don't expect a little more water will hurt the shoes any more than this muck and mire has already."

She pushed a chair over to Rate, and he gladly sat down. He was losing the feeling in his feet and legs. He watched as his mother hurriedly dragged a foot tub before him, then took water from the reservoir. She added some cold water thinking mildly warm water would probably be better than water which was hot.

Ralph put his feet in the tub. At first he felt nothing, then gradually, the warmth of the water penetrated his icy clothing. In a short time, he could remove the skates, then came the shoes which were indeed a sad looking sight. It was going to take a lot of tallow to keep them pliable after they dried out.

Miney appeared with a towel, fresh underwear, and pants.

"I'll change this muddy water, but you can just soak your feet in some fresh water. I'll make it warmer this time. Land sakes, Ralph, you are half frozen. Just look at the way you are shaking. I'll get a quilt and we'll wrap you up good. If we don't, you're going to get pneumonia," was the dire prediction.

For once Ralph didn't argue. He was perfectly willing to let his mother coddle him. He didn't feel as though he'd ever be warm again.

When Miney had him tucked in a warm quilt, his feet in warm water, she made him a cup of hot cocoa. Goodness, that boy was always a trial. She just hoped his constitution was strong enough to keep him from getting bronchitis or something worse. Of course, she had a lot to be thankful for, the accident could have been worse.

The season warmed, and for once, Ralph did not hate to have the ice leave the river. He hadn't escaped having a severe cold, one which kept him in bed for two days--on the weekend so he had not had to miss school. Ma hadn't even reprimanded him for his carelessness; he guessed she was just glad he hadn't got pneumonia.

There were times when Millie took Ralph with him when he went to buy livestock to butcher for the market. Ralph didn't mind except he often wished his father was a mite more talkative. Often they drove for several miles without a word passing between them. At these times, Rate wondered what his father was thinking, for surely the man had thoughts even if he was unwilling to share them.

It had been one such day in early spring. Ralph was doing the driving while Millie sat lost in thought. They had a load of grunting, squealing hogs and were headed for the slaughterhouse.

Finally, Millie noticed where they were. He spoke to his son. "Rate, stop at Charlie Randall's."

"All right, Pa."

They drew up in front of the Randall house. As Millie climbed down from the wagon, Charlie came from around the corner of the house. The men had been talking a few moments when shouts and cries assailed their ears. Several children came running around the house, shouting at each other.

Just then, Mrs. Randall came out the front door to see what was causing all the commotion. By then, the horde of children had crossed the front yard and were headed for the back yard once more.

Charlie scratched his head, a perplexed look on his face. He looked at his wife, and with a determined sigh, said, "Toot, we got to do something. Your kids an' my kids are pickin' on our kids."

With a nod to Millie, he followed the children to the back yard. Ralph could hear his voice above the clamor; then suddenly, all was quiet. Rate wondered what was going on. Didn't sound like anyone was gettin' a lickin'.

Millie said a few words to Mrs. Randall, then clambered back on the high wagon seat. Millie was chuckling as though he found the situation extremely funny.

"Think Charlie's got his hands full," he commented.

"How many kids they got?" inquired Ralph.

"Nineteen, I think. Charlie had kids by his first wife, she had kids by her first husband, and they had some after they were married. His kids and her kids are about the same ages. Think there's only three or four who are old enough to have left home. Think it requires more patience than most men have in them to manage a family of that size."

Ralph agreed. There had been times when he wished he could have had a brother, but he wasn't sure he'd like having a whole bunch of brothers and sisters. Of course, if there had been another sister, he'd have had one more to tease. He smiled a moment at that thought. Still, all in all, he was satisfied with life as it was. Besides, there was no way to change it.

CHAPTER 15

When the warm days of late spring arrived, Ralph was impatient for school to be out for the summer. Of course, he enjoyed playing baseball, but the time spent in the classroom suddenly seemed dull. There was so much a young boy could be doing in the wondrous outdoors. Being confined in a classroom certainly cramped his style.

After school and on Saturdays, he tried to cram as much living into these hours as was possible. Normally, he was glad to work at the meat market, but even that time seemed confining; he felt antsy, as though he could hardly wait until his chores were done. He knew better than to shirk them because Pa would have been quick to notice and some form of punishment would certainly have followed.

One Saturday, Rate, along with George and Harold Lusk, went bullfrogging on the millpond. They had a flat-bottomed boat which they poled slowly among the lily pads and other aquatic life. They waited quietly until they heard the unmistakable hruumph of a bullfrog, then they cautiously moved in that direction.

They took turns poling, the other two perched on each side of the boat armed with long wooden spears. It took agility to spear a bullfrog, but the boys were patient and soon had several on the bottom of the boat. For a lad who became easily bored in the classroom, Ralph could work at this for a couple of hours, and the time flew past. He always felt there was a challenge here, he was pitting his expertise against the natural wariness of the frogs.

Ralph returned home with several frogs. Miney looked at them and shook her head in dismay as Rate proudly exhibited his catch. In his enthusiasm, Rate did not notice his mother's lack of response at first.

"See, Ma, I got enough so we can have frog legs for supper. You know Pa really likes 'em. Guess Blanche isn't that fond of them, but she eats 'em."

"Yes, I'd say there is enough for a meal."

Ralph looked at his mother skeptically. "You don't seem very pleased."

"I'm sorry. Of course I'm pleased. You do right well with your hunting and fishing. It helps with the grocery bill."

"What's wrong then?" he asked suspiciously.

"Nothing. You'd best get them cleaned."

Rate left with a pan to put the frog legs in when he had severed them from the body. Ma sure acted strange. He'd just keep watch and see if he could discover what was wrong.

Miney had begun supper. The potatoes were boiling, and she had the pan on the stove melting the lard in preparation for the flour-breaded frog legs. She was unaware that Ralph was peeking around the corner of the doorway to the dining room surreptitiously watching her every move. He saw her give a shudder as she began placing the legs into the pan of hot grease. He could hear the sputter as they began frying. His mother had a mighty strange look on her face. He edged closer. He could see nothing wrong.

"Ma, something's bothering you."

Miney jumped. She gave him a glance, then turned back to the pan.

Ralph watched in fascination as the legs jerked and kicked like something alive. "Golly, Ma, look. Do they always do that?" he asked, excitement in his voice as his eyes were glued to the large, cast iron skillet.

"Always." She gave a shudder. "Now, you know why I dislike frying them. It seems like they are alive. It just sends shivers down my spine. I've never got used to seeing them wiggle."

"Aw, Ma, you know they aren't alive. Wonder what makes 'em do that? Bet if I asked Miss Finch, she'd know."

The legs had finally become still, and Miney moved to turn them in the pan. She didn't rightly care what made them behave in such a fashion. Guess she just didn't have the curiosity Ralph had. She was thankful there quite likely would be no more frog legs for another year. Of course, they did make mighty fine eating, she admitted grudgingly.

The wagon Millie used to haul livestock was low-wheeled with the axle off-set allowing the floorboards to be much closer to the ground than a regular farm wagon. it had a stanchion at the front for hauling cattle; the side racks were high enough to discourage a hog or sheep from attempting to scale the sides.

Millie had noted the floorboards were becoming worn, but he had not taken the time to repair them.

Millie had made arrangements to pick up a good-sized bull from a farm several miles north of Elsie. He knew it would spoil the better part of a day, so he decided to send Ralph to pick up the animal. He gave the boy the needed cash with explicit instructions as to the location of the farm.

Rate had no problem locating the farm, and the farmer helped him load the bull. Not only did they safely close the stanchion, but they left the lead rope on and tied that to the wagon rack. The bull seemed placid since he had walked up the tailgate, into the wagon, docilely. Still, one never quite trusted a bull. A person lived longer that way.

Before they had gone very far, the bull became restless. When Rate looked back, the huge beast tossed his head, and danced as far sideways as he could in the confining space. Rate thought he heard a cracking sound, but he gave it no more thought as the bull settled down once again.

They were about two miles from Elsie when Rate heard a sharp crack, and there came a bellow of terror from the bull. Rate glanced back from his perch on the high spring seat. Ohmigosh, the bull had broken through the floorboards. He was down on his front legs, snorting with fear.

Rate pulled in the horses. As soon as the forward movement stopped, the bull gingerly got to his feet, carefully extricating himself from the broken floorboards. He snorted his displeasure, moved, and one leg slipped back into the hole. Something had to be done before the animal broke a leg.

Rate crawled down, tied the lines to a ring on the rack, then surveyed the scene. Pa knew those floorboards were getting bad. Why hadn't he taken the time to fix them? Better yet, why couldn't they have broken when Pa had the wagon out?

The door in back, which also served as a ramp, was fastened in place by a big iron pin passing through an eye on each side of the door which meshed with a corresponding eye on the frame of the wagon. If he removed the pin, the door could be taken off. It was heavy, but Ralph thought he could lift it. If not, he could tip it end for end.

In only moments, he had the door off. It was heavier than he had realized. He struggled to tip it up into the wagon where it leaned against the side racks. He contemplated his next move. If he unfastened the stanchion, the bull could back out, but Ralph decided he darsent untie the rope because there was no way he could hold the bull if the animal decided to run. He decided to retie the rope, giving the animal as much slack as he could, then he'd unfasten the stanchion and see if the bull would back out of the wagon.

At first, the bull was contrary, and although he was loose, he refused to budge. One hind foot was in a splintered hole, and the bull just stood there as though he couldn't lift that leg out. Finally, Rate whacked him on the end of his tender black nose; he snorted, shook his head, and backed a couple of steps. Rate yelled at him, and when the bull discovered he was able to move more, he continued backing. He nearly lost his balance when his hind legs slid off the back of the wagon. He backed another step or two, then stopped. Wouldn't you know? The large animal had reached the end of the rope, and his front feet were still in the wagon. So there he stood, half in, half out, roaring his displeasure.

Ralph was in a quandary. What should he do?

After contemplating the situation for a time, Rate decided to see if the bull would walk on his hind feet if he was careful to keep the team at a very slow pace.

The strange cavalcade moved at a snail's pace to Elsie, then west to the slaughterhouse. Every so often, the bull bellered in protest, but Ralph kept moving steadily forward. Several youngsters called to him, laughing at the spectacle, but Ralph looked neither right nor left, pretending not to see or hear them. He was glad he met only a couple of rigs and those were driven by no one he knew. What an embarrassing situation! He bet Pa would think the episode funny, but that was just because he hadn't been the one to have all the trouble.

At last, school was out for the summer. The bright skies and warm days were like a tonic to Ralph and his friends. While most of the boys had a few chores each day, they still had plenty of time to do the things they liked.

Ralph was home for meals, but other than that, Miney saw little of him. He went to the store for her when asked, mowed the lawn, and spent time working at the meat market. Still, he managed a lot of time to be with his friends.

Mary Jane Scott was well past middle age. She lived by herself north of town, and sometimes did light housework for Miney. Somehow, her working for his mother never failed to surprise Ralph because it was generally known that the first place Mary Jane went when she came into town was the saloon for a shot of whiskey. Most women wouldn't have been caught dead in such a place. Perhaps Mary Jane figured that at her age, she could do as she pleased regardless of what people thought. Since his mother was so set against a person imbibing spirits of any kind, Ralph often wondered why she accepted Mary Jane's behavior.

Whether Miney had work for her or not, the woman usually showed up at the Setterington household just about dinner time, knowing Miney would invite her to eat with them. This happened at regular intervals during the spring, summer, and into the fall until the weather turned quite cool.

One day, Mary Jane showed up just as Miney was putting on a kettle of potatoes. Miney hurriedly added another potato, and she asked Mary Jane to sit while she continued preparing the meal. Miney wrinkled her nose at the unmistakable odor of whiskey on the woman's breath. Miney felt the woman might better have saved her money to buy material for a new dress since this one was quite worn and had been patched in several places. Of course, one must give Mary Jane credit because the dress was spotlessly clean. Well, Miney thought, perhaps she should give the aging woman one of her second best dresses the next time Mary Jane helped her with some cleaning.

They sat down to dinner on the stroke of twelve. Mary Jane took the platter of meat, observed it closely as if attempting to decide what it was, then took a piece and passed the platter on. Ralph noticed her hesitation and almost snickered.

At the end of the meal, Ralph could no longer contain himself. "Mary Jane, do you know what kind of meat that was?"

She thought a moment, then said, "No. I'm afraid not."

Grinning mischievously, Ralph said, "It was turtle. I caught it yesterday," he added proudly.

An odd expression passed over the woman's thin face. She contemplated this bit of information a moment. Then, she gave him a slow smile, and said, "It was tasty, Ralph, very tasty."

Ralph smothered a laugh. From the expression on her face, Ralph knew Mary Jane would have passed up the meat if she had had any inkling as to what it was. People sure were funny. Turtle was even better than frog legs, and it certainly came in way ahead of chicken or pork. It didn't have a fishy taste either. Well, at least the elderly lady had admitted it was good, and she hadn't been irritated because they had fed her something she hadn't tasted before. Probably that was because she didn't want to jeopardize future meals. Ma said she didn't have much money so these were likely the best meals she got. Ma was a right good cook, and with a husband who had a whoppin' big appetite, she always had plenty of food on the table.

Shortly after school was out, Millie decided he and Miney would go to Stockbridge to visit his parents. Since Blanche was working, she would be unable to go. Millie decided Rate was old enough to assume some of the responsibility of running the butcher shop. After all, the boy had turned fourteen in December, plenty old enough to handle things with the help of George Page. Millie decided to warn George about his drinking--he was to remain sober the few days Millie would be gone.

Millie took his son aside and explained there was plenty of beef in the cooler to last until he returned. However, if they had a run on pork, they would certainly need more. There were hogs penned at the slaughterhouse, so all Rate would have to do was butcher one. Rate had seen his father do this countless times; therefore, he knew the exact procedure to follow.

True to Millie's prediction, they ran very low on pork, and George and Rate came to the conclusion Rate had better butcher a hog the next day.

Ralph went to the slaughterhouse in the early morning. He built a fire to heat water in the huge, black, cast iron kettle. He knew Pa always took four pails of boiling water to one of cold for the scalding barrel.

Ralph singled out a hog, drove it into the narrow chute where he could catch its legs to drop it on its back. Without too much trouble, he managed to stick it neatly with the long, slender-bladed knife used for this one purpose. From here, the carcass was dragged onto a platform.

The wooden scalding barrel was set on a slant in front of this platform enabling the carcass of the hog to be slid gently into the hot water. This was a crucial period. If the hog was left in the water too long, it set the hair so it wouldn't scrape off no matter how hard one worked. If it wasn't in the hot water long enough, the hair wouldn't scrape either.

Rate slowly slid the hog head first into the barrel until only the hind feet protruded from the water. All was going well. He counted to himself just the way Pa did. There. Enough time had elapsed. He took hold of the rope around the hog's back legs and pulled. The hog barely budged. Rate pulled again, bracing his feet and pulling with all his might. The hog slid up a short distance, but no matter how he tugged, it would come no further. Ralph hadn't realized how much more difficult pulling the hog out of the barrel would be; after all, it looked easy when Pa did it.

Now, Ralph was desperate.

He decided to set up the windlass to see if he could then drag the hog onto the platform. Golly, he bet the hair was set good by now. Why hadn't he thought of the windlass earlier?

Just then, he noticed a man approaching. It was Hand Manross. With a quick glance, Hand surveyed the scene, realizing the cause of the difficulty.

"Havin' a mite o' trouble, Rate?" he asked, giving the boy a knowing grin.

"Yup. Can't pull this blamed hog out o' the barrel. Tried my darndest."

"Here, I'll give you a hand. Let's see if we can't get it out."

Since Ralph had the windless almost in place, Hand finished the job, and with little effort, pulled the dripping hog from the barrel. He reached out and attempted to pull a few hairs from the hot carcass.

"Rate, it 'pears to me the hair is set."

"I know. I just couldn't get it out. Never thought o' usin' the windlass in the first place." Ralph looked disconsolately at the hog. "Sure will have to shave ever bit of it, so guess I'd better get at it. Can't sell meat with hair still sticking to it." As an afterthought, he added, "Much obliged for your help."

"Glad I came by. Saw the rig and thought your pa might be back."

"Naw. He won't be here until Saturday."

Hand nodded his head and moved off while Rate set about to take care of the carcass. He'd have to hurry. He'd intended to be back to the market by noon, but it didn't look as though he'd make it. Blanche would probably yell if he missed dinner, but that couldn't be helped either. She'd better not yell at him or he'd tell her where she could go. He was in no mood to have his sister complain.

Ralph had learned his lesson. He hated every moment of shaving the hair off the carcass--it was ever so much more time consuming than scraping the hide with the large scraper designed for this purpose. He'd not mention this to Pa. If Hand kept his mouth shut, there'd be no one to tell Pa what had happened. Rate knew full well his father would have found the situation comical. In fact, he could have sworn he could hear his father's laughter now. Guess he hadn't been as responsible as Pa had thought. Well, he'd certainly never make this mistake again, that's for damned sure.

The day was unseasonably warm. In fact, there might be a storm brewing, but Rate headed for the river as soon as he had run an errand for his mother. He hadn't had to go to the meat market. In fact, he didn't go there very often now. The week after Millie returned from Stockbridge, he had sold a half interest in the market to Walter Lusk. Rate had a sneakin' suspicion this was the reason Millie had taken the trip to Stockbridge--he'd wanted to ask his father's advice. Now that Rate was older, he often wondered why Pa found it so difficult to make a decision on his own, always felt the need to ask Horatio's opinion. Well, whatever the reason, he guessed he was glad Mr. Lusk had come into the business. Bet he'd not be asked to butcher any more hogs on his own.

There were times when Rate liked being by himself. He had found that if he was to study wildlife--and this was high on his list of things he enjoyed most--it was much easier to move quietly to observe something if he had no one with him. With no one to break his concentration, his watchful eye caught the movement of many of the wild creatures which inhabited the meadows and woodlots.

It was not only downright hot, it was also humid. There wasn't much of a breeze either. The leaves hung limply on the trees. The earth was moist in spots from yesterday's shower, but the sloping, sandy banks of the Maple River had been dried by the sun.

Rate moved cautiously, hoping to get a glimpse of a red fox. He knew where the vixen had her lair. He supposed she would have whelped by now, and he was wondering if he might catch a glimpse of her pups--they usually had four.

He stopped. Something moved a few feet ahead of him. He was part way up the high, sandy bank. He edged forward. It was only a turtle. Golly, if he wasn't so far from home, he'd catch it and they could have a nice meal tomorrow. What was that turtle doing? It was behaving strangely. The turtle was using her head to hollow out a place in the sand. Rate stretched out on the ground, parting the grass in front of him, as he silently watched the procedure. It finally dawned on him that this was a female turtle. When she had the spot shaped to her liking, she laid her eggs in the hollow. Rate was surprised that this process took so little time. He knew she had undoubtedly laid at least twenty-five eggs, maybe more.

When finished, the turtle worked diligently to make certain all of the eggs were completely covered with a layer of sand. When they were covered to her satisfaction, she began to make her way back down the slope to the river. Rate knew the summer's sun would hatch the eggs in a couple of months, and the young turtles would head immediately for water. The western bank would have sun until after midday; he thought it amazing how nature provided for her creatures.

Now that Walt Lusk and Millie were partners in the meat market, Rate and George saw more of each other than ever. Some days, their fathers had jobs for them to do at the market. Rate thought it was ever so much more fun to have someone with whom to share the work.

One such day, George and Rate were sent to take a barrel of spoiled salt pork to get rid of it. Neither man explained in detail what the boys should do, so the boys simply took the barrel to the dumping ground and dumped it. Neither Millie nor Walt asked them about it when they brought the empty barrel back to the market.

A couple of days later, Ren Burdick, the village health officer, went to investigate the smell. He found the pile of meat, covered with flies and maggots; he held his nose because at this close range, the stench was terrible.

Ren went back into town and paid a visit to both meat markets asking if they had dumped any meat.

Walt, not knowing what the boys had done, said, "Honest, Ren, Millie and I haven't dumped any meat lately. If we do, we bury it. Wasn't us."

Ren shook his head. If neither of the butcher shops had dumped the meat, there was no way of telling who was responsible.

"Guess I'll just have to go bury it. Can't have that mess stinking up the whole village for God knows how long," he said with a sigh.

When Millie related the incident at the supper table, Ralph volunteered no information. He felt a little sorry for Mr. Burdick, but neither Pa nor Walt had told the boys they should *bury* the meat. They had simply said to get rid of it, and the boys had done it the quickest way possible. Guess he'd know better next time, if there ever was a next time.

The Fourth of July was only a couple of days away. Rate, along with his friends, was more excited over the holiday than ever before. There was to be a balloon ascension this year. Rate and his cronies had never seen one before. The boys had discussed what it must feel like to float high above the houses and trees. Some went so far as to indicate they would like to be a passenger. Ralph wasn't sure he would go that far. He'd have to watch an ascension before he decided if riding the basket of a hot air balloon appealed to him.

Ralph was around bright and early on the day of festivities. Before he could get out of the house, his mother had made certain he changed into clean clothes. One thing he could always count on was Ma checking to make sure he was clean even if he was fourteen. Sometimes, he wondered if she'd ever think he was old enough to be responsible for his appearance. He wondered if other mothers were the same way.

There wasn't much doing as yet because it was still early. Farm folk had chores to do before they could head for town.

Golly, the ascension was to take place just west of the main four corners. Ralph looked skeptically at Doty's Hotel and Bates' dry goods store on each side of the wide street. Must be they expected the balloon would go straight up, at least for a spell, if it was to clear either of these structures. He noted there was scarcely any breeze, and what little there was, came from the southwest; that ruled out the hotel. Must be there wasn't enough wind to cause the balloon to drift since it scarcely fluttered the leaves on the trees.

Rate watched from the boardwalk as several men set about taking the balloon off the flatbed of a truck. The basket was set to one side, the ballast sandbags hanging from it's sides.

Each man seemed to know what he was doing. Some positioned the folds of the gray balloon west on the street; two men made preparations for a fire in the middle of the street. Guy ropes were strung out. A man glanced at his watch, nodded to a companion who ignited the fire.

Rate wanted to ask questions. He had been joined by Brownie McNall, Don Besley, and George Lusk. The boys edged closer. Rate noted the ropes were soot stained as was the neck of the balloon. In fact, none of the equipment looked any too clean; even the men wore soot-stained clothing. The men had made a ring of soot blackened stones to contain the fire. Must be they took these stones with them wherever they went.

The boys stepped gingerly over the ropes and moved to inspect the basket. It looked solid enough, but Rate decided it wasn't very big although he supposed there was plenty of room for one man.

The boys were fascinated as the balloon began to writhe and move, a section of it expanding with a pop; it seemed like a giant coming alive. It was going to take a long time to fill. The men must have done it so often they knew exactly how much time was involved since the ascension was billed to take place promptly at noon.

Now, the balloon was partially upright. Men were holding guy ropes while still more ropes were added.

"Hey, kid, wanna help?" The man was looking directly at Rate.

"Sure. Whaddaya want met' do?"

"Hold this rope. Think you can do that?"

"Sure can."

"It's important. We can't have the balloon taking off before we're ready."

Ralph nodded. That made sense.

"How come he picked you," asked George. "I'm bigger."

"I dunno. Maybe I looked smarter." He gave an impish grin, then hurriedly added, "Guess I was closest, that's all."

The other boys eyed him enviously. Some people had all the luck.

As the balloon filled with hot air, it strained to go aloft. The soot-blackened rope rubbed across Ralph's chest. Gripes, look at that smear of black. Well, it couldn't be helped, the darned rope was hard to hold steady.

Just before noon, a sizable crowd had assembled, and a rather small man climbed into the basket. The barker was explaining how the man had nerves of steel, anything to keep the crowd's interest these last few moments before the ascension.

Finally, zero hour came. Steadily and gracefully the mighty balloon lifted majestically into the summer sky; the man in the basket waved to the crowd below. Although it had risen perpendicular to the earth, the air currents now sent it drifting lazily northeast.

Golly, it hadn't been all that great thought Ralph as he hurried home for dinner. Still, he did wonder how far the man would travel and how high above the earth the balloon would take him.

Mina had given Ralph permission to be late for dinner because she knew how badly he wanted to see the ascension. Millie and Blanche had not been interested, and she guessed she had more important things to be doing. Still, she could well understand Ralph's curiosity.

They were seated at the table when Miney heard Ralph come into the woodshed where he stopped to wash up. She had put a plate of victuals in the warming oven, so she rose from her chair to fetch his plate to the table. Just as she turned around, Ralph came through the door.

A horrified look came to Miney's face as she beheld her son. With an exclamation, she put his plate on the table with a bang.

"Land sakes, whatever happened to you?" All eyes turned to look at Ralph.

"What's wrong?" he asked innocently.

"Have you taken a look at yourself?" asked Blanche with a smirk.

"Why should I? What's wrong? Have I got two noses?" he asked his sister as he slid into his chair.

"Ralph Setterington, you are filthy. What have you been doing? Your clean clothes look like they belong to a chimneysweep. How in this world will I ever get them clean?" A look of despair was on Miney's face. His light blue shirt would have to be boiled, and then she wasn't certain the black spots would be removed entirely. If she couldn't get it clean, it would go for the rag bag even though it was almost new.

Ralph looked down at his front. Golly, there were a couple of black marks where the rope had pulled across him when the balloon swung a little, but what were those specks? They looked like spots of soot. Well, he had been on the windward side of the fire, but he hadn't noticed anything at the time. Guess probably he'd been too busy watching the balloon to be worried about a little dirt.

"Gosh, Ma, I'm sorry. They needed someone to hold the guy ropes an' one of the men asked me. Honest, I didn't know I was gonna get dirty. It just seemed like a good idea. It got me where I could see everything that went on."

For once, he actually did look contrite.

"Think you better go scrub your face. From the looks, you could pass for colored," said Millie, his eyes betraying his feelings.

Mina started to say something more, but Millie interrupted her.

"He didn't do it on purpose. I'll admit he's a sight for sore eyes, but yelling at him won't change a thing.

"No, I suppose not. But, Millie, that's one of his good shirts."

"Can't be helped. At least this situation won't be cropping up again. Be thankful for that."

Mina gave a sigh. What Millie said was true, but she bet he'd sing a different tune if he was the one who had to wash the clothes. Still, Ralph *had* looked sorry. Why was it he always attracted trouble of some sort?

CHAPTER 16

Usually, the boys went to the swimming hole back of Cobb's because there they simply stripped to the skin with no one to bother them. However, some of the time of late, they swam in the channel by the bridge, a pair of old pants served as their swimsuit. As long as the mill wasn't in operation, the current wasn't swift enough to put them in any danger. By now, most of them were strong swimmers.

For some reason, George Lusk had never quite mastered the art of swimming. He wasn't afraid of the water, but somehow, when he tried to stroke, he sank like a rock. He could float, but he got tired of doing that because he dared not go where the water was over his head. He was envious of the good times his friends had in the water, but for want of something better to do, he usually accompanied them to the river.

The main attraction at the gristmill was the iron bridge. Someone had had the brilliant idea that diving off the bridge would be lots of fun. They took turns standing on the railing, then diving into the channel. It was glorious. Wes Payne even crawled up to the first support and dove from there, but no one else was quite that brave--or foolish--Ralph included.

George sat disconsolately watching his friends. Golly, that looked like such fun. He knew he could dive, and he could surely float after he surfaced; it was the swimming back to the bank he wouldn't be able to do.

Suddenly, he had an idea.

"Rate. Rate, com'ere," he shouted.

Ralph swam over to the bank and treaded water while he looked up at his friend, wondering what he seemed to be so excited about.

"Rate, I got an idea, but I need your help."

"Doin' what?"

"Well, I want to dive off the bridge like the rest of you fellows. It looks like a lotta fun. I want to give it a try."

"How'd you expect to get back to the bank? You know you can't swim," Ralph stated bluntly.

"I know. But supposin' someone was there to pull me out?" George's hopeful expression was not lost on his friend.

"I dunno, George. I never tried haulin' someone with me. I'm not sure I could do it."

"That's not what I mean."

"Well, what *do* you mean?" Ralph had climbed out to sit by his friend. Now, he looked at him expectantly.

"What if you took that old rowboat out there, an' when I surface, you jest stick out an oar for me to grab. That way you can pull me over to the boat. C'mon, Rate. It'll work. I know it will."

"I dunno, George. It's sort of risky."

"No, it isn't. What could happen?" he asked confidently.

"What if you can't get into the boat?"

"I'll jest hang on while you row me over to the bank."

Ralph considered the proposal. He had always felt sorry for George because his inability to swim made him miss out on a lot of fun. If George could float in shallow water, he should be able to float when he surfaced. The greater depth of the water would make it even easier as long as he didn't panic.

"All right, we'll try it. If anything goes wrong, some of the others could likely help pull you out."

"Thanks, Rate. Knew you'd understand."

In a few moments, Ralph was in the old rowboat heading for the channel.

"All right, George. I don't want to get closer or you might come up under the boat. Ready?"

"Yup."

The other boys shouted words of encouragement to George as he climbed up on the railing.

George balanced himself, hesitated a moment, then dove. He broke water several feet from where Rate waited with the rowboat. He flopped over on his back and waited until he heard Rate's shout.

"Here, George. Grab hold."

Rate held an oar out to his friend who grabbed it and hung on while Rate hauled him over to the side. As George pulled himself into the boat, it rocked dangerously; but neither boy seemed to notice. The spectators cheered at their success.

George dove off the bridge several more times, and Ralph was always there to hold the oar out for him to grab. On several other occasions during the summer, the boys repeated this activity. Neither boy realized they were doing anything dangerous. Both had complete confidence in the other. In their estimation, this was the purpose of good friends.

Now that Ralph didn't have to work very often at the meat market, he was free to work for others. He rather liked this because some people paid better than Pa, and everyone paid better than Ma.

Ralph drove on certain days for the livery stable south of Doty's Hotel. It was run by Truman Armstrong and Ed Hawes. Ralph was always a little skeptical when Truman sent him out because he remembered the mare Truman had given him to drive for the sleigh ride one winter. However, Ed was completely reliable, and Rate did enjoy driving. He'd have done it for nothing. Getting paid was just the frosting on the cake.

Drummers—traveling salesmen—came to the hotel, and since they did not know the countryside, they wanted someone who knew his way about to drive them. They usually paid fifty cents a day. Of course, the day varied in length, but they seldom set out at a time Rate called early, and they liked to be back by four or five in the afternoon.

On one such occasion, Ralph was driving a man to Ovid to catch the train there. He was a short, pudgy little man with a narrow-brimmed, flat-crowned, woven straw hat crammed on his head. He hadn't seemed one bit friendly, and Ralph had taken an instant dislike to him.

They were proceeding at a slow trot which steadily ate up the distance. However, the man kept taking his watch from his vest pocket to check the time. Periodically, he mopped his face with what had been a white handkerchief although Rate didn't figure the day was all that hot. Finally, the man complained because Ralph was going too slow--he'd never get to the depot in time. His tone was caustic and Ralph's irritation grew. The man behaved as though Rate didn't know what he was doing, like he'd never driven somewhere before.

Ralph was driving a young mare. Truman had cautioned him not to use the whip on her because she liked to run. Rate gave this advice a moment's consideration, but when the man opened his mouth to find fault for the third time, Rate gave the man a knowing grin and touched the mare's rump lightly with the whip.

The mare surged forward and broke into a run; Rate braced himself as the buggy swayed and bounced. The man made a wild grab for his hat, but it flew from his head and out of the buggy. Ralph spoke soothingly to the mare and pulled her in. He started to turn her around.

"What are you doing?" gasped the man, once again mopping his face with the dirt-streaked handkerchief.

"Going back after your hat. Didn't figger you'd want to lose it permanently." Rate's eyes danced with merriment, but his face was expressionless.

"You just stop her right here. *I'll* go back after my hat. Why she'd be likely to take off in the wrong direction. Then where'd we be?" He glared at Ralph, then backed clumsily out of the buggy.

Rate snickered to himself. She might like to run, but she behaved well and had been no trouble to stop.

"Whatever you say."

The hat was further back than the man had realized. He was sweating profusely by the time he returned. When he clambered ponderously back into the buggy, he said nothing, but he gave Rate a dark scowl, his heavy brows drawing completely together.

Ralph thought the incident extremely funny. The man was puffing like he was not accustomed to walking more than a few feet at a time. Guess he had been badly frightened because he never looked at his watch again nor did he complain about Ralph's driving. At the station, he snatched his suitcase and waddled through the door of the depot without a word or a backward glance. Rate figured it was a good thing he had been given his pay in advance. He bet if this man ever came back to Elsie, he'd ask for another driver. At the thought, Ralph laughed to himself; he turned the mare and headed for home at a slow trot. Sure took all kinds to make up the world.

Ralph and Volney McNall, better known as Brownie, had mowed away a load of hay during the morning, and each had been given fifteen cents for his work. Rate figured it was a fair amount since it hadn't taken him and Brownie all that long to finish the job. One had worked on the wagon, the other in the mow.

Both boys had gone home for dinner, but now they were headed north out of town. Each had a bright new cane pole resting on his shoulder. The fifteen cents had been more than enough to purchase the equipped pole, so each lad chomped on a piece of stick candy as they sauntered along. They were going fishing for bullheads under the railroad bridge.

"Did ya notice who's comin' our way?" asked Brownie as they passed the last house on the street.

"Ralph Boone. I'd know his walk anywhere. Wonder where he's been."

The lad in question was coming across an open pasture field at an angle. He walked swiftly as though in a hurry. Boone was almost a head taller than Rate, heavy in the shoulders, and was noted for his strength. By comparison, both Brownie and Rate looked small and weak.

"Hard to tell. Wherever it was, bet he was up to no good."

"Ever notice how he's usually by himself? Guess no one likes him much. Can't say as I blame 'em any."

"Hey, Boone, where ya been? Robbing some little old lady?" called Brownie.

Even at this distance, the boys could see Boone bristle at those words. He clenched his fists as he strode to meet them.

"Rate, there's two o' us an' only one o' him. Let's clean his clock."

"Good idea. I owe him. Thought I'd wait till I was big enough to do the job myself, but today suits me fine."

"You two callin' me a thief?"

"Naw. We're just callin' ya a bully. Figgered some little old lady would be more your style than someone your own size," volunteered Brownie.

"Take that back."

"What for? You gonna make me?"

Brownie laid his pole off to one side where Rate had already placed his.

"What's the matter, Boone? Scared?" taunted Rate.

"Of you two? I could lick both of you with one arm tied behind my back," he bragged.

"Prove it," dared Brownie, putting up his fists.

Boone threw caution to the wind and moved to hit Brownie. The lad ducked, and Boone's fist only caught his shoulder. Before Boone realized what was happening, Rate's fist caught him in his eye with enough force to snap his head back. Now, Boone roared his anger. Since he only picked on those smaller than himself, he did not know how to cope when the odds were against him. He had never learned any finesse, had always depended on brute force to overpower an adversary.

He dove at Rate, carrying him to the ground, but Rate got in another punch as they fell. Boone's nose started to bleed. He hit Rate on the chin, but by then, Brownie was on his back raining blows on his head. The boys rolled over and over on the ground. Boone was flailing out in desperation, most of his punches going wild. The other two were more calculating. He was definitely getting the worst of the deal.

Finally, the big boy struggled free and lurched to his feet. He started to run blindly toward town.

"What's the matter, Boone? Can't fight no more?" shouted Brownie derisively.

"Always knew you were yella at heart," yelled Rate.

Boone stopped and looked back at the two boys; his nose was still bleeding, both eyes looked as if they might turn black, and one was definitely swelling; he had other scrapes and bruises on his face.

"I'll remember this. I'll get even. Just you see," he threatened.

"You an' who else? Wait'll we tell the fellas how well you fight," laughed Rate.

"Boy, I don't know when I've ever seen anyone so mad. Think he'll try to catch us alone," asked Brownie, a worried frown on his face. Given Boone's size and reputation, it was a sobering thought.

"Naw. He's all bluff. He'll get razzed so much about this, he'll think twice about comin' after anyone. Bet he won't be seein' out of that eye for the next couple o' days," said Rate with a satisfied chuckle.

Both boys picked up their poles and continued on their way as though nothing had happened.

That night at the supper table, Millie noted the bruise on Rate's chin and a scratch on his cheek.

"Been fighting today?"

"Sort of," Rate admitted.

"Who with?"

"Ralph Boone."

"You tackled him by yourself?" asked Millie, surprise in his voice. He knew Boone was taller and heavier than his son.

"Naw. I'm still too small, but Brownie McNall and I showed him a thing or two.

Guess this partly pays him for shovin' me down the stairs that time." Millie nodded his head in agreement.

Miney looked first at her son, then at her husband. No need for her to say anything because neither would listen. Ralph's voice contained an unmistakable note of pride when he explained to his father how badly the Boone boy had come off.

Fighting was something Miney would never be able to understand. She'd like to impress upon Ralph that fists were not a way to settle a problem, but with Millie there to egg him on, her words would fall on deaf ears. There were just some things about men that Miney realized she would never, never understand.

Elsie, although a small village, was certainly a thriving one. They even boasted of having a shooting gallery owned by Frank Johnson. Frank was a mail carrier, but there were several routes out of Elsie, so it required no more than half a day to run his route. Therefore, immediately after dinner, Frank could be found at his business establishment on the south side of Main Street just over half a block to the east of the four corners.

A gasoline engine provided the power to move the targets which were in the form of ducks, geese, and deer. Besides the moving targets, there were large and small still targets, clay pipes, and hanging targets which Frank set in motion by hand. The rifles provided used .22 shorts. A thick steel plate in back of the targets kept the bullets from being a danger to anyone.

Frank offered three shots for a nickel. A prominently displayed sign stated that if anyone was lucky enough to ring a bell with his shot, that person received three free shots. Of course, the bell was attached to only two or three of the more difficult targets.

For the most part, Frank didn't have to give free shots very often.

Ralph and Curly Sherman had begun spending one or two Saturday afternoons a month at the gallery. Shortly after Rate had received his rifle, he had gone there, but Frank had tried to discourage him by saying he was too young. Ralph had argued and cajoled until Frank had let him try his luck. The lad had hit a stationary target, but had missed his attempts at a moving target. Rate had figured he'd practice, and the next time he'd do better. This had been almost two years ago.

Ralph and Curly were on their way down Main Street. Each boy had a little spending money, so the first place they headed was Frank Johnson's shooting gallery.

As they stepped in the door, they heard, "Oh, no, not you two." Frank gave them a weak grin as he sadly shook his head.

"Hello, Frank," they chirruped.

"Let's see. Both of you are broke," he said hopefully.

"Aw, Frank, ya know you're glad to see us. Ain't we your best customers?" asked Don with an impish grin.

"That's right, Frank. Bet we're more regular than anyone else in town," said Rate with a little chuckle.

"Suppose that's true," he acknowledged.

"Then act like you're glad to see us and set 'em up. Me an' Rate, we're expectin' to have a little fun."

"At my expense," grumbled Frank.

Both boys laughed as they each gave him a nickel and picked out the rifle they intended to use. Frank loaded each rifle with three cartridges and handed it back. He started the engine and threw the lever which set the targets in motion.

The rifles cracked, targets tipped, and two bells rang.

Don and Rate laughed and nudged each other; their complete confidence showed as they presented their rifles to Frank for him to reload. They delighted in the fact that the next three shots cost them nothing.

Frank set up a row of clay pipes. Rate took the first two and Don took the next two; then, they both hit a target which they knew would ring a bell.

"Whyn't you boys have a heart? Soon's I set up these clay pipes, you jest come along an' break 'em," complained Mr. Johnson as he set up a new batch. "Aincha got no other place to go?"

"Now, Frank, look at the advertising you get. I've heard some say that your rifles are rigged so no one can win. When they see us using different rifles for each round, they know just how honest you really are." Rate gave the man an engaging grin.

"Humph. Don't see no one here now, do you?"

"Not this very minute," Curly conceded, "but he's right, Frank. Don't we often have a bunch standin' around watching?"

"That's jest because they enjoy seein' me get took. Especially by a couple o' brash teenagers."

"Quit bellyachin'. You're the one who made the rules," laughed Don.

"Never expected a couple o' younguns like you could be so lucky. Ain't none of my other patrons who can ring a bell more than once or twice a session. If all my customers was like you, I'd go out of business."

The boys laughed at his displeasure. They stayed for the better part of an hour, shooting regularly, but the only money they spent was the initial nickel apiece.

"Well, Frank, guess it's time for us to mosey on," said Ralph.

"Aincha gonna miss us?" asked Curly, a devilish expression on his face.

"Like a hole in my head. No offense, boys, but don't hurry back. You already cost me a day's wages."

Frank watched them go with mixed feelings. Sometimes, he doubted if he broke even when those two showed up. Certainly was a good thing more of his patrons weren't as accurate as those two scalawags. Still, they were a good-natured pair, and he admitted he liked both of them. He wondered how much practicing they did each week. Bet they went through a lot of ammunition. He remembered when Rate was only twelve or so, he'd not been very good. A couple of years sure had made a difference. They were a mouthy pair, never without a quick answer; yet, he admitted, they were not really disrespectful.

Rate realized summer was passing quickly. Sure had been a fun one for the most part. Just last week, Curly Sherman, Rollie Swarthout, and George Naegle had gone with him to Owosso to the Ringling Brothers, three-ring circus. It was the first time his parents had let him go to something that far away with a group of his friends. Getting older certainly had its advantages.

Ralph had thoroughly enjoyed the circus; however, he felt there was too much to watch all at the same time. He was used to the little, one-ring circus which came every year to Elsie, and he felt a degree of loyalty for the Silver family. Still, the big circus had had a lot more acts, grander costumes, and just fancier trappings all around. The big top had been gigantic. The acrobats and the aerialists had been something to watch all right. He had liked the jugglers and the animal acts.

Rate had been pleased because his parents had allowed him to go. Some of the time they could be mighty nice. He guessed they realized he was growing up. Course Pa was not often the one to tell him he couldn't do something; Ma was the worrier of the family, always afraid he'd get hurt. Of course, he must admit there had been a lot of minor scrapes, and that cut from Pearl's newly shod hoof had been no picnic for her. Still, he'd never had any broken bones. The way he saw it, Ma hadn't had all that much to worry about.

CHAPTER 17

For some time now, Millie had been keeping an eye out for a mate for Pearl. Millie was one that liked his teams to be a matched pair; they looked much nicer, and Millie took great pride in his horses. Via the grapevine, he heard that the hardware dealer in Oakley, a man named Eagan, had a mare the same size and color as Pearl. Oakley was a far piece, but Millie figured it would be worth the trip if he got the mare.

Millie and Rate drove to Oakley, contacted Eagen, and bought the mare. Millie had been prepared to haggle over the price, but the man had asked $150 which seemed reasonable enough. Millie had looked her over and found her sound. Her teeth said she was an eight-year-old. She was a bargain.

It was already past noon, so Rate and Millie went to the only restaurant to get themselves a meal before starting for home.

At first, Millie was going to drive the new mare, Gyp by name, but then he changed his mind. He decided they'd drive Pearl and put Gyp on a lead at the back of the open buggy.

All was going well. Both horses trotted effortlessly. They were overtaking a buggy traveling at a snail's pace ahead of them. Just as Rate pulled out to pass, something on the top of the buggy ahead flapped in a gust of wind.

Gyp went wild.

She jerked on her lead rope, then came forward and jumped, her front feet landed in the back of the buggy. Pearl, hearing the commotion behind, began to plunge and kick; she backed up, nearly throwing Gyp to the ground which only frightened the mare more. It seemed as though one horse was going one way, one the other. If they kept this up, it would be a miracle if one or both didn't break a leg. Ralph expected the thills of the buggy to break at any moment.

Millie managed to jump from the buggy, and dodging flailing hooves, grabbed Gyp's rope. At the same time, Ralph fought to calm Pearl and bring her under control. The back of the buggy went off the road, into the shallow ditch, and both Ralph and Millie heard the crunch of breaking wood.

As if the sound had been a signal, both horses quieted. Pearl behaved as though nothing unusual had happened. Gyp was covered with nervous sweat, but she was at least manageable now.

Several spokes on the rear wheel of the buggy had been broken and would have to be replaced. Ralph walked back to Oakley to find someone who could make the repairs.

It was long past suppertime when Millie and Ralph finally arrived back in Elsie. There had been no other incident although Gyp remained skittish and nervous.

Mina had kept their supper warm although she was becoming increasingly anxious as the time passed. Millie was just never late for meals. She had felt mightily relieved when they trooped into the kitchen.

Long after supper, Rate could hear his parents talking. He was busy reading, so he didn't pay much attention. Then, when he got up to go upstairs, he heard his father's voice.

"My Godfrey Jones, Miney, but I wish I could wake up in the morning and find that mare dead. She's like a stick of dynamite with a short fuse." Millie sighed audibly, and Rate noted the discouraged tone in his father's voice. It wasn't often Millie sounded so depressed.

Ralph couldn't hear his mother's reply, but he knew his mother would be thinking of all the money that was wasted buying a horse which Millie was reluctant to drive. Ma often failed to understand things except in terms of money.

How right Millie was in his appraisal of Gyp. She was wild. Ed Hawes and Truman Armstrong took her to the livery stable to try to use her. They always had to hook her up with a jerk rope if they were to control her at all. They dared not drive her single. If anything went wrong, or if something unusual happened, she'd try to get away. By now, Millie realized why Eagen had sold her so cheaply.

So much for having a mate for Pearl. It no longer seemed important.

Don Sherman's parents had moved from their farm on the Ridge Road to a farm just north of the cemetery. Rate decided that if he had to live in Elsie, he was glad Sherman's had moved. He saw more of Don now that he didn't live all that far away. Of course, most of the time Pa had no objection to him taking

Pearl, but if Ma wanted the buggy, then he had to walk. Besides, sometimes he and Don arranged to meet elsewhere if they were going fishing or hunting.

It was a Friday night, and Don had driven into town. They'd visited with several boys, played some cards, thought about visiting the card parlor and pool hall, and just generally had a good time being with friends.

Ralph was spending the night with Don, and the moon was already far into its nightly course when the boys headed home. When they reached the millpond, Don drew in the horse a moment as they gazed at the moonlight rippling on the water. It was a quiet, serene scene.

"Look, Rate. Over there. A flock of ducks. See 'em?"

"Maybe you're right. They're in the shadows, Curly, so it's kinda hard to tell."

"What say we go get some guns an' have us some duck to eat?"

"Sounds good, Curly. Think they'll be here when we get back?"

"Sure. They won't leave till dawn."

"Guess you're right. Okay. Let's try it."

Curly spoke to the horse, and they were once more on their way, up the slope to turn the corner by the cemetery. They pulled into Sherman's yard, and while Don went quietly into the house to get a couple of shotguns, Rate stayed in the buggy holding the lines; the horse knew this was home and kept attempting to move toward the barn.

Curly was back as silently as he had gone. He turned the horse around and headed back for the bridge.

"See, they're still there," said Don.

"You sure those are ducks?" asked Ralph as he tried to peer more closely into the shadows.

"Course I'm sure. We'll shoot a couple o' times, then we'll wait for the current to carry 'em to the shallow water by the dam."

Both boys shot where they thought they'd be the most likely to hit one or two ducks. They returned the shotguns to the buggy and scrambled down the bank to the river. They slipped out of their shoes, rolled up their pantlegs, and waited patiently.

Several minutes elapsed, but no ducks came floating down the river.

"Rate, don't it seem like we should have seen a duck by now?"

"Yup. Maybe they caught on the dam. I'll take a look."

Ralph moved upriver to peer more closely where the water fell over the edge of the dam. There'd been ample rain of late and the water was higher than it was some years this late in the summer. No, nothing was caught here.

After waiting a little longer, the boys gave up and went home.

Early the next morning, they were back, hoping to find the ducks still there. They heard no telltale quacking as they stole closer. Finally, they could see the river, but no ducks floated on the quiet water.

"Don't that beat all? Rate, I know we're here early enough. Where'd those damned ducks go?"

"Maybe there weren't any."

"Whadaya mean? I saw 'em. So'd you."

"We saw what we thought were ducks. They were in the shadows. I know I couldn't see all that well, an' neither could you."

"We saw somethin'. You'll have to agree to that."

"Yes, but I don't think it was ducks. Look." Rate pointed close to the bank a little upriver from where they stood. "I think that's our ducks."

"Well, glory be. You might be right," conceded Curly.

An old stump floated in the water, bottom side up, its roots spread wide. Here and there, a piece of root protruded from the water; a dark object which in the darkness might have resembled a duck. The stump was caught on something, so it was quite stationary except for a gentle bobbing up and down.

"That's a good one on us. Imagine. Shooting at an old stump," said Don with a chuckle. He shook his head as though he found it hard to believe they had done this.

"At least no harm's done. Guess after this, we'd better do our shooting in daylight when we can see what we're shooting at."

Don nodded his head in agreement. Still, he'd been awful certain last night.

Frank Clement had a shoe repair shop and a gun shop on the east side of Ovid Street. Rate passed it every time he went up town for his mother. He often stopped in to chat. He liked Frank. The man was quite a story teller, and he was also known to distort the truth a smidgen. Because of his stories, Frank was popular with the kids, and he always had a kid or two hanging around the shop. During the school year, they stopped in after school.

Miney wasn't quite taken with the man because she knew he was often careless how he handled the truth--she hesitated to say he was an out and out liar. However, because of this quality, she strongly disapproved of Ralph's friendship with the man. On more than one occasion, she had voiced this disapproval, but she realized that nothing she had said thus far had kept Ralph from frequent visits.

Rate came into the gun shop, letting the screen door bang behind him.

"Hiya, Frank."

Frank looked up from a rifle he was working on.

"Afternoon, Rate. What brings you by?"

"Nuthin' special. Didn't have anything better to do."

As Rate watched the man replace the trigger guard, he told Frank about shooting at the tree stump. Frank had a good laugh. He always had a good sense of humor; this was one of the characteristics Ralph liked about him. Frank was always fun.

"Haven't seen you since I went fishin' last week, have I?"

"Nope. Have any luck?"

"Sure did. Caught a nice mess o' bluegill, but that wasn't the best part. I done caught me a bass this big." He measured off at least three feet.

Ralph laughed before he said, "Frank, if it was that long, it sure wasn't no bass. Sure you know your fish?"

"Well, maybe it was only this long." He measured off about twenty inches, his eyes alight with good humor.

"More likely it was like this," said Rate, holding his hands a foot apart.

"Maybe it just felt that big. Sure did put up a fight. Ever been bass fishin'?"

"Nope. Haven't ever been to a lake. Do all my fishin' in the river and at the creek north of town."

"Someday, I'll have to take you. Bet you'd like bringing in a good bass."

Frank had moved to the back of the shop where he sighted guns. He placed the rifle in a vice, put up a new target in front of a container of sand which had a steel plate behind it. He looked down the barrel, adjusted the vice, then fired the gun. He then checked to see where his shot had gone. The gun was shooting off-center and down to the left.

"I'm not as good at this as I used to be. Eyesight isn't good enough."

"Whyn't you let me do it for you."

"Think you could?"

"Don't know why not. There's nothin' wrong with my eyesight. Just ask Frank Johnson if you don't believe me," added Rate with a grin.

Frank laughed at this.

"Seems I've heard tell how you and that Sherman boy keep Frank outta clay pipes. Maybe you *could* do this if I showed you how."

Frank showed Rate how to adjust the sight. They fired the rifle a few more times, adjusting the sight each time. When Ralph was finished, the gun would hit the bull's eye every time. Frank told him he had a natural knack for working on a gun. Ralph beamed.

Frank's praise was warmly received. This sure was some different from working for Pa. Frank tried to pay him, but Rate declined the offer. Frank ended by saying, "I know you don't own a shotgun, but if you ever want to use one, I'll have one you can borrow, an' I'll provide the shells. Deal?"

"Deal."

The offer pleased Ralph greatly. He didn't often need a shotgun, but once in a while he liked to go rabbit hunting in the winter, and sometimes, he liked to see if he could rid the countryside of a few pesky crows. He knew Frank would keep his end of the bargain.

Even though Millie now had a partner in the butcher shop, he and Walt had continued to let Ralph try out the tallow, and they still gave him the bones. Rate figured this was because trying out tallow wasn't a great job, the pay was small for the time spent, and he figured neither his pa nor Walt had wanted to do the work. Rate always scorched it a little, but Aberly, the hide man, was generous and gave him top price anyway.

Millie spread and salted the cow hides to preserve them, and when he had a stack of hides about three or four feet tall, he would give Aberly a call. Besides the hides and tallow, the man bought the bones too.

This time, there was a huge pile of legs and heads. Rate and the man were good-naturedly haggling over the price when the man made him an offer.

"Rate, I've got a single harness here. It's in right good shape. An' take a look at the bridle. Ain't them rosettes pretty?" The man held up a bridle. The rosettes had the Odd Fellow emblem under the curved glass.

Golly, Pa was an Odd Fellow. The harness looked nearly new. Pearl's harness didn't look this good.

"I dunno, Mr. Aberly. That's a big pile o' bones."

"I know. That's why I offered to trade. This ain't no cheap harness, an' thet bridle is wuth as much as the harness. Whadaya say?"

Rate thought a moment, his eyebrows drawn together. Then, his face broke into a smile.

"I'll take 'em. Sure hope Pa thinks I made a good trade."

When Millie looked over the harness and bridle, he nodded his head with satisfaction. The boy had done quite well, but Millie failed to tell him so. He merely said, "'Pears to me it's a good harness. Think it might be better than the one we use on Pearl. 'Spec that's why you wanted it?"

"Yup. Intend to use it on Pearl all right."

Millie nodded and left; as usual, his feelings were carefully bottled inside. No need to give the boy the big-head.

Golly darn. Pa didn't act like he'd made a good swap. Wonder why. There was just no figgerin' Pa out. Well, whether Pa thought he'd done well or not, Rate figured it was a good deal. Bet Pearl would look right smart in her new harness.

Horatio and Lovina hadn't stayed long in Stockbridge. They now lived on Madbury Street in Detroit, and much to Miney's chagrin, Lovina wrote to Blanche regularly. It wasn't the idea that Blanche received letters from her grandmother which bothered Miney, it was their content. Each letter made some mention of the fact that Lovina thought a large city a much more exciting place for a young woman to live. While she made no mention of Gerd Pershing, the young man Blanche saw on a regular basis, she often spoke of some "nice young man" she had just met who was Blanche's age. This made Miney fume. She knew that her interfering mother-in-law was doing her darndest to get Blanche married off. Of course, anyone Miney liked would scarcely meet Lovina's approval.

Whether it was because of Lovina's persistent letters, or whether Blanche herself decided she wanted a change, Blanche gave Mr. Netzorg notice, and made plans to move to Detroit. Once more Miney's world toppled. Her resentment of Lovina grew, but for once, she kept her thoughts to herself. Blanche could be as stubborn as Lovina, and Miney did not by word or deed want to alienate her daughter.

Sometimes, Miney felt she understood Blanche less and less as the years passed. Miney would have found it difficult to meet the public each day clerking in a store, but Blanche enjoyed the work. She said it presented a challenge. She liked to see how many sales she could make each day.

The whole family went to the train station to see Blanche off. Rate was taken completely by surprise when his sister gave him a big hug. Blanche was all right. He guessed he'd miss her. Now that they were older, she no longer tattled on him. She even knew he was learning to play pool, but she hadn't breathed one word to Ma.

He wondered how Gerd was taking this. Gerd had come by the house last night, and Rate had thought he looked like he'd lost his last friend, but Blanche hadn't seemed to notice. She was so excited about moving to Detroit, she had failed to notice that not everyone was pleased. Rate knew Ma was upset, but in her euphoria, Blanche hadn't noticed that either.

Miney waited impatiently for Blanche's first letter. When it came, she told them she had a job at Crowley's. She was finding city life exciting.

Miney carefully reread the letter. She guessed she would have to accept the fact that Blanche was not cut out for life on a farm or in a small village. Miney felt Lovina was to blame for this. That woman filled Blanche's head with all sorts of notions. It was as though Lovina felt Blanche belonged to her, not Miney; but of course, it had been that way from the moment of her birth. Mother Setterington had always interfered. If only Millie had had some backbone where his mother was concerned. But he hadn't. It was too late now to change anything. She would just have to learn to live with it and hope Blanche came home for visits.

This was another election year. The Republicans had met in Chicago to nominate Secretary of War, William H. Taft of Ohio. The Democrats once again nominated William Jennings Bryan.

As the campaign began in earnest, Millie read the excerpts from speeches made by both candidates which were printed in the Owosso paper.

"Maybe I won't bother to vote this year," he said to his wife.

"Why not? You always have before. At least since you went through all that rigamarole of taking out your citizenship."

The first time Millie had tried to vote, he had been required to fill out a form which asked where he had been born. When it was noted that he had been born in Canada, he was told he was not a U.S. citizen; therefore, he was not eligible to vote. Millie had assumed that since he was only two when he came here, he was a citizen. Horatio had renounced his allegiance to Queen Victoria, but had never taken out citizenship papers. No one bothered to ask Millie where his mother had been born. Since Lovina had been born in the United States and had never given up her citizenship, Millie was automatically a citizen. Millie was not aware of this, so he did as he was told, and finally, on the fifth of November, 1892, he officially became a citizen of the United States.

"This time, I'm not *for* either candidate. We've had too many years with the Republicans in the presidency."

"But Millie, you supported both McKinley and Roosevelt."

"I know. Seemed the right thing to do at the time. But it don't pay to have one party in power for such a long spell. They get where they forget who voted them into office. I just wish the Democrats could have come up with someone other than Bryan. That man is a born loser. Seems like there should be a Democrat somewhere who'd have made a likelier candidate."

Millie turned back to his paper, and Miney knew he was finished speaking. No use to ask him questions because he'd be likely to ignore them. She didn't pretend to understand politics. Women did not have the right to vote; therefore, what she thought of a political candidate made no difference. Still, it was not like Millie to want change in anything. She wondered what had made him decide they needed a change in the White House. Goodness, there were times when

Millie was more complicated than usual. He must have his reasons, but she'd wager she'd never learn what they were.

School started, and once more Ralph felt it restricted his activities. He usually went to school-sponsored parties, and he watched the weekly football games. However, football was not his sport. He'd much rather have been playing baseball.

Ralph was on his way up town for his mother. He decided there was no particular hurry, so he stopped at the gun shop to see Frank. After exchanging a few words, Frank reached up to take a .22 Savage repeater from where it hung on the wall. He tossed the rifle to Ralph who deftly caught it in midair.

"What do you think of this one, Rate?"

Ralph noticed the clip wasn't in, so he hefted the gun, put it up to his shoulder, brought it down to look at it more carefully.

"Not bad, Frank, not bad."

He raised the gun as though drawing a bead on a target and snapped it off. To his surprise and horror, the gun fired! A shell had been left in the chamber. The bullet hit a metal plate, ricocheted, narrowly missing Frank, and struck the clock on the wall, taking a nick out of it but not damaging the works.

"Jeepers, Frank, I'm--I'm sorry. I checked for the clip. Honest. I never dreamt there was anything in the chamber." The lad was visibly shaken, his face several shades paler than normal.

"It's all right, Rate. It was my fault. I should have checked it when I took out the clip. Guess we've both learned a lesson. Never assume a gun's empty unless you've checked it yourself."

"Like Pa's always sayin' 'bout experience teaching a dear school. Well, guess I was the fool today. I can tell you, it won't happen again. I've learned my lesson," Ralph stated emphatically.

Frank took the rifle and hung it back on the wall. Rate noticed the man's hands were trembling, but he said nothing. Ralph felt that his own were none too steady. It had been a sobering experience. What if he had killed Frank by his carelessness? He'd make certain there was never another time. For as long as he'd been handling guns, he should have known better. He was glad Frank didn't hold it against him. He'd hate it like the dickens if Frank didn't want him around.

CHAPTER 18

Blanche's letter upset Miney. Blanche had quit her job at Crowley's because Mac, Miney's brother-in-law, had not thought Crowley's was a good place for her to work. After all, it wasn't a prestigious store; he considered it run-of-the-mill. It made no difference that Blanche had been satisfied with her work and had liked her fellow workers.

Mac had been instrumental in getting her a job he considered much more suitable. As a result, Blanche was now working at Siegel's, a spiffy woman's store. That would have been all right except Blanche hated it. They catered to the wealthy, and Blanche found many of these women haughty and filled with their own importance which made them completely obnoxious to the young girl. Blanche had never learned to tolerate anyone who put on airs.

When would her in-laws quit interfering in her daughter's life? Miney felt terribly resentful although it did her not one mite of good. She hated to think her daughter was even a tiny bit unhappy. From the time Blanche was a small child, her happiness had been at the top of Miney's list. She realized she had never been that concerned about Ralph's happiness. Of course, Ralph had never been one to complain, or share many of his thoughts with her for that matter; thus, she rationalized that she seldom knew if something made Ralph unhappy.

Blanche had always been vocal about her feelings. She had often criticized her grandmother's domineering ways, but that had not stopped her from moving to Detroit. Miney found this difficult to understand. Personally, she liked being as far away from Lovina as possible. The older Ruby got, the more she was like her mother, so Miney was glad to be shed of them both. Even Ruby's daughter was becoming a pain the older she got. Couldn't rightly blame the girl. It was the influence of Lovina, thought Miney a little maliciously.

A few weeks later, Miney felt vastly relieved when she received a cheery letter from Blanche stating she had quit her job at Siegel's and now worked in the notion department at Hudson's. She explained that it was ever so much nicer working there. Besides, Aunt Ruby had a girl Blanche's age staying with her, and she and Blanche were having a very good time together. The tone of the letter left Miney with ambivalent feelings. She was relieved because Blanche sounded so happy, but she felt sad because she knew the odds against Blanche ever returning to Elsie to live were enormous.

Election day came, and the country proved that once again Bryan was a loser.

Millie had not gone to the polls, but had reiterated his opinion that neither candidate deserved his vote. He said he wasn't sure the country was ready for four more years of Republicanism. However, Millie's pessimistic outlook was countered by his what will be, will be, philosophy.

There was more than just a nip to the air, and there had been a few snowflakes during the early morning. It was enough to remind everyone cold weather was just around the corner. Miney discovered she dreaded the thoughts of winter more each year--a sure sign she was getting older. She always hated it when the first killing frost left her late-blooming flowers on stiff, dried stems. Spring, when she could enjoy her garden, seemed a long way off.

Claude Conklin often did custom butchering for farmers or villagers. Instead of his customers bringing the animal they intended to slaughter to him, he traveled to their home. Once in a while, he asked Rate to help him with some butchering.

Claude had run into Rate on Thursday night after school.

"Rate. How about helping me butcher a beef come Saturday?"

"Sure. Where 'bouts?"

"Herb Putman wants one butchered. Shouldn't take too long. Thought we'd do it early in the morning. We'd be back afore noon."

Herb Putman lived about a mile north of the farm where Rate had been born. Dressing out a beef wouldn't take all that long if Herb had the critter in the barn waiting for them. Sometimes, farmers turned the cattle out for a spell in the morning while they cleaned stables, and they often never thought to keep the one to be slaughtered in the barn. Occasionally, the beast was easy to entice back into the barn, but more often than not, they were nothing but trouble. Around the stable, cattle were wary of strangers to begin with, so they couldn't see the door of the barn even though it stood wide open. It was always exasperating attempting to coax the animal back where it belonged. Well, maybe Herb would be ready for them this time.

Luck was with them. Herb had the animal tied on the barn floor. Claude handed Rate the rifle saying, "I'll give you the honors. You're a better shot than I am."

The cow stood immobile although she watched Ralph suspiciously. He took careful aim and fired. She stood a moment as if nothing had happened, then crumpled slowly to the floor. Claude moved quickly to slit her throat, the blood soaking the chaff on the cement floor. A block and tackle was rigged and her hind legs impaled at the large joint on the sharpened ends of a heavy, rounded piece of oak, smooth and shiny from years of use. Both Rate and Claude knew just what to do as they began skinning the animal; they pulled her higher and higher to keep the work area at a comfortable level while they systematically worked quickly with no lost motions.

The carcass swung just as Rate slit her open further to pull the large paunch out of the abdominal cavity.

"Damn!"

"What's wrong?" asked Claude.

"Nothin' much. I nicked myself a little on the shin. Nothin' to worry about. One thing about you, Claude, you always carry a sharp set of knives."

"Guess maybe I *am* more particular than some. Makes the job easier."

The two worked well together. The heart, liver, and tongue were placed in a large pail; the innards were shoved to one side; the head and legbones were tossed to a couple of dogs who began to growl at each other even though they had plenty to share. The carcass was sawed in half from the tailbone through the neck. It now hung in two halves where it would age for ten days or so before being cut up to can.

"One o' you want the tongue?" asked Herb. Rate looked at Claude who shook his head.

"Sure, I'll take it," said Rate.

A tongue wasn't worth much. Sometimes, Pa gave one to a good customer, but Rate really liked them. Since Pa had a partner at the meat market, he didn't bring near as much home now. Guess maybe he and Walt sort of divided up these parts that were near worthless or else they used them to promote better customer relations.

Rate's cut had bled only a little, and he had shrugged it off as nothing to cause any concern. His mother hadn't ever known of the incident because he hadn't wanted her fussing. It seemed to him she had been worse since Blanche was in Detroit. He guessed probably that was because she missed her daughter, and Ma was happiest when she was fussing over someone. At least it seemed that way to him.

The first of the week, Millie decided that come Saturday, they'd bring the sheep home from the south forty. His renter would take care of them during the winter months for a share of the spring crop of lambs. Millie told Ralph to make no plans since it would take both of them to get the sheep rounded up and headed for home. Once on the road, the older ones would realize where they were going, and the younger ones would follow their lead.

It turned cold the latter part of the week, and Saturday morning dawned bright and frosty. It had been a cloudless night, and the temperature had dropped to single digits. Frost clung to the trees where it sparkled in the rays of the rising sun.

Since they would be driving Pearl, Rate was the one to harness her. When he came to put on the bridle, he dipped the bit into a pail of water to take the frost out of the metal so the mare's tongue wouldn't stick to the bit. If it hadn't been so cold, he could have cupped his hands around the bit and blown on it; the warmth of his breath would have warmed it sufficiently. However, this morning, he was taking no chances since it was so cold.

Actually, Rate didn't mind the cold. He had begun wearing his winter underwear a few weeks ago. His thick woolen stockings kept his feet warm. A stocking cap was pulled over his ears, meeting the collar of his heavy coat and he wore lined gloves. No wind stirred the glistening branches. Rate felt complete contentment as he and his father left the village.

They drove directly to the south forty. No one had lived here since Millie, Miney, and Rate had spent one summer here. Millie had been talking of selling the place, but thus far, it had been nothing but talk.

As usual, the main part of the flock rounded up easily enough, but there were always one or two stragglers who were determined to go off on their own.

Ralph chased a couple of young ewes around the old granary. Those darned sheep were as nimble as goats. Ralph pursued them over a pile of junk, barking his shin in the process. He had no more chased them back to the main body of the flock when two more made a dash for the farthest corner of the pasture. By the time Rate had them back where they belonged, he was winded.

He watched as the bell weather swung into the road behaving as though she knew exactly where she was going; the rest of the flock fell in behind, content to follow her lead.

Millie and Rate headed for the buggy to follow, hoping there would be no stragglers to chase down.

Something about his son caught Millie's eye.

"Boy, you're bleeding to death," he said quietly, a frown creasing his face. "What happened?" He pointed to Rate's leg.

Ralph looked down at his right leg--the one he'd cut last week--and noted his sock and shoe were covered with bright, frozen blood.

"Golly, Pa, I didn't feel anything. I don't know when it happened."

"Get in the rig. I'll drop you off at Clark's where Lena can tend you until I get these sheep taken care of. Had you hurt that leg before?"

Rate told his father about last Saturday. Millie said nothing, only nodded his head with understanding. He felt concern, but none of this showed. Besides, it wasn't likely to be as bad as it seemed at the moment.

Lena hadn't known what to do. She'd put a bandage over the cut, but it had still bled in spite of her efforts, and the bandage was soon soaked. Even pressure helped only as long as it was being applied.

Millie came back as quickly as possible. He helped Rate into the buggy and they headed for town. He propped Rate's leg out straight, hoping this would help stem the flow. Millie didn't like the pallor of Rate's face, but he said nothing. No need to alarm the lad. Pearl needed no urging to set a fast pace, and for once, Millie let her have her head.

When he reached the house, he stopped in front instead of going across the street to the barn. When Ralph climbed out of the buggy, he crumpled to the ground.

"Pa, I can't stand up. My--my knees are like water."

Without a word, Millie scooped his son up in his arms and strode to the door. Miney had noticed their arrival and opened the door as Millie reached it with his burden.

"Land sakes, Millie, what's wrong?"

Call Doc Beale immediately. Rate's bleedin' from a cut on the leg. Tell Doc to hurry. There's no time to waste."

Miney had never heard such a tone in Millie's voice. The note of urgency was there, but there was also something else--fear. Millie laid Ralph on the couch while Miney ran to the phone on the kitchen wall. She prayed the doctor would be in.

They were in luck, and within a short time, the doctor arrived, little black bag in hand. He clucked to himself as he removed the sodden bandage Lena had put on Rate's leg. A whimper came from Miney, and her face blanched--she was almost as white as Ralph. Blood still flowed from the small cut.

When Dr. Beale was finished stitching, the flow had stopped, and blood barely oozed from between the stitches. Rate watched as the doctor placed a bandage on the leg. He hoped this healed better than the last cut, the one where Pearl had struck his leg with her shod hoof. The doctor hadn't even bothered to wash his hands before he worked on Rate's leg, so the lad was rightly skeptical. Rate hadn't thought the man's hands were any too clean; there was dirt under his fingernails. Ma would have scrubbed her hands before touching a wound of any kind. He guessed Ma was just a lot more persnickety than a man.

Miney was more upset than she let anyone know. Ralph's deathly pallor cut deeply. Why was he always getting himself hurt? Sometimes, she wondered if he would live to be a man. In contrast to Ralph, Blanche had been no trouble at all. Except for her asthma, she was healthy as a horse. She'd never had another attack of appendicitis, and because she had been in Chicago when it occurred, Miney seldom remembered it. Blanche had had her share of the childhood diseases, but they had never been severe. Thank heavens for Blanche. Miney wasn't at all certain she could have coped with two like Ralph. Still, Pa had always said the Lord never sent us more than we could bear. She told herself that her father was right, but there were fleeting moments of doubt.

Rate was still weak by Monday. Miney had made him spend his time on the couch. She fed him carefully, giving him what she considered especially nourishing food which was easily digested. Rate chafed under her coddling although he did not voice his thoughts. From her behavior, he guessed his mother did love him. It was just that she loved Blanche a whoppin' bit more.

This had been some experience. Rate realized he must have lost a lot of blood and that was why he had been so weak. Golly, Pa had carried him almost as easily as when he was a child. He bet some men would have needed help. Because of his weakness, Ralph gave some thought to death. He guessed bleeding to death would be an easy way to go.

As Ralph had feared, the cut was slow to heal and proud flesh appeared at one end. However, the first time the proud flesh was burned off took care of the matter, and the leg healed. At least he had only missed a couple of days of school. He was sure thankful for that. It was bad enough to do his work daily, but having to catch up was for the birds.

Ralph was in the kitchen and overheard his father talking to his mother. "Miney, I just don't think Old Mikey is going to winter through."

"What do you intend to do?"

"I'm not sure. Would you like a robe?"

Miney had a strange look on her face, and she eyed her husband a moment before answering.

"Somehow, it just doesn't seem right. Old Mikey has been so faithful, would it be right to skin him?"

Just then, Ralph came in, a determined look on his face.

"You're not gonna skin Old Mikey. I'd hate seeing his hide as a robe." He would have said more, but Millie interrupted.

"Haven't said one way or the tuther. No need to get your dander up. We could use a good robe. Look at it this way, would you rather have a robe or have his hide go with the carcass to God knows where? Or perhaps you'd rather bury him and have it rot away in the ground. Those are your options. Which are you going to choose?"

Ralph had no answer for his father. He turned and left.

"My, that boy sure sets a store on that horse, don't he?"

"Yes, Millie, Ralph has a great liking for animals. I can understand his feelings. We've had Old Mikey since before Ralph was born. Ralph sometimes hates to let go. I don't think he wants to admit how old Old Mikey is. I'm sure he has never considered the fact that the horse will die some day."

Old Mikey was thirty-two years old. Horses were considered "old" if they reached twenty, so this put Old Mikey in a category by himself. From a distance, he didn't show his age, but up close, the white hairs around his velvety nose and under his jaw were sharp against the usual blackness of his hide. His eyes were no longer clear and bright, and he was slower to rise if he had been lying down for any time. He was like an old man with rheumatism, it took him a while to get started.

Rate went to his room to contemplate the situation. He knew that when horses reached Old Mikey's age, their teeth were not as good and often they got indigestion. Nearly always, this proved fatal. If left to themselves, they died a slow, extremely painful death. Most farmers were humane and put them out of their misery. Rate hated to think this might happen to Old Mikey. Rate had loved the horse from the earliest he could recollect. Old Mikey's glossy black coat was accented by a white stripe down his nose and four white feet. At a young age, Rate had thought him far prettier than the traditional bays, sorrels, or blacks with no white to break up the monotony. Well, maybe Pa would winter him through and come summer, on pasture, Old Mikey would do well.

Rate had been taking boxing lessons from Reverend J.B. Buffin. Each morning, he had to take milk to the minister's house. Of course, the man paid Miney a small sum each week for the milk, but he had begun the boxing lessons to compensate Ralph for his time and effort.

Ralph was an apt pupil. In fact, he was getting quite good. The minister never realized Ralph had an ulterior motive. Rate had a couple of scores to settle, and he figured the better he was at boxing, the easier it would be. He figured he still owed Bion Clement, and there was always the specter of Ralph Boone. Since he and Brownie McNall had trounced Boone, the bully had pretty much left them alone. Still, Rate wanted to take on Boone by himself.

Ralph was getting pretty cocky at one of his training sessions. Instead of boxing for the fun of it, he was pressing pretty hard. Finally, he seized the advantage, waded in, and caught the minister with a solid right to the chin. Before Ralph knew what was happening, two blows came at him with such speed, he could not defend himself; the third blow knocked him clear across the study. As Rate shook his head in disbelief, he heard the minister's voice as if from a distance.

"Rate, you asked for that." There was a pause, then the man asked, "You all right?" He made no move to help the lad rise.

Rate got to his feet, gave the man a lop-sided grin, and said, "Yeah, I'm all right.

You sure pack a wallop. Guess I'm not as good as I thought."

"You were just getting too big for your britches. We are doing this in fun. There is an art to boxing. I do not intend your fists to become lethal weapons."

Ralph nodded. He guessed he had a lot more to learn. He had the notion that if Reverend Buffin knew why he was interested in boxing, the lessons would be immediately terminated. Well, he'd watch himself from now on, and he'd not get too aggressive. He'd simply make every effort to improve his style. As he'd often heard his father say, ignorance is bliss; therefore, he guessed the Reverend was a lot happier not knowing what his real motive was.

Ralph went often with his father to the farm. Each time, his first action was to check on Old Mikey. The old horse always got an extra ration of oats when Ralph was around and the choicest bits of hay--no stems which would have been tough to chew. He was rewarded by seeing the horse do reasonably well. While Old Mikey lost some of his body weight, he didn't deteriorate in any other way. Ralph heard no more talk of having Old Mikey killed.

Christmas was especially good for Ralph. Reverend Buffin, knowing of the lad's interest in reading, presented him with three books of The Leather Stocking Tales by James Fenimore Cooper: *The Deerslayer, The Pathfinder,* and *The Last of the Mohicans.* Ralph was elated. There was nothing he liked to do better on a cold, blustery winter's night than curl up with a good book.

Miney and her sister, Lorin, had both had a letter from Mary in Chicago. Mary had said that Jap wasn't doing very well. It was more than his rheumatism which had kept him from working for the past few years. Lorin and Miney both thought that in her letter, Mary sounded very discouraged. Even the fact that Lelah, her youngest daughter, was soon to have a child did not seem to cheer her. And everyone knew that Mary adored babies.

Miney felt a great deal of compassion for her sister. She knew it would be difficult for her if Millie was seriously ill. Of course, Mary was almost thirteen years older than she, and Jap was two or three years older than Mary. For the umteenth time, she wished Mary and Jap had never moved away from Elsie. Miney would have been glad to give her half sister moral support as well as whatever else Mary needed. She couldn't go to Chicago; but then, she guessed Hattie would give her mother all the support she needed.

Winter held a firm grip on the land almost through the month of March. Then, as so often happens, the weather warmed and spring seemed to arrive in a matter of days. The river ice broke up, the spring flooding came and went so rapidly it caused no problems.

Rate and Wes Payne had been discussing the fact that each year some boy braved the cold waters of the Maple River to be able to brag that he had been the first one in swimming for the season. They had decided this was to be the year when they were to claim the dubious honor. Saturday morning, the boys met about midmorning and headed for the river.

Back of Cobb's, the river was its narrowest, so this was where they headed.

The sun shone brightly, but the air was cold. When the boys reached the river bank, they stared for a moment at the dark, swiftly moving water. It looked cold and foreboding. Still, they had made up their minds that today was to be the day.

Quickly, they stripped to the skin, being careful to place their heavy winter underwear where they would be able to slip back into it with the minimum of effort.

With a grin at each other, the boys dove in. The icy cold momentarily took Rate's breath away. Lordy, the water was colder than he had anticipated, and the current much more swift. He struck out with a firm stroke for the opposite bank. Unless he hurried, his extremities would become numb, and this in turn would hamper his movements.

He could hear Wes a short way off, but he wasted no effort trying to speak. He made the turn to go back. The bitter cold was creeping into his body, and the other shore seemed a long way off. Besides, he was fighting the current, trying not to be swept downstream. He hoped Wes was all right. He couldn't hear him, yet he was sure they had made their turn together.

Ralph wanted to rest a moment, but knew he didn't dare. it would take only a moment for the current to carry him a number of yards off course. Golly, this was much more difficult than he had imagined. He was tiring fast. Each stroke was becoming an effort. He tried not to panic. He counted to himself. Stroke, stroke, stroke. Just as he began to wonder if he would ever make the bank, he felt the current ease and knew he was almost to the bank.

Gasping, he hauled himself upon the still cold ground. His teeth were chattering, and he felt as though he would never be warm again. He noted with satisfaction that Wes was almost to the bank, so he began to haul on his winter underwear. His hands were frightfully cold, his fingers stiff, and he had trouble fastening the buttons. Some, he left undone. At least the sun had kept his clothes from soaking up the cold from the moist earth, or maybe it was just that anything would feel warmer than his body.

By the time they were both dressed, their spirits had returned, and they began to laugh over the experience.

"Think we'll ever feel warm again?" asked Wes.

"By the time we hike back to town, we'll be all right. Guess the water was colder than I thought."

"Yeah. I even began to wonder if I was gonna make it all the way back."

"Me too," admitted Rate. "Well, no one else has been fool enough to try it, so guess we get the honors this year."

"You're right there. I'll tell you one thing. I'm not going swimming again until midsummer when it's good and warm."

"Me either. I wouldn't admit this to another soul, but I figure it was a fool idea.

We're just lucky we made it."

Wes nodded in silent agreement.

Now that Ralph didn't spend as much time at the meat market, he had more time to himself. He often did odd jobs for some of the village residents thereby earning a dime, or if he was lucky, a quarter. He spent more time at the gun shop even though his mother continued to complain about Frank Clement, the owner. Ma had never come out and forbid him going there, so it was perfectly easy to ignore her criticism – he sort of let it go in one ear and out the other. Of course, he was of the opinion that because he had heard Pa tell her there wasn't any harm in his going there, she didn't actually want to oppose her husband. Still, this didn't keep Ma from having her say. He guessed in many ways, his mother would never change.

Millie sold the south forty. Rate had no idea how much money had been involved because Millie, in his usual taciturn way, had not volunteered the information, and Ralph figured it would do no good to ask. Pa could be darned close-mouthed sometimes. Pa was always saying, "Keep your mouth shut, your eyes open, and you'll find out." Ralph supposed this meant ears too. He often found out more by listening to Pa talk to Ma or someone else than by asking questions. Miss Finch had always said we learn a lot by asking questions, but he guessed she hadn't counted on there being folks in this world like his pa.

Shortly after the sale of the forty, Ralph learned the barn was being moved a half mile north to where Ed Houston lived on the Ridge. He had gone out there to watch the workmen jack up the barn in preparation for the move. He would liked to have been able to watch when moving day came, but he couldn't keep coming back every day, and a couple of the men he spoke to had no idea when the move would be made.

A few days later, at the supper table, Millie mentioned that the barn had been moved the half mile to the Houston farm. Rate knew a moment of disappointment, but then he hadn't really expected to be present to watch the moving process. Sure would have been interesting though.

The following week, the community had the first severe thunderstorm of the season. The lightning came in bright flashes, cutting a vertical path to the earth; the thunder crashed like giant cymbals. At times, the wind blew viciously, sending pieces of roofing sailing through the air, rending limbs from numerous trees, rolling pails across yards, leaving clutter and debris in its wake. The residents of Elsie heaved a sigh of relief with the storm's passing; fortunately, there had been no lightning strikes in the village.

However, the farmland residents were not as lucky. Houston's barn which had not yet been dropped down on the foundation, had been struck by lightning and burned to the ground. When Millie told his family, Rate said nothing, but thoughts swirled through his head. He felt sorry for Mr. Houston. All that work of several days destroyed in a few hours, to say nothing of the money lost. It just seemed an awful shame. If, as Ma always said, God was a just and caring God, why had He chosen to burn that particular barn? If Ma was right, God controlled everything in the world. It didn't seem right for Him to send Mr. Houston so much grief. Where was the justice in this act? Was there a God, or were these storms simply a freak of nature? Something no person nor deity controlled.

Rate became aware that his mother and father were still discussing the storm. There had been plenty of wind damage, but most of it had been minor.

At least Mr. Houston had not lost any of his other buildings, and there had been no report of any other fire. Of course, both Pa and Ma were mighty grateful nothing had happened at the farm or here in town. A few small branches had littered the yard, but that was all, nothing to complain about.

CHAPTER 19

Although Blanche liked living in Detroit, she found living with her grandparents a pain much of the time. Sharing their home seemed worse since she was older. Perhaps that was because she felt that at twenty, she was old enough to be her own boss, a state not truly accepted in the Setterington household. However, the small amount of money she made clerking would not have paid room and board in a neighborhood as nice as the one where her grandparents resided. Besides, living in a single room held little appeal for her. She was certain the advantages of living on Medbury Street offset the disadvantages--at least most of the time.

Of course, Grandfather wasn't the one she found irksome; Grandmother amply filled that category. Blanche had met several young people at church, and on occasion, one of the boys would call her. Naturally, Grandmother was always the one to answer the phone. She would dutifully call Blanche, a pleased look on her face. "It's a nice-sounding young man," she'd say with a knowing smile.

However, Lovina never moved far away, but made a point of listening to Blanche's conversation. Then, to irritate her granddaughter further, she'd tap Blanche on the shoulder several times with a rigid forefinger saying, "Ask him up. Ask him up." When Blanche would scowl and shake her head vehemently, Lovina would reply in a defeated tone, "You're going to be an old maid." She would at last walk off, sadly shaking her head. One would have thought that being an unwed woman was comparable to an early death. Perhaps in Lovina's mind, it was.

Blanche knew her grandfather sold insurance and dealt in real estate. She sometimes listened to her grandfather in awe. She told herself that whatever that man put his mind to, he was a whopping big success. Somehow, he just always seemed to make money. At times, Blanche couldn't help comparing her father with her grandfather. There was something which drove Grandfather to be a peg above everyone else, but Blanche realized her father did not have this driving force, this need to make money. He was content to have what he termed a "good" life, he did not care if others were looked upon as more successful. He measured success by his own standards and was at peace with himself.

Blanche had had a letter from Cleon Rummel telling her he intended to be in Detroit for a few days. He asked if he might see her. She had known Cleon most of her life and considered him a friend, not a beau. She made the mistake of telling her grandmother that Cleon was doing pretty well for himself since he had become employed in the bank. He had just had a raise and now made $100 a month.

Obviously, Lovina thought this sounded pretty good, and in rather strident tones, she let Blanche know she thought Cleon was a good catch. Blanche knew better than to argue or try to explain that she had no romantic interest in Cleon Rummel. She was quite certain he felt the same about her.

Before Cleon's visit was over, Blanche vowed she would bite her tongue off before she would confide anything to her grandmother about the success of any young man she might know. Cleon had been invited to supper, and Blanche simply could not believe how her grandmother fawned over him. Blanche had found it all terribly embarrassing until she caught her grandfather's eye and noticed the humor there as he gave her a most undignified wink. She gave him a fleeting smile in return which said she understood. Thank the good Lord for Grandfather. Somehow, knowing he viewed the situation in a humorous vein lessened her anger at her grandmother. Besides, Cleon behaved as though he was enjoying the attention. Surely, he realized her grandmother's motives, but he gave no indication as he thanked them for an enjoyable evening. Blanche was actually relieved when he left.

Why was it Lovina felt she had to run everyone's life? She still ran Pa a good share of the time. Of course, Uncle John had rebelled, and Aunt Ruby was plain spoiled; Lois, although she was only six, was becoming a dictatorial, obnoxious little girl. Of course, like her mother and grandmother, she could also be charming. Still, it never seemed to Blanche that Lovina interfered with Aunt Ruby nearly as much, and thus far, she only spoiled Lois. However, Blanche wondered what her grandmother would be like when Lois reached an age where she would become interested in young men. Too bad Grandmother couldn't run the lives of Uncle John's girls. it might take some of the pressure off her, thought

Blanche irritably. Of course, since Uncle John and Aunt Grace had turned out to be the black sheep of the family, so to speak, Grandmother didn't see those grandchildren. Blanche gave a little sigh of envy, then immediately felt contrite. After all, over the years, her grandparents had been very good to her, it was just that Grandmother could be so exasperating.

Blanche felt a little envious of Aunt Grace. She had never let Grandmother intimidate her. She talked right up to her, she dressed any way she wanted, even if her mother-in-law did disapprove. It was no wonder Grandmother didn't like her much and felt Johnny had married beneath him.

* * * * * * * * * * * *

Miney had no more than entered the house when the phone rang. She would liked to have washed her hands, but she didn't feel she could take the time. It was Lorin. Mary had called from Chicago to tell her that Jap had died. It was the 28th of July. Mary had tried to call Miney, but had had no answer. Miney explained that she had been working in the garden.

Lorin said that Jap's body would be returned to Elsie where they already had a lot in the village cemetery. Their son, Claude, was buried there, as well as twin daughters who had lived only a few days. Lorin said Mary was doing as well as could be expected. Miney was not surprised. Mary had always been very capable and able to accept whatever adversity had come her way. Miney was not certain she would be as capable under similar circumstances.

When told, Blanche had wondered if Lelah, her husband, and her baby, who was only four months old, would accompany Aunt Mary. She guessed she'd like to see Lelah; they had been close a few years back, more like sisters than cousins. However, Lelah's marriage had brought about changes. They no longer had much in common. Blanche had not given marriage more than a passing thought. She knew for certain she didn't want children, at least at this early age. Grandmother might be afraid she was going to be an old maid, but Ma kept telling her there was plenty of time, and that she should enjoy her youth before she took on the heavy responsibilities of being a wife and perhaps, a mother. Blanche wondered if her mother ever wished she had been older when she married. It was common knowledge that Ma hadn't wanted children, but Ma had certainly been a good mother. She was certain that Ralph would agree with her even though he knew Ma showed partiality.

Since the funeral would be on the weekend, Blanche came home from Detroit, partly because Aunt Mary was her favorite aunt, and partly, she supposed, because she did want to see Lelah.

It seemed that she and Lelah had very little time together, and even then, the old camaraderie seemed to be lacking. Lelah asked about Blanche's work, but Blanche felt she did this to be polite, not because she was really interested. Little Beatrice occupied much of Lelah's time. Blanche still had not acquired more than a tolerance for a baby this young, but she guessed Lelah was happy, and that was all that mattered.

Ralph had felt like an outsider. Aunt Mary had talked to him for a few minutes, but there were old friends and neighbors who wished to extend their condolences, and she couldn't ignore them. He felt in the way. Hattie had taken some time for him; he knew she sensed his discomfort, and being Hattie, had done what she could to make him more comfortable. Trouble was, there was no one in the family near to him in age. Besides, he didn't remember Aunt Mary all that well. It seemed to him as though she looked a lot older than he remembered. Of course, he had been pretty small when he had last seen her. Maybe he just didn't remember too well.

* * * * * * * * * * * *

At Sunday School and Church, Blanche had become acquainted with a young girl her own age who worked at Studebaker. Maude's weekly salary was far better than Blanche's, Because Blanche had shown such an interest, Maude promised to call her if she heard of any job openings. They liked the idea of both of them working at the same place.

Several weeks passed, then one Sunday, Maude asked, "Blanche, why didn't you come this week to apply for the job I called about? Now, it is too late. They've hired someone else."

"What job? You mentioned nothing last Sunday."

"True. But I called Tuesday. Your grandmother answered the phone. She assured me she would give you the message."

Blanche's lips drew into a thin line.

"Ohhh. That woman! Maude, she never gave me the message. She interferes in everything I do. Just wait until I get home. I'm going to have this out with her."

"I didn't mean to cause any trouble."

"*You* didn't. You knew I wanted the job, and I appreciate the fact that you called. Oh, why did I have to be blessed with such an interfering soul for a grandmother? Anyway, none of this is your fault."

Blanche seethed all the way home. Her grandparents were talking, and no one noticed how quiet Blanche was. Sometimes, Blanche thought, she came close to hating her grandmother. Right after dinner, she would bring the matter out in the open.

Blanche cleared the table mechanically--she had been told often enough just how her grandmother wanted it done. Like everything, there was Grandmother's way and the wrong way. Actually, Blanche was going over in her mind just what she was going to say to Lovina once they began doing the dishes. Even in a war of words, Blanche knew she must be well prepared when the enemy was her grandmother.

Just as Lovina began carefully washing the thin, etched glassware, Blanche took a deep breath before she launched her attack. It was now or never.

"Grandmother, Maude said she called this past week. Was there a reason why you didn't mention it?"

Blanche's voice was deceptively calm.

"Oh, didn't I tell you? I'm sure I must have. She said it was not important." Lovina continued washing dishes as though the matter was settled.

"I suppose whether it was important or not depends on one's point of view. You were supposed to have told me about an opening for a job at Studebaker. Why didn't you?"

"Oh, that. My goodness, Blanche, why would any respectable young girl want to work in a factory of all places? I knew you'd realize it is a highly inappropriate place to work. I suppose that is why I forgot to mention it."

"Grandmother, you *knew* I would be interested. It was an office job so don't make it sound as though I would have been working in the factory part. Maude makes much more money than I do clerking. I've explained all this to you. What makes you think you must make my decisions for me? You have no right, no right at all." Blanche's eyes showed the fury she felt.

"Blanche Setterington, don't you take that tone with me. No granddaughter of mine is going to work in some office alone with a man. It isn't respectable." She gave Blanche a look that said the matter was settled.

Grandmother, I am not some ten-year-old whom you can order around. I am twenty years old, old enough to know my own mind and to make my own decisions without any interference from you."

Blanche's brown eyes stared into her grandmother's blue ones. Lovina's face was inscrutable. Never had Blanche spoken to her grandmother in such a tone before. Clearly, it had taken Lovina by surprise. She was not accustomed to having anyone disagree with her.

"I only do what I think best for you. Is this the thanks I get?" She eyed her granddaughter as if she was making some attempt to understand her.

"I do not need your help. I cannot keep you from voicing an opinion, nor do I want to, but I *will* make my own decisions. I hope you will remember this in the future."

Blanche carefully folded the towel, hung it in its proper place, turned and left the room. Her knees felt weak, and she noticed her hands were shaking. Grandmother had looked furious although she had said no more. Well, Blanche thought, I was furious too. I vowed a long time ago I'd have enough backbone to stand up to her and not be like Pa and Ma. Well, I guess I just did. Grandmother's like an elephant, she'll never forget. I just hope she bends a little and understands I must make my own decisions.

It had been unusual for Lovina not to have the last word. She had watched Blanche's departing figure with mixed emotions. She recognized a part of herself in this strong-willed granddaughter; therefore, she felt respect with a little bit of pride thrown in. She sighed audibly. All she wanted was the best for Blanche. Perhaps she wasn't keeping up with the changing world. This new century was still very young, but everywhere one looked there was change in the air. Lovina wondered if her own mother had ever felt this way.

Lovina decided she should be more careful about meddling in Blanche's affairs. However, this was a fleeting thought, forgotten almost as soon as it was conceived. After all, Miney had never been one to guide Blanche, thus it was up to Lovina to see that the girl turned out as befitted a Setterington. It never occurred to Lovina that Blanche's goal in life might not coincide with hers. After all, she was older and much more informed than a "child" just turned twenty.

For several days, a tension existed between Blanche and her grandmother. For once, Lovina sensed that Blanche's feelings ran deep, and she was not going to forget the incident quickly. A less domineering person might have backed off, realizing she could not control this granddaughter, but Lovina, while admitting she had lost the battle, never doubted she would win the war. Defeat was not a word in her vocabulary.

Lovina had never paid much attention to the fact that Blanche had been keeping rather steady company with Gerd Pershing of Ovid. She never considered him in serious contention for Blanche's hand because he was only a cheesemaker. After all, *her* granddaughter would certainly marry someone with a more prestigious means of earning a living.

Blanche delayed telling her grandmother as long as she could that Gerd was making a special trip to Detroit to see her. Cleon's visit was still fresh in her mind. However, she was certain Gerd would not rate the same attention Cleon had been given. In fact, she dreaded the derogatory comments she knew her grandmother would make. Gerd was a very nice young man, and Blanche did not want him made uncomfortable by her grandmother's caustic tongue. She knew Grandfather would treat Gerd well, but then, even Grandfather had a way of intimidating those who did not know him. To Blanche, he simply looked dignified; to others, he looked overly stern.

Blanche had an idea why Gerd was coming to visit. She hadn't written very regularly although his letters came every week--not love letters, but still they often showed a wistful longing. Blanche had been having such a good time with Mabel Baker, a girl her own age who stayed with Aunt Ruby, that she often put off writing to anyone except her parents.

When Blanche had left for Detroit, she had hinted rather strongly that her stay would quite likely be a short one. Knowing her mother hated having her gone had given her second thoughts about staying with her grandparents for any prolonged length of time. Somehow, she imagined that to her mother, it looked as though she was taking sides in the constant conflict between Miney and her mother-in-law. Now that she was older, she realized more fully just how miserable her grandmother often made life for her mother. Yet, in all fairness, she doubted that Lovina understood this and did not intentionally cause Miney pain.

While Gerd had let it be known he did not like having her move so far away, he had been somewhat mollified by this assertion of a short stay. Lately, every letter had asked when she intended to come home. Well, she had never really promised, had she? She was not about to return home when she found life exciting here in the city. Besides, she was not at all certain marriage was for her. Perhaps that was because she felt Lovina was too pushy. After all, her grandmother had been twenty-two when she and Grandfather were married, so Blanche couldn't understand why she should be in any hurry. Actually, twenty-two seemed much too young. Blanche did not want to be tied down with the responsibilities she knew marriage would bring. No one had ever explained to her how a woman got in the family way; Blanche only knew it happened *after* a woman got married. She was certain she was not ready for motherhood, if she would ever be. Blanche had never been around many babies, and those she had seen, held no appeal.

When Gerd came, Blanche learned he had tickets for the baseball game where Donnie Bush was the fans' favorite. Although Blanche had never been a truly dedicated baseball fan, she supposed it was a good way to spend the afternoon. The weather was warm, the sun shone brightly, and it did seem good to see Gerd now that he was here. She read the longing in his eyes and felt a small twinge of guilt when she considered how seldom she had written.

Of course, when her grandparents had met him, Blanche had not failed to note the disapproving look in Lovina's eye. She knew Gerd had felt uneasy which was to be expected. She was certain he had heard many stories about her grandmother although he would have been far too polite to mention them. In a small village like Elsie, it was impossible not to know the reputation her grandmother had, and Blanche was certain there were those in Ovid who were equally informed since Ovid was only six miles away. Everyone, it seemed, recognized Lovina as an interfering soul, yet they were quick to recognize she also had a compassionate nature--mostly outside the family.

Blanche decided she was not going to let her grandmother spoil their day. She felt it was her duty to see that Gerd had a pleasant day too.

After the ballgame, Gerd took Blanche to a very nice restaurant for supper. This was a special treat. In fact, it was the first time a young man had taken her to anything but a lunch counter for a meal. Blanche did her best to hide her nervousness. She was so afraid she'd make some social blunder and embarrass both herself and Gerd.

They were walking along Medbury Street, with about a block to go before reaching her grandparents' home, when Gerd stopped and turned Blanche to face him. She noted his serious expression, even his eyes looked sad.

"Blanche, we have to talk."

"All right. What about?" Her tone was intentionally light.

"Us."

"Us?" Blanche decided this was not a topic she wanted to discuss, but she could think of no way to avoid it.

"Yes, Blanche, us. When you came to Detroit, you indicated it would be for only a short time. Well, the weeks have stretched into months, and when I mention your coming home, you avoid making an answer. What I want you to tell me is, are you really coming home?"

He watched her intently while she struggled to find the right words.

"Blanche, if you don't come home soon, we're going to break up. I don't want a city girl for a wife."

Blanche looked a little startled. Gerd had never actually asked her if she would marry him, but he certainly seemed to have taken it for granted. Somehow, that fact grated. She did not like being taken for granted. She guessed what really mattered was that she liked having Gerd for a friend, she liked going places with him, but it ended there. In no way could she envision herself being married to him.

She gave a sigh of regret as she looked him in the eye and spoke with candor. "I'm sorry, Gerd, but I'm not at all certain when I'll be coming home. If that means you no longer want us to be friends, I think I understand."

"That's not what I want at all. You must know that. It's just that I can't see any future for us if you continue to live in Detroit."

He sounded defeated. Blanche honestly had not realized he cared this much. Although nothing had ever been said between them which even hinted of marriage, perhaps she should have been able to read between the lines of his letters. She guessed she was an ignoramus where men were concerned. Now, how could she gracefully handle this situation?

"Gerd, I'm truly sorry if I have misled you in any way. Frankly, I don't know what I do intend to do with my life. I do know that I don't expect to be a store clerk forever. However, I am enjoying life right now. Mabel is as content as I am. We have fun together. I don't want to give this up and return to Elsie. Perhaps I *am* a city girl at heart. At any rate, marriage is out of the question. At least for now."

"I guess that says it all, doesn't it?"

"I'm afraid so."

They walked in silence to her grandparent's house. At the door, Gerd took her hand for a moment.

"Goodbye, Blanche. I hope you continue to be happy."

Before Blanche could answer, he turned and ran down the steps. He hurried along as though he was being pursued. He did not look back. Blanche felt as though a chapter of her life had ended. She liked Gerd a lot, but marriage was not for her. She was young, she was healthy, and she was happy. There was no need to have a man in her life.

Blanche knew her grandmother would be glad she and Gerd had broken up; however, Lovina would be quick to present a list of several eligible suitors. Blanche dreaded even the thought. She supposed Grandmother meant well, but Blanche was so tired of always being at odds with her. She wished Grandmother would give her credit for having some intelligence, thereby being perfectly capable of managing her own affairs.

Some of the time, Aunt Ruby was just as bad. Of course, Aunt Ruby had never earned a dime in her life, so Blanche felt her aunt could not understand why any woman chose to earn her own keep. A proper young woman waited patiently at home for some man to take her under his wing and support her. Of course, Blanche felt the drudgery of housework, the responsibility of raising numerous children, being at her husband's beck and call presented a grim picture.

At this last thought, she laughed. Grandmother had never been at anyone's beck and call, much less Grandfather's. But then, who would want to pattern herself after Lovina Setterington?

Blanche squared her shoulders and entered the house, ready for the barrage of questions she knew would come from her grandmother.

CHAPTER 20

Old Mikey had been on Rate's mind of late. Last year, Pa had talked of having Old Mikey put down and having his hide made into a robe. Old Mikey had lost weight during the winter months even though Ralph had given the loyal old horse extra oats every time he went to the farm, and he always made certain Old Mikey had the choicest bits of hay. Still, it had not been enough.

Rate had felt certain that Old Mikey would return to robust health during the summer months when he had nothing but tender grass to eat. It hadn't happened. While his coat became glossy and smooth once more, his weight did not return to normal. He looked his age.

Every time Ralph went to the farm, his first action was to check on Old Mikey. Deep down, he knew the days of the old horse were numbered, but he hated to face the facts. It just seemed that Old Mikey should go on forever.

Then came the day when Ralph failed to locate Old Mikey. He rushed to his father demanding, "Where's Old Mikey, Pa? What have you done with him?"

Millie paused with his work and said, "He's up to Clark's."

Ralph asked nothing further. He heaved a sigh of relief. Ed often borrowed Old Mikey for some small job. Well, he'd hurry with his chores and cut across the fields to the Clark farm to see Old Mikey, sorta make certain Ed was feedin' him right.

When Ralph came over the pasture fence by Clark's buildings, Ivan and Milford both noticed him. The boys were younger than he, but he liked them well enough.

"Rate, Rate," yelled Milford, running to meet Ralph. "Guess what we've got to show you."

"What and where?"

"Come see," said Milford, heading for one of the buildings.

Ralph looked at Ivan and winked as he followed the exuberant small boy.

When Milford pointed and said, "There." Rate's stomach did a flipflop. There, tied in a square, was the hide of a horse, and from one corner, a small amount of glossy black hair showed. Rate knew at one glance whose hide it was. Poor Old Mikey. Pa had lied to him. Pa knew all along that Old Mikey was dead, and that he'd been skinned.

Rate stayed only a few minutes. He made his excuses and hurried home. The nearer he got, the angrier he became.

"Pal Pa! Where are you?"

"Over here." Millie sat mending a piece of harness.

"You lied to me, Pa. Old Mikey's dead, an' you knew it. You lied to me. You told me he was up to Clark's. An' he's dead an' you skinned him," accused the overwrought boy.

Millie had eyed his son during this outburst, his face expressionless. "Done?" Rate nodded.

"Now, back up a little. I told you Old Mikey was at Clark's. He is. Ed buried him. I didn't skin him. Merval Keenan did. Now, you never asked if he was alive. You've known Old Mikey was getting in bad shape. He'd never have wintered through, and we can use the robe. I'm sending it off today to have it done."

"I'll never use that old robe for anything."

"The choice is yours," said Millie as he began to work on the two pieces of leather.

Rate knew his father was done speaking. Leave it to Pa to crawl out of something. Rate still felt his father had lied to him, but strictly speaking, he supposed Pa hadn't. It was just that Pa never volunteered one blamed thing. Pa knew very well why he had asked about Old Mikey. Would it have hurt Pa one little bit to have told him the entire story instead of letting him learn the truth by the Clark boys showing him the hide? Sometimes, Pa could be callous, never realizing how something made him feel. There were times when he wondered if Pa even cared. Of course, he guessed having Old Mikey buried was better than having the carcass hauled off to a rendering works.

Resentment grew, and it was to be quite some time before Ralph would no longer harbor ill feelings toward his father.

When the finished robe came, Ralph scarcely gave it a glance. Let Pa and Ma use it if they wanted; he'd keep warm without it.

Since Ralph often chummed with Reverend Thompson's two sons who were near his age, he felt he knew the preacher quite well. Actually, he really liked the man. For a man of the cloth, he was not one to push his religious beliefs like some Ralph had known. In fact, he was just a regular guy when he wasn't in church or calling on the shut-ins. He always showed an interest in young people, but he was never one to lecture. Ralph appreciated that quality, especially since he figured he got enough lecturing from his mother.

It was a Saturday afternoon when the Reverend came by. Neither Millie nor Miney were home. Pa, of course, was at the meat market, and Ma had gone calling-- he wasn't sure where since he hadn't paid that much attention. Rate was meeting some of the fellows a little later. He had just finished doing some yard work for his mother.

Reverend Thompson had wanted to speak to Miney, but when he learned she was not at home, he spent a few moments with Ralph. He had come to the back door, so he noticed the pairs of boxing gloves which hung on the woodshed wall.

"Ralph, I hear you are getting pretty good at boxing. Is that so?"

"I don't know how good I am, but Reverend Buffin has been giving me lessons. He's the one that's good. I'm not in his class, I can tell you." Rate recalled the time the minister had put him in his place in short order.

"I used to box a little while at the seminary. I was not all that good, but it served as an outlet for a young man's energy. I was never very good at any sport to be honest with you. Guess I wasn't too coordinated," he said with a little laugh. "How about it, Ralph. Want to put the gloves on with me?"

"I dunno, Reverend. Maybe just for a few minutes. I have to meet some friends shortly."

"That's all right, Ralph. I just want to see if I remember anything I was taught. It's been quite some time you know."

Ralph took down the boxing gloves, doing his best not to show his reluctance. Should he let the pastor knock him around a little, defending himself in a haphazard manner, or should he be aggressive much as he would be with anyone not a minister? Guess he'd just wait and see how good the man was.

Ralph held back, letting Reverend Thompson make the first move. The Reverend jabbed a couple of times with his right; Ralph deflected the punches easily.

Now, the Reverend feinted with his right, but swung with his left. His movements were mechanical, and Ralph sensed what he was going to do before he did it. His footwork was slow and uncoordinated with his hands. Ralph agreed with the pastor's own assessment--he wasn't very good. Sure didn't hold a candle to Reverend Buffin. He was clumsy, and Ralph felt sorry for him--at least temporarily.

They had sparred for several minutes when Ralph decided he was tired of pussy footing around. He threw a couple of quick punches. The Reverend was too slow to block either of them.

"Ralph, you really are pretty good. You've got speed. That's what makes a good boxer--speed."

Just then Ralph sent a left crashing through the minister's inadequate defense. The man stumbled slightly, so instead of making contact with his jaw, Ralph's punch landed squarely on the man's nose. Immediately, blood spurted from both nostrils.

"Jeepers, Reverend Thompson, look what I've gone and done. I've given you a nosebleed." Rate pulled his gloves off and grabbed for the towel by the wash stand. "Here, take this before you get blood on your clothes. I'm sorry, sir. Golly, I only intended to hit you on the chin."

"Don't worry, Ralph. It was my own clumsiness. No harm's done except to your mother's towel. See, the bleeding has almost stopped." He took the towel away to show that only a small amount of blood oozed from one nostril. "It will stop in a moment."

The Reverend was right. The towel was a mess. Rate could just hear his mother voice her complaint. Why was it everything always had to go wrong?"

"Here, Ralph. I'm all right now. You pack quite a wallop. Now, so your mother won't be upset over her towel, let's rinse it out in cold water. If it is done before the blood dries, we can get the blood out so no one need know." He gave Ralph a conspiratorial wink.

Rate grinned.

"I just brought in a fresh pail. It's pretty cold."

"Good."

The minister filled the wash basin and began to dip the towel up and down, now and then squeezing it gently.

"Here. Let me do that. After all, it was my fault you got the nosebleed."

"All right. I'll let you finish. I think you'd better change the water first. I'll be on my way. Guess I've learned my lesson. I'll stick to preaching. It's a lot safer."

The Reverend left, and Rate rinsed the towel twice more in fresh water. Looked pretty good to him as he held it up and surveyed it critically. He just hoped his mother's eyesight was no better than his. Funny thing about mothers, they could spot dirt or a stain where there wasn't any. Well, he'd done his best. He spread the towel out on the rack, hoping it would dry before his mother returned.

Several days later, Rate was spending a couple of days with Don Sherman. When together, neither were content unless they were busy doing something; often the "something" got them into some sort of trouble. Of course, now that they were older, they had become more adept at keeping most of their activities from their respective parents. Neither boy lied; they simply did not tell what they felt their parents did not need to know. Had either set of parents questioned them, they would have answered each question carefully but truthfully.

They had been debating what they should do for amusement when Don suggested, "Let's go shoot a crow."

Since this sounded like a good idea to Ralph, the boys each took a shotgun and some shells and headed for a spot on the river flats where the timber had been cut off leaving nothing but stumps and a few small bushes.

Each lad picked out a stump to stand on about a hundred yards apart. They began to scan the sky for crows. For the moment, no crows or any other birds were visible. Rate waited patiently, his gun held securely in the crook of his arm. A woodlot was near by, and Ralph felt certain it wouldn't be long before one or two crows came their way.

Don was bored. Any other time he bet there'd have been a dozen crows circling above them. Don rested the stock of his gun on the stump, taking no notice of the fact that he had pulled the hammer back to enable him to get off a quick shot when a crow appeared. Absently, he began to twirl the gun around, his eyes still scanning the sky.

Rate was startled by the blast of a shotgun. He had seen nothing at which to shoot. He turned toward Don. His eyes widened in fear at what he saw. He jumped down from the stump and ran toward his friend.

Don's sweater jacket was on fire, and Don was attempting to get it off, but in his haste, was making little headway. Rate grabbed a sleeve, pulled it from Don's arm, then helped him get the other arm free. Luckily, wool does not burn rapidly.

It was obvious to Rate that Don was unhurt although his face was blackened from the powder. They had torn the sweater off before he had suffered any burns; therefore, Rate began to laugh. The look of disbelief on Don's face only made him laugh harder.

"That's right. Laugh, you damn fool. When a man's dying, laugh."

In between bursts of laughter, Rate managed to reply.

"You aren't hurt, you dummy. Course your sweater isn't much good and your face is black. You are lucky that's all that's wrong. How in heck did it happen?"

"Well, I had pulled the hammer back so I could get a shot off faster than you. Then, since I didn't see anything, I rested the stock on the stump, and I was sorta twirling the gun around when it slipped off the damned stump. Kinda dumb, wasn't it?" he asked sheepishly.

"Like Pa says, experience teaches a dear school, but a fool can learn no other. Guess that fits you today. Go on down to the river and clean up or your mother will have heart failure when she sees you. What are you gonna do with the sweater?"

"Bury it, I guess. Ma won't miss it right away if I'm careful. If she asks, I'll just tell her I lost it. She'd have a conniption if she knew what really happened."

Ralph nodded his head in agreement.

They found a spot where they could dig in the soft dirt with a couple of sticks and buried the sweater in a shallow hole. After Don had washed up, they headed back to the Sherman farm. The desire to shoot crows had vanished.

Instead of coming in the back door as they normally would have done, they quietly entered by a side door. Don stopped and listened, then said, "I think I hear Ma out in the garden. Let's get these guns put away, and then we can go out by the barn. Won't hurt if she sees us coming from there."

"I'd suggest you wash up better. You still have black marks on your neck. You know how mothers are. She'd be sure to notice."

Rate took care of the guns while Don washed up. Still moving quietly, they left by the same door and circled to the barn, carefully avoiding the garden. Neither boy wanted to explain to a parent what had happened. Both knew the accident could have been a disaster. Of course, with a degree of fatalism, their thoughts turned to more important things.

Miney may have been strict with Ralph in many ways, but she had always allowed him to bring a friend home to sleep over whenever he wanted. There were times when she didn't know she had an extra mouth to feed for breakfast until the boys showed up in the kitchen. This never bothered her since there was always plenty of food in the Setterington household. Miney might be cautious with her money, always looking to get the most for every penny, but she had learned early in her marriage that food must be abundant to satisfy her husband's voracious appetite.

Ralph had been with a group of boys for the evening, and somehow, it was decided Niles Smith would come home with him to spend the night.

It was later than usual, so the boys slipped quietly up the back stairs. They carefully avoided the step that squeaked, silently eased open the door to Rate's room, but just as Ralph was gently closing the door, there came the expected call.

"That you, Ralph?"

Once again his mother had proven how acute her hearing was in some instances.

"Yes, Ma," he answered in a resigned tone.

"What time is it?"

"About twelve."

Ralph had just closed the door when, in the stillness of the darkened house, the downstairs clock struck the hour of three. The boys started to chuckle, then afraid his mother would hear them, they covered their faces with a pillow to smother the sound.

Finally, Niles managed to whisper, "Think you'll be in trouble for lying?"

"Didn't really lie. Said it was about twelve--that could mean a little before or a little after."

"Three hours after?"

They broke out laughing again.

"If she asks, I'll tell her she might have missed the first strikes because we were talking."

Niles chuckled.

"Does she always know when you get home?"

"Never fooled her yet."

"Wonder what she'd have done if I'd answered instead of you?" "Probably woke Pa to check on an intruder."

This comment set the boys laughing again as each envisioned his own version of what Millie would look like trying to apprehend an intruder in his nightshirt.

Miney said nothing to Ralph the next day, so he assumed she had not heard the clock strike. Golly, how come she could hear his every move and miss something as loud as the clock? Sometimes, Ma was a mystery.

Ralph had been to Chapin and was headed for home; it was late, but a full moon shed light upon the countryside. As was his custom, as soon as he set Pearl on the road for home, he promptly went to sleep. Both horse and driver were accustomed to this arrangement. Pearl knew where she was going as well as Ralph did. She was completely dependable.

Rate was awakened by the whistle of a train. They were still some distance from the tracks, but he could sense Pearl's apprehension. The mare was deathly afraid of trains. Not long ago, Millie had driven her to Ovid where he had made the mistake of attempting to drive her alongside the train which was stopped at the station. Pearl went wild and began to back up. Millie used his rawhide whip to no avail. Even though he cut the hair off much of her rump, she continued to back. The buggy hit the side of a boxcar, shattering the thills. It had taken Millie and a couple of other men to get the frightened mare away from there so she could be quieted down. Of course, Pearl had always given Millie.more trouble than she gave Ralph.

The whistle sounded again. Even in the dark, Rate could tell they were a considerable distance from the crossing. He made no move, spoke no words. His senses were alert to Pearl's every move. She stopped. Her ears were pricked forward, listening intently. She remained motionless while the freight roared past. It was a long freight, and several minutes went by before the light on the caboose signaled its end. Pearl turned her head slightly in the direction of the receding train; then she moved cautiously forward, every muscle tense, and carefully crossed the tracks. She then settled into her easy trot as though nothing unusual had happened.

Rate was proud of her. His thought was that she was smarter than some humans. Sure was his lucky day when Pa traded for her even if he had hated to have Gyp go.

School resumed, and in many ways, Ralph was glad to be back in the classroom. It was the same old story, some classes he liked, and some he would have gladly done without.

Each student had a desk in the large assembly room where he kept his books. This was also the study hall. Rate happened to have a desk behind Clara Mentor. Actually, it was most unwise to have a girl seated in front of him.

It had been a rainy, windy, fall morning. There were umbrellas hanging with the coats along the hallway, and while a few students left their rubbers beneath the hook holding their coat, most of them placed their rubbers under their desks. They were easier to locate this way. Sometimes, in the hallway, one or both rubbers were kicked a ways down the hall when students passed to classes. Boys especially were rather adept at sending a rubber hurtling down the hallway thus making it difficult for a student to sort out his own.

As often happened, Rate was somewhat bored. He had finished his assignments– at least as much as he intended to do. When he moved his foot, he felt something. Peering down, he saw Clara's rubbers which she had neatly placed beneath the desk seat. An impish smile appeared on his face as he looked about the room to locate the teacher who was monitoring study hall at this time.

Moments before the bell would ring to dismiss the students for noon, Clara reached under her desk to retrieve her rubbers. She went home for dinner, and she fully intended to slip her rubbers over her shoes before the bell rang.

She took one look at them, then with an exclamatory oh, jumped from her seat and began to pound Rate over the head with her rubbers. Rate blocked the blows with his hands, laughing softly as he did so. Neither heard the bell.

"Something wrong, Clara?"

"You, Rate Setterington, you know what's wrong. I suppose my rubbers turned themselves inside out."

Other students began to laugh as Clara continued her tirade.

"Just you wait, Mr. Smartypants. I'll get even with you some day. Just see if I don't."

"I'm shaking in my boots."

"Oh, you make me so mad." She stomped her foot to punctuate her statement.

Ralph had noticed the study hall teacher coming their way to investigate, so he moved quickly to the double doors and headed down the stairs to the first floor. Golly, he really hadn't thought Clara would be this upset. Maybe she'd be cooled off after dinner. He didn't think she'd tattle on him. At least, he hoped not. He really didn't want to be in trouble this early in the year.

Millie had belonged to the Odd Fellows Lodge for a number of years, and while they had lived in town, had gone quite regularly to their meetings. This Saturday was no exception. Since it was often after eleven when he came home, Miney never waited up for him.

Millie was quiet at breakfast, but that was hardly unusual. He was often taciturn, at least until he had satisfied his hunger.

Millie pushed aside his empty plate, took a sip of coffee, then announced, "I won't be going to any more Odd Fellow meetings."

"Why, Millie, whatever do you mean?"

"Just what I said. I'll not be going to any more meetings, and I don't intend to renew my membership."

"But I thought you liked attending meetings," said a puzzled Miney.

"I did. But I won't associate with a drunk man on the street, and I won't sit beside one at Lodge."

"Oh."

Rate would liked to have asked who was drunk, but knew better. Ma looked as though she was dying to know who had offended Pa, but from the set look on Pa's face, it would do her no good to ask.

Rate thought about what his father had said. He guessed he could understand his father's feelings all right. Pa never drank except maybe for a glass of cider that was getting hard which wasn't at all like beer and whiskey. Rate had seen very few drunks, but those he had seen, he thought were disgusting. He recalled seeing George Page sleeping off a drunk. Pa was certainly justified to feel as he did. Kinda made him proud to know Pa didn't drink and make a fool of himself.

Rate knew that almost every year Guy Sherman, Gene Cooley, Fred Wolf--he ran the saloon and hotel at the east end of town--and Ren Vincent would take the train to the north country deer hunting. The men could take two deer each of either sex. They stayed at a lumber camp and were usually gone a week or ten days, depending on how good their luck was finding deer.

Ralph, along with several of his friends, tried to be at the depot when the men came home. The boys would try to guess how many deer the men would have, which man or men would fill their quota, and how many of the deer would be bucks.

While Rate liked to hunt small game, he had never had the desire to hunt deer. Maybe he'd have felt differently if deer had caused crop damage on their farm. Perhaps the men liked being away from their wives for a time and in the company of men exclusively. He guessed that didn't sound so bad--no women to pester you to clean your feet, comb your hair, wash your hands, and the list was endless. Of course, on the other side of the coin--no one to cook your meals, no one to bake pies or cookies. Guess there were certain advantages to having women around. Anyway, the men seemed to come back exceptionally good natured even if they only had a couple of deer between them.

Millie knew his renter intended to move off the farm come the last of February. Ralph knew it too. He wondered what Pa would decide to do. There was no use to ask because Rate knew his father would not confide in anyone until after he had made his decision. He had, however, heard his father tell his mother that the meat market wasn't bringing in enough money to continue to support two families. When Miney had asked what he intended to do, Millie had not answered. Miney had learned one thing over the years: it would do no good to press the matter; dragging words from Millie was like pulling teeth from a chicken--impossible.

Then came the day when Millie announced, "Well, I sold Walt my half of the market today." He looked first at Miney, then at Ralph. They were sitting at the supper table, and Miney had just passed the fresh apple pie.

"Isn't somebody going to say something? Cat got your tongue?"

"I don't rightly know what to say," came from Miney. Once again Millie had made a major decision without consulting her or at least asking her opinion. It rankled.

"Gee, Pa, what are you intending to do?"

"Something that should please you. Boy, we're going back to the farm come March."

"Golly, Pa, that's great. I'm getting big enough to help you with a lot of the field work. Bet I could even learn to plow."

Rate's eyes shone. Town had been all right, and he hadn't been unhappy here, but there was no place like the farm. Land was what was really important. Farm animals could be exasperating at times, but Rate had always welcomed the challenge. Did a man's heart good to raise good livestock and grow good crops. Rate just knew there was nothing in this old world to compare with living on a farm.

"Miney, you haven't said how you cotton to the idee."

"Since you've already decided, I don't guess it matters a great deal what I think. I've enjoyed being in town, close to church and stores. Still, I always liked the farm even if It does mean much more work for me. I don't know what Blanche will think, but then, she is seldom here since she moved in with your mother in Detroit." A note of bitterness crept into Miney's tone.

"You sound as though you think it is Ma's fault that Blanche prefers city life." As usual, Millie bristled at the idea that someone was blaming his mother for anything.

"No. It's just that Mother Setterington encourages it. She likes having Blanche with her. She's trying to marry her off, and of course, no one in Elsie would suit your mother. Anyway, none of that matters. We're moving in March, and that's that."

Millie failed to note how disheartened his wife sounded.

Miney began to clear the table. There weren't many victuals left over-- a potato and a smidgen of gravy. She'd have to add a thick slice of bread to the potato and gravy to give Bruno his supper. One thing about having a husband with an appetite like Millie's, one never had to worry about what to do with the leftovers.

Millie had been up town to get the mail. Now that he didn't have to open the meat market every day, he was often restless. He still went to the farm each morning, but there wasn't much to do at this time of year. He took care of the sheep and helped the renter with the horses, but this took less than half a day from the time he left town until his return. This meant his afternoons were free. Some days, there was kindling to split, but the winter's wood supply had been corded in the woodshed long before snow flew. Therefore, out of boredom, Millie usually walked to the post office each afternoon, and more often than not went to some of the business places looking for someone with whom to pass the time. Sometimes, he even found someone willing to play a game or two of checkers.

He came in the house rather quietly, hung up his Mackinaw and hat, then continued into the dining room where Miney sat with some mending, her chair drawn up close to the window for the best light.

"Did we get any mail?"

Millie hesitated, then said, "Only a letter from Pa."

"None from Blanche? I had hoped for a letter today. She has not written very regularly lately." Then as if she finally absorbed what her husband had said, she asked, "What did Father Setterington want?" Father only wrote when it concerned business, otherwise, Mother Setterington was the one to write.

"Wants to know if I have any money to loan. I swear, Miney, that man has a nose for money like a hound for rabbits. I never told him I sold the butcher shop, so what made him think I'd have any spare cash? He knew I sold the forty on payments."

"How much does he want?"

"Here, read it for yourself." Millie dropped the letter on Miney's lap. With a pensive look, he sat in his favorite rocker.

Miney took the letter from its envelope, a frown on her face. Money matters always worried her. Even though Millie had always been a good provider, Miney worried for fear the time would come when they would not have money for the necessities of life. She didn't ask for much since she had learned to be frugal from her mother, perhaps the only one besides Lorin who had.

The letter was written on the German American Insurance Company letterhead. This was a fire insurance company based in New York. Father Setterington had sold both insurance and real estate since moving to Detroit.

Detroit Nov 13th/09

Dear Millie

Have you any money that you will not want to use for a while say about four months am making a loan and can pay you 6 per cent for say about 8 hundred or $1000. 00 Dollars.

If you have check or certificate and should send it to me, just write on the back of it,- Pay to the order of H. Setterington and sign your name.

I suppose you will be on the farm before long, hope you all keep well. Blanche seems real well, your ma is well except her cold, or coff and hope she may be entirely well before long, let me hear from you as soon as you can.

With Love to all
Father

It seemed to Miney as if Father Setterington had known Millie had sold the market. How did that man always know everything? Mina hadn't even told Blanche, partly because she thought Blanche might not like the idea of them moving back on the farm even if she was living in Detroit. After all, Blanche did come home once in a while although not nearly as often as Miney would like.

Father Setterington might be extraordinary when it came to business, but Miney could not help feeling a little smug as she noted his mistakes in punctuation. Just proved the man was far from perfect in everything.

Miney folded the letter, returned it to its envelope, then looked at her husband as she realized the importance of the letter--at least to Millie.

"What will you tell him, Millie? Do we have extra cash?"

"Reckon so. At least we could send him the $1000.00 for a short time with no hardship. I've got money for taxes, and there's no other major expense coming soon. Six per cent is a fair offer, but I'd bet my bottom dollar that Pa will get at least ten. Even where I'm concerned, he'd have to make a sizable profit."

Millie paused. Miney realized her husband would hate to tell his father no, yet she felt certain he was sorely tempted.

"Guess it wouldn't hurt to earn a little extree cash. Leastwise, Pa's word is good, and we'd get every cent due us."

Miney knew the matter was settled. Millie would send his father the money. Well, one thing was certain, Father Setterington did have a knack for making money. He had proven that time and time again. Trouble was, the man couldn't understand why Millie and John didn't have the same acumen. She knew Mac irritated Father Setterington because he always had some get rich quick scheme which never really panned out. Mac would have been in financial trouble more than once if Father hadn't been there to bail him out. Miney had always believed Father would have let Mac suffer a little except that Lovina was like a she-bear with cubs where Ruby was concerned. At least Millie had never depended on his father financially. Of course, money had been the straw that broke the camel's back in John's relationship with his father.

Life with the Setterington men certainly was different. Pa had never been obsessed with making money, and he had been far more religious. He had been a severe task master, but her mother had never complained. Of course, Ma had never been one to complain about anything or any one. Miney felt she had had a good life. Ma and Pa had not had the material advantages that Father and Mother Setterington enjoyed, but theirs had been a happy family.

Miney had had a letter from Blanche indicating she would be home for Ralph's birthday, the week before Christmas. What Blanche failed to tell her mother was that she was coming home for longer than the rest of the year.

Blanche had made up her mind that she was going to go to business school. In spite of her grandmother's objections about her working in an office, Blanche had given the matter a lot of thought. She felt office work would be preferable to standing on her feet all day waiting on customers, some of whom were a real pain in the neck. There were times when she found it difficult to be pleasant.

Pa had said he would pay her expenses if and when she decided to go to school. She had saved some money of her own--this had been one of the advantages of living with her grandparents--so she wouldn't be entirely dependent on her father.

When Millie met Blanche at the station, he teased her about the amount of luggage she had.

'"Pears like you accumulated something extree whilst in Detroit. Don't remember there was this much when we drove you to the station to leave."

"Oh, Pa, it's just that I kept buying things--clothes mostly. And I'm not going back--at least not soon. That's why I bought this telescoping bag. Of course, I never really expected to fill it." Blanche gave a little laugh. "Just shows how good a judge I am." Millie made no comment, and Blanche was relieved. She was not at all certain how her father and mother would view her plans.

At supper that night, the night of Ralph's sixteenth birthday, Blanche made her announcement.

"Pa, Ma, I've finally decided what I want to do with my life. I've decided to enroll for classes at The Business Institute. I want to become a stenographer. They say there are plenty of openings for their graduates, and the pay is better, the hours shorter, than clerking. I don't want to begin in the middle of the year, so I won't be going back to Detroit until next fall. Guess you'll be stuck with me until then."

"Some birthday present," retorted Ralph.

"Oh, little brother, you know how much you've missed me."

"Like a hole in the head," he replied, but Rate's grin belied his words.

Miney had tears in her eyes when she spoke.

"Blanche, it will be good to have you home even though you will leave again next fall. Why we've got the rest of the winter, spring, and all of summer to enjoy." "When did you make this decision?" asked Millie.

"Actually, a month or so ago."

"Does your grandmother know?"

Blanche eyed her father a moment before replying.

"Grandmother knows I'm not coming back. I didn't feel I had to discuss my future plans with her. She would only argue and tell me what a mistake I'm making. After all, it is my decision and is really none of her business."

"It would have been best had you told her," was Millie's stern reply.

"Pa, when will you realize I have no intention of letting Grandmother run my life. After all, I'm over twenty years old, plenty old enough to make my own decisions. If mistakes are made, the will be mine, not hers. I have my own ideas about the kind of life I want, and I hate having Grandmother pointing out where every idea I've ever had is wrong."

"That's not quite fair, Blanche. Ma has always had your best interest at heart." Millie's tone was mild, but the reprimand was there.

"I suppose, in a way, you are right. But Pa, you know Grandmother never listens to anyone, simply assumes she knows best. She may have good intentions, but I resent having her interfere."

Miney had listened to this exchange with some apprehension. In Millie's mind, she wasn't sure who would take precedent in an all out battle, his mother or his daughter. Miney derived more than a little satisfaction knowing her grown-up daughter had enough gumption to stand up to Lovina Setterington. My, all these years she had wanted to tell her bossy mother-in-law she would run her life as she pleased, but had never quite dared. Of course, she not only had been intimidated by Lovina, she had known that in any disagreement, her husband would take his mother's part. Somehow, this had always rankled, and at times she had resented both Millie and his mother. Now, Blanche was showing her mettle by refusing to let Lovina run her life. Good for her!

Millie looked as though he intended to say more, but then busied himself with cleaning his plate. Miney felt relief. She doubted if Millie would ever bring up the subject again. This was not his way. What's done, was done.

Blanche felt the first hurdle had been cleared. She knew her father disliked the idea that his daughter might have asserted herself with *his* mother. Well, Pa, thought Blanche, you'll just have to get used to it. I'm sure Grandmother and I will have many more disagreements along the way.

Rate had given his sister a devilish grin. He could imagine how Grandmother would accept Blanche's decision. Grandmother did not think office work was respectable--especially for a granddaughter of hers. However, he knew when Blanche had that determined look, she could be just as stubborn as Grandmother. The whole affair might prove interesting.

No one in the family quite realized how much Miney's world improved with her daughter home. Christmas was truly a wonderful day because Miney knew Blanche would not be leaving with the coming of the new year. Her work load seemed ever so much lighter, and not just because Blanche was there to help with the household chores. Miney even noted with satisfaction that Blanche and Ralph were getting on remarkably well. She guessed Ralph was growing up too, and the little-boy pranks no longer appealed to him. Life could hardly be more rewarding.

In fact, Ralph and Blanche had gone on a couple of sleighing parties together. The parties had been sponsored for young people by the Baptist Church, so there had been a wide range of ages. Since Ralph had not yet begun to keep company with any girl, he had no objection to his sister being one of the crowd. Mostly, she had her own friends, and if there were two sleighs, like as not, they were not even on the same sleigh.

Millie had come in just in time for supper. The day had been cloudy and darkness had come early. As usual, there had not been much conversation until Millie had taken second helpings of the steak, potatoes, and gravy. He was buttering a slice of Miney's homemade bread when he looked at Ralph with a stern face but a twinkle in his eye.

"Richard Fizzell was with me today. Pearl was driving nice as you please when we heard sleigh bells behind us. Funny thing, Pearl took off like a scared rabbit, paid no attention to the lines. The cutter swayed a little and Richard was hangin' on for dear life, yelling, 'Pull her in, Millie. Pull her in.' Course, he didn't know I was tryin'. Then, all at once, Pearl stopped, cocked her head to listen, then moved forward like nothing atall had happened. Course we didn't hear no more sleigh bells either. Boy, do you run that horse a little?"

"Gosh, Pa, whatever makes you think that?"

"Just a hunch. Well?"

"I can tell you this. Pearl's never let another horse pass her. Nooossir, that mare always has to be first."

"Thought so," chuckled Millie.

Ralph felt better when he heard his father's chuckle.

Guess there were times when Pa remembered what it was like to be young. Still, one could never outguess him. Rate figured Pa had thought it funny because Richard was afraid. Ralph knew nothing like a runaway horse would upset *his* father.

Rate knew that while he was looking forward to returning to the farm, Blanche was not. She liked being in town where girls she had chummed with were only a block or two away. Of course, some of them had married, but they still had time in the afternoons for callers, especially when the caller was a former schoolmate. Some had hundreds of questions to ask about "the big city." They enjoyed hearing

Blanche talk about her various jobs, often relating some humorous exchange with a customer which had not been funny at the time. There were often parties for this group of young adults which Blanche thoroughly enjoyed.

One Saturday, as Blanche and Miney were finishing the dishes, Miney asked, "Are you going somewhere this evening?"

"To a party at Hazel's. I intended to tell you because Elzie Call will be calling for me."

"Elzie Call?" Miney stopped scrubbing the frying pan and looked at her daughter. "But 1--1 thought he was keeping steady company with Mildred Chamberlin."

Blanche shrugged her shoulders.

"I wouldn't know," she hedged. "Anyway, he asked me if I would go with him tonight, and I said I would."

Blanche did not meet her mother's eyes. Miney had the feeling Blanche knew all along that Elzie and Mildred had been keeping company for months. True, Blanche had been in Detroit, but this was the sort of thing that everyone in a small town knew. Miney wondered what had happened to break up Elzie and Mildred. Goodness, she hoped no one would think Blanche was at fault.

"Well, I don't suppose it's any of our business why he isn't seeing Mildred any longer. He isn't, is he?"

"Oh, Ma, how would I know? He's a nice young man who just happened to ask me out. I had no reason not to accept."

"No, of course you didn't," agreed Miney as she returned to scrubbing the pan. "As far as I know, they were never engaged, it was just that people expected they would be."

Neither said anything more. Blanche was glad Elzie had asked to take her to the party. It wasn't like when she was in high school when boys and girls simply went to parties as a group. Now, they were paired off in couples, and Blanche was determined not to be the odd one. True, she had accidentally run into Elzie a couple of times just lately, and she had been very pleasant--he was easy to be pleasant to-- and perhaps that was why he had asked her out. Certainly wasn't her fault if he wanted to take her rather than Mildred. She fully intended to enjoy the evening and sincerely hoped Elzie would enjoy it too.

As usual, Miney worried about what people would think. Bet Tillie Lance would be here first thing tomorrow to put in her two cents about Blanche going out tonight with Elzie. She was certain to hint that it was Blanche's fault that Elzie had not taken Mildred. Spare me, thought Miney. Besides who really knew what was on the mind of young people?

In her day, a young woman was likely to marry her very first beau. Now, it seemed, they often dated several before making their choice. Other than Gerd Pershing, Blanche had not dated anyone steadily. Miney was not certain if this was good or bad. Well, at least Blanche had not plunged into marriage as soon as she finished school, and Miney was thankful for that.

The more she thought about Tillie, the more worried she became. Lawsy, she would like to slam the door in Tillie's face, but that was not possible because Tillie never bothered to knock, simply waltzed right in, and without so much as a howdy-do would take off like a four alarm fire on her latest gossip. That Sunday was a church going day didn't matter. She'd just show up a little earlier. No use believing Tillie wouldn't know Blanche was at a party. Why that woman would know who was there and with whom, and be able to tell what sort of dress each young woman wore. When it came to knowing the personal business of the townspeople, Tillie stood head and shoulders above everyone else.

Maybe Elzie and Mildred had had a little spat, and Elzie had asked Blanche to the party because he was miffed with Mildred. If this was so, he probably would not ask Blanche out again, and she was worrying for nothing. Miney felt some better after she convinced herself that this was a one time happening. At least Blanche would have a good time, and that was the important part of the situation. Her daughter's happiness was always Miney's first concern.

Since they would be moving to the farm soon, Blanche decided there was no need for her to look for a job. She was not about to make the drive from the farm each day. Blanche had become accustomed to riding street cars if the distance was too far to walk; therefore, the prospects of having to care for a horse each day held no appeal. No, she'd stay home and help Ma with the extra work with which a farm wife had to contend.

Miney had been right about Tillie Lance. According to Tillie, Blanche had been most unladylike and had flirted outrageously with Elzie who had simply had his head turned because a young woman who had lived in Detroit was treating him so special. Tillie felt sorry for poor Mildred who hadn't stood a chance against the wiles of a "city" girl.

Miney fumed, but knew that anything she might say would make no difference. She knew Tillie was voicing her opinion all over town. What's more, she knew there would be those who believed the woman. Well, after they were back on the farm, Tillie would find it rather difficult to make Blanche the subject of her gossip, Miney thought with a sigh of satisfaction.

Moving day came, and while Millie viewed the work involved as nothing much, it was bone-tiring for Miney. There were so many small details that a man never even considered. To Millie, the furniture was the big item, he scarcely thought about all the dishes that had to be carefully packed and unpacked, all the jars of canned fruit and vegetables as well as jams and jellies, and a few jars of canned beef. True, there was not as much this late in the season, but Miney had canned goods to last until there was fresh produce from the garden. Of course, all the empty jars must be moved to be there when needed for this year's crops.

Miney was grateful for Blanche's help. She even acknowledged that Ralph helped in many ways. He and Millie saw to setting up the beds, and Ralph brought the heavy boxes to the cellar where she could place the canned goods in the order she wanted them. It was just that she never got a chance to sit down. If she wasn't actually doing something, she was directing what someone else was doing. Miney decided she hated moving. For a moment, she even felt some compassion for her mother-in law who had moved to Elsie from Canada, and had moved three or four times since. Of course, this sympathetic thought was fleeting as Miney reminded herself how pleasant it was with Lovina in Detroit.

Once again Ralph had three and one-half miles to drive to get to school. He still used the barn across from the now vacant house that had been Grandma Smith's. He wondered if Pa would sell the place. Technically, it belonged to Ma, but he knew she would do whatever Pa wanted.

Ralph hated to think of the place being sold. Although Grandma Smith had been dead a long time, he still associated the house with her. In his mind's eye, he could see her sitting by the window, her knitting needles making a soothing, clicking sound. He wished she could have lived longer. She and Aunt Lorin never seemed to care because he was a boy, they treated him just as well as they did Blanche. There were still times when he missed Grandma, and he guessed Blanche missed her too.

Ralph thoroughly enjoyed being back on the farm. His share of the chores had increased since he was now sixteen, but thus far, Pa hadn't bought many cows, and the sheep weren't much work now that lambing time had passed. Of course, he had always enjoyed taking care of the horses.

With spring just around the corner, Ralph even enjoyed the drive into town. Spring was a good season. While it was still too early for planting, the fields of wheat had already turned green, and the pastures and hay fields were beginning to show growth. Ralph enjoyed seeing things grow. There was something extremely rewarding about seeing the fields come alive, all the more so when they were filled with something which you had planted.

Yup, he guessed there wasn't a better place to live than on a farm. At least not at this time in his life. For the present, he was perfectly content.

Baptist Church   Elsie, Michigan

The Grist Mill